GENESIS

Inside & Out

(1967-2000)

By Robin Platts

We acknowledge the financial support of the Government of Canada through
the Book Publishing Industry Development Program for our publishing activities.
Published by Collector's Guide Publishing Inc., Box 62034, Burlington, Ontario, Canada, L7R 4K2
Printed and bound in Canada
GENESIS — Inside & Out (1967-2000)
by Robin Platts

ISBN 1-896522-71-8

GENESIS

Inside & Out
(1967-2000)

By Robin Platts

Table Of Contents

Acknowledgements

I'd like to thank the following people for their invaluable assistance and support:

Mick Barnard, Marcus Bicknell, Nick Davis, Steve Hackett, David Hentschel, Anthony Phillips, Daryl Stuermer, Paul Whitehead and Ray Wilson for subjecting themselves to interviews.

Also, very special thanks must go to Billy Budis, Marijeanne Gorectke, Øystein Hage, Anne-Marie Hill, Barbara Jeffries, King Lerch, David Stopps and Steve Waxman. Many thanks to everyone at Collector's Guide Publishing for making this happen, and to Mary Standell for her endless support.

Photo credits to Phil Anderson for some of his live concert photos. KAOS2000 Magazine www.kaos2000.net.

Introduction:

"I like music that takes me on an unexpected journey," says Steve Hackett. "People say to me, when they like something, 'This music is very visual.' And they don't mean 'visual' in terms of, 'this would make a great video.' They mean it's very visual within itself or that it transports you. It takes you somewhere else. It's music to dream to."

For more than thirty years, Genesis has been making music to dream to. Hackett, who was their lead guitarist from 1971 to 1977, helped the group develop a style that put them at the forefront of the "progressive rock" movement. Genesis has been many things to many people. From a schoolboy pop group to progressive rock pioneers to chart-topping megastars, their sound has changed, but the name has remained. Incredibly resilient, the group endured personnel changes that would have finished most other bands. Instead of splitting up, the band reacted to the departure of key members by pushing in new directions, usually to greater commercial success.

Their music has been loved and loathed, sometimes by the same listeners. Many fans turned on by early progressive fare such as *Supper's Ready* and *The Cinema Show* had a hard time getting to grips with the lightweight pop the band was turning out by the mid-80's. Likewise, many of the newer fans who discovered Genesis through radio-friendly toe-tappers like *Invisible Touch* or *That's All* were undoubtedly baffled if they ventured deep enough into the group's back catalog to discover such titles as *The Return Of The Giant Hogweed* or *The Fountain Of Salmacis*. There are also plenty of fans who can find something to enjoy in each of the band's eras, who will defend 1997's post-Phil Collins release CALLING ALL STATIONS just as fervently as 1973's FOXTROT.

What makes a great Genesis song? The answer is subjective, but it has little to do with how long the song is, whether it's a simple love song or a mythical epic. Genesis are at their best when they really seem to be trying hard to create music that is different, possessing an indefinable quality that makes it a Genesis song. Their best work is visual, evocative, romantic, challenging and unique. The drum-machine driven hit single *Mama* is just as inventive as the Mellotron-laden sci-fi epic *Watcher Of The Skies*. The stripped-down, straightforward ABACAB LP is in many ways just as challenging an album as the expansive, obscure THE LAMB LIES DOWN ON BROADWAY.

The Billboard Guide To Progressive Music suggests that "Progressive music always looks forward, striving to be new and different, dissenting vigorously from the current musical establishment." Certainly this describes the best Genesis music. The group sounds weak, on the other hand, when it gets stuck in a musical rut, or begins to repeat itself. Sometimes the band seems to progress and regress on the same track. The 1992 hit single *No Son Of Mine* starts off in fine, inventive form, with a rhythmic pattern that incorporates a very strange sampled sound from Mike Rutherford's guitar. But, after that great setup, the track lapses into a sort of Genesis auto-pilot and soon sounds too much like a number of previous Genesis or Phil Collins solo numbers.

At the time of writing, founding members Mike Rutherford and Tony Banks seem to be doubtful about whether Genesis will continue. After more than thirty years, it could well be time to close the Book of Genesis for good, but you never know . . .

In this book, I've attempted to tell the story of Genesis by examining their music, how they made it and how their approach has changed over the years. This isn't a biography in the usual sense. If you want to find out about Phil Collins' marriages, you'll have to look elsewhere. But if you want to find out about how these great songs and recordings came together, about the group's recording sessions and concerts, keep reading.

Chapter 1: The Charterhouse Boys

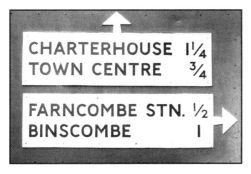

In 1974, one of the British music weeklies did a feature that referred to Genesis as "The Charterhouse Boys". The privileged environment of Charterhouse — a boarding school near Godalming, Surrey — was an unlikely setting for the formation of a rock and roll band. No fighting in the streets, no girls, no working class "credibility." Not very rock and roll, but then Genesis was never a rock and roll band in the usual sense. Growing up in that setting in the 60's, all the while tuning in to the radio hits of the day and dreaming about girls, they inevitably came up with something very different. They were isolated at Charterhouse, situated some twenty miles South East of London. And they remained somehow isolated even after they graduated, doing their own thing without paying too much attention to the rest of the world.

In September 1963, a student named Tony Banks arrived at Charterhouse. Tony had been studying classical piano for several years, but was starting to lose interest. Now thirteen, and in possession of a transistor radio, Banks preferred to channel his musical abilities into pop songs. After a friend showed him how to play the Beatles' *Eight Days A Week*, there was no looking back. Whenever he had a free moment, Banks would seat himself at the piano in the Charterhouse dining hall and play songs like *I Put A Spell On You* and *Try A Little Tenderness*. Beside him, supplying the vocals, was his friend Peter Gabriel. Gabriel had arrived at Charterhouse at the same time as Banks, and they soon became close friends. The pair's shared love of music provided some relief from the strict atmosphere of a school that Gabriel later referred to as "a repressive, middle-class institution."

Gabriel was especially fond of blues and soul. In his adolescence, he aspired to be a drummer and manned the skins for a young combo known as the Spoken Word. Years later, Gabriel's bass drum would figure in Genesis' live act, adding another bizarre dimension to the group's performances. At 13, Peter was already writing his own songs, his first effort being a ditty entitled *Sammy The Slug*. Rather than just aping the pop songs he was hearing on the radio, Gabriel immediately gravitated towards more unusual subject matter. Before long, he and Banks were writing songs together.

Banks and Gabriel had a good friend by the name of Anthony Phillips, who played in a band with a student named Michael Rutherford. Prior to his arrival at Charterhouse, Phillips — "Ant" to his friends — had played in a group called the Spiders. That group was "very, very primitive, doing Beatles copies, really," Phillips explains.

> "Only two or three of us could play. A couple of us couldn't really play and just strummed along in the background — mainly on the same chord! A very good

friend of mine called Rivers Job was the main protagonist with me, and we were really keen on all the kind of pop stuff around at the time. We used to get sheet music from my mum, who used to very kindly send them down — the latest Beatles songs and stuff. We just used to learn them all and then do them. It was pretty basic."

Upon his arrival at Charterhouse in April 1965, Phillips put together a band called Anon. Ant played guitar in the group, alongside Rivers Job (bass), Rob Tyrell (drums) and Richard MacPhail (vocals).

"By that stage, we were reasonably competent at copying the Shadows, Beatles and Stones," says Phillips. "And, in this band, everyone could play! Mainly copies (i.e. cover versions), but we did a couple of our own things. And we did a few recording sessions in the holidays. We were quite a competent unit, actually."

Needing a second guitarist, Anon soon recruited Rutherford, who had been at the school since 1964.

Anon's early repertoire relied heavily on Stones and Beatles covers, with a strong blues influence brought in after MacPhail witnessed a particularly inspiring John Mayall and the Bluesbreakers gig in London. (In fact, Rivers Job would go on to pursue the blues as a member of Savoy Brown in 1968.) The group's style began to change in 1966, when Phillips and Rutherford started writing their own songs. Suddenly, the repertoire was half raucous blues covers and half originals. These self-penned numbers pointing to the duo's future musical style. On some of the originals, Mike and Ant began to develop a unique sound, based on the interplay between their 12-string acoustic guitars.

"It was kind of strange really," Phillips recalls, "When Mike and I were starting to write as a pair. On the one hand there was this primitive second-rate blues, and then we were also kind of dipping our toes in the water of what turned out to be quite an original style, which was the two-acoustic-guitars thing. And we couldn't really tell the difference — it's kind of amazing to think. On one hand stuff was really sort of bad imitations and on the other was stuff that was going to be groundbreaking."

For Gabriel, Banks, Phillips and Rutherford, music was an escape from the bleak atmosphere of Charterhouse. The most appealing thing the school had to offer them was the chance to sing hymns in its chapel. Hymns and classical music were the only forms of music condoned by the school, and the future members of Genesis found things to like about both forms. Both influences would definitely come to bear as the quartet began creating music of their own. In fact, several years later, Rutherford and Phillips wrote a hymn entitled *Take This Heart*. Appropriately, it was recorded by the Charterhouse Choral Society and released on a Charisma Records compilation called BEYOND AN EMPTY DREAM.

The highlight of Anon's career was an end-of-term concert at Charterhouse, in July 1966.

They headlined the bill, the opening act being another young Charterhouse combo called the Garden Wall. The Garden Wall was Banks and Gabriel's vehicle, which featured Chris Stewart on drums. For the end-of-term concert, the Garden Wall line-up was fleshed out with the addition of Anthony Phillips on guitar and Rivers Job on bass. Tony Banks played a grand piano, and the charismatic Gabriel sang and cast flower petals out over the audience.

"I can remember the Headmaster sitting at the school concert with his hands firmly stuck in both of his ears because he couldn't take the noise," says Phillips. Clearly, there was no support or approval from the Charterhouse establishment, but the young musicians didn't let it put them off. In the years to come, Genesis would practically make a career out of ignoring the lack of encouragement they got from most agents, publishers and record companies. The more the music business powers stuck their fingers in their ears, the more determined the group became to carry on.

Anon split not long after the end-of-term show, but Phillips and Rutherford continued to collaborate. By early 1967, the duo were keen to record some of the songs they had written together. That April, they arranged to record some demos at the four-track Chiswick studio of a friend named Brian Roberts. Roberts' setup was by no means a professional studio, but it was good enough to help the budding songwriters capture their ideas on tape.

Mike and Ant invited along Tony Banks, who played a Farfisa organ on the session. The original plan was for Phillips to sing lead on the demos, but his vocals left something to be desired.

> "I never really considered myself a singer at all," he explains. "I was never the singer of (Anon). In fact, Mike was, at one stage. I used to give him a real hard time when he couldn't hit the high notes! I guess what happened was, when we started writing our own stuff, it was a sort of singer-songwriter thing. You know — you wrote something and so you sang it. And Mike and I did these demos together and we both sang. I think probably I sang a bit more than he did because maybe I wrote slightly more — or at least I started the ideas more than he did, generally, at that stage."

> At the demo session, "Tony Banks brought along Peter to do this one song of theirs (She Is Beautiful), which turned out to be by far the best. I can't remember if he ended up doing the vocals on the other songs. I mean, he was a proper singer and I wasn't."

The songs recorded at that first session were Don't Want You Back (also known as Don't Wash Your Back), Patricia (which later became In Hiding), Try A Little Sadness, She Is Beautiful, That's Me and Listen On Five. One of these recordings — the instrumental Patricia — was finally released in 1998, on the GENESIS ARCHIVE box set.

As the two songwriting teams evolved into a group of sorts, it was decided that Gabriel

9

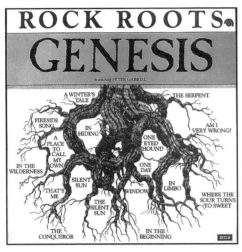

EARLY GENESIS RECORDINGS WERE REPACKAGED ON THIS MID-70'S RELEASE.

would sing lead on all the material. However, Phillips was a prominent backup vocalist throughout his days with Genesis, often singing in unison with Gabriel, as Phil Collins did later on. Occasionally — on parts of *Let Us Now Make Love*, for instance — Ant's voice could be heard on its own.

Although they had put a viable band together, Gabriel, Rutherford, Banks and Phillips were by no means a professional performing outfit. The group, such as it was, was more of a vehicle to present their songs, in the hope that other artists would record them. "We thought these masterpieces were ready to be recorded by thousands of Number One recording stars," said Gabriel years later. Still schoolboys, they were isolated at Charterhouse, but eager for their songs to reach a wider audience than their schoolmates.

GENESIS ANTHOLOGY SONGBOOK

Enter Jonathan King. A Charterhouse alumnus, King had become a pop music sensation in the years since he graduated. Although he was involved in many projects, King's claim to fame at the time was the pop hit *Everyone's Gone To The Moon*. Was this the sound Banks, Gabriel, Rutherford and Phillips aspired towards? Probably not, but it didn't really matter. King was in the pop business and a visit to the school by this Charterhouse "old boy" was an opportunity not to be missed. Lacking the confidence to approach the great man directly, the budding songwriters gave their demo to a go-between who handed it to King.

"Whatever did he see in us?" asked Tony Banks three decades later, in an essay for the ARCHIVE box set. King has said that what struck him in particular was Gabriel's voice, quirky and soulful even at the age of seventeen. In the 'Genesis History' video documentary, King said he thought the tape was "absolutely fabulous, because I thought the guy had a great lead voice and they were really interesting songs." King was looking to become a producer and envisioned these young hopefuls as the start of his production career. Clearly, they were eager to break into the music business and he could control their sound more easily than he could with a more developed act. Although he didn't really advocate the "progressive" inclinations that would ultimately bring Genesis success, Jonathan King was there at exactly the right time.

Chapter 2: The Silent Sun

AD FOR THE 1974 REISSUE OF FROM GENESIS TO REVELATION

In the summer of 1967, Jonathan King invited the young hopefuls up to London to meet with him. Shortly thereafter, King paid for the group to record another demo tape. This second effort included *She Is Beautiful*, *Try A Little Sadness*, *Where The Sour Turns To Sweet* and *The Image Blown Out*. A couple of songs from this tape were released in the late 90's: The *Image Blown Out* and *She Is Beautiful* were tagged on to the umpteenth reissue of FROM GENESIS TO REVELATION, and the latter was also featured on the ARCHIVE box set. They apparently had no shortage of material to choose from. In a 1970 interview, Gabriel claimed that the four songwriters had written 300 songs by the time they met King.

King was very pleased with the tape and decided that the young combo was ready to make a record. He soon got them a deal with Decca Records, the label to which he was signed as a recording artist. In fact, such was his enthusiasm for the band that he tried to get them to sign a five-year management contract with him. When the group members' parents found out about this, they interceded, since the would-be pop stars were still minors. The contract's duration was altered to a more sensible length of one year.

King wanted to simplify the group's sound as much as possible. "I told Tony Banks to cut his rather self-indulgent keyboard solos by three quarters, which he resented," he told *Q* many years later. King felt the emphasis should be on a straightforward acoustic guitar-and-piano mixture, with none of the "organ rubbish" that Banks was inclined towards.

In August 1967, the still-unnamed group made their first attempt at recording a single. By this point, Rutherford had switched from guitar to bass and ex-Garden Wall man Chris Stewart was drumming. Under King's supervision, they recorded *Where The Sour Turns To*

Sweet and *From The Bottom Of A Well* at Advision Studios, for a planned single release. The recordings were deemed unsatisfactory and were shelved, but King didn't lose interest in his young protégés.

In October, the band recorded another demo tape, at Regent Sound and Central Sound in London. Titles on this effort included *Hair On The Arms And Legs, Fourteen Years Too Long, Lost In A Drawer, Sea Bee, Hidden In The World Of Dawn, Barnaby's Adventure* and *The Mystery Of The Flannan Isle Lighthouse.* The new batch of songs was more ambitious and less poppy, hinting at the true nature of the group. Although none of these numbers would make it onto a record, the demo versions *Sea Bee, Hidden In The World Of Dawn* and *The Mystery Of The Flannan Isle Lighthouse* eventually appeared on the ARCHIVE box set. These early efforts reveal a group working within mid-60's pop conventions, yet grasping for something more.

> "It wasn't yet the progressive era," Anthony Phillips points out. "This was around the time of *Sgt. Pepper*, you've got to remember. So we were well into some of the *Strawberry Fields* / *Walrus*-type tracks, the more interesting ones. We were writing long, rambling pieces."

King was much less keen on these numbers than he had been on the group's previous efforts. At the beginning of December, the group received a letter from Joe Roncoroni, of King's Jonjo Music company, explaining that Jonathan and his associates were "not very impressed" with the new songs. "The previous batch you did are, in our opinion, much better," the letter explained. This was not the response the group was hoping for.

> "We weren't so much into the more poppy area," says Phillips. "Jonathan King's area was the three-minute pop single. He was very successful with a sort of sound and molding certain types of groups into a kind of package that worked. It was fairly light level pop. He was a very clever man, although he always claimed he only knew seven chords. We respected him enormously and, obviously, we did everything he said. I suppose he was being practical, looking back on it. He tried to instill in us that we needed to hone things down. These rambling five-minute epics weren't going to get us anywhere, at that stage. And it was probably right, in a way."

According to Phillips, the Banks-Gabriel writing team was much more adept at turning out the type of pop numbers King liked than he was. "I hated it. I really kicked against it."

Not surprisingly, then, it was Banks and Gabriel that delivered the first number deemed worthy of release. King liked the Bee Gees, so Tony and Peter penned a pastiche of the Brothers Gibb, a catchy tune entitled *The Silent Sun*. It worked. King decided that *The Silent Sun*, was good enough to be their first single. Recorded towards the end of December 1967, at Regent Sound A in London, Gabriel even did a Robin Gibb imitation on the second verse. At the same session, the group recorded the Phillips-Rutherford song *That's Me*, which was chosen as the flip side.

Before they could release the record, the quintet needed a name. King dubbed them Genesis. From his point of view, the name was a reference to the fact that he envisioned this group as the beginning of a successful production career for himself. The genesis of a great producer, perhaps. King had previously suggested the name "Gabriel's Angels"; Peter was all for the idea, but apparently the others didn't share his enthusiasm.

Decca released *The Silent Sun* on February 22, 1968. The *New Musical Express* called it "a disc of many facets and great depth, but it might be a bit too complex for the average fan." The single also got a positive review in *Melody Maker*, which predicted it would be a hit. The charts didn't beckon, as it turned out, despite some airplay from prominent disc jockey Kenny Everett. Sadly, the television viewing public never got a chance to see the coordinated outfits that the band members had bought on trendy Carnaby Street, anticipating a *Top Of The Pops* appearance.

> "Mercifully, it wasn't successful," says Phillips. "I think if it had been successful, it would have been the end of the band. The band would have got stuck, would never have developed a really original sound. It would have got stuck in a kind of neo-Jonathan King style. It would still have come through, but I think a lot of the more interesting stuff would have been sort of cut off at the hip, would never have had the chance to develop. Because once you become successful at something, and make money, a whole industry springs up around you and they expect you to carry on in the manner to which you've been accustomed. So it would have been much more difficult to branch out. It's a very good thing that we weren't successful, I think, with very kind of slick and simple singles."

Undeterred by the failure of *The Silent Sun*, Genesis came up with a new batch of songs, which they committed to tape on March 13, 1968. At a demo session at Central Sound Studio, Denmark Street, London, they recorded *Hey!*, *I'm Here*, *2:30 Park Time* and *There Was A Movement*. (One of these recordings, *Hey!*, eventually surfaced on the ARCHIVE box set.) Presumably, King and Decca were less than thrilled with these new ventures, since none of them were chosen for any of the group's releases.

King still encouraged the group's efforts, and another single appeared in May 1968 — *A Winter's Tale*, backed with *One-Eyed Hound*. This second waxing proved no more successful than the first, although it did get a favorable review in the *New Musical Express*. The *NME* deemed it "an absorbing disc . . . The soul-searching lyric is impressive and gripping — and, while the melody could have done with a little more substance, it's a platter I can thoroughly recommend."

By this point, Phillips and Rutherford were eager for the group to turn professional, but Banks and Gabriel were not convinced. Tony planned on attending university, while Peter was eager to go to film school. And, during the summer, Genesis had its first spot of drummer trouble.

> "Jonathan King decided we all had to leave school if we were going to play in the band," Chris Stewart told the *UK Telegraph* many years later. "My folks were against me leaving: they said no. So I was booted out. Jonathan sent Peter

Gabriel to me with a pre-written letter resigning all my rights to the songs we'd recorded in return for £300. It was a lot of money at the time and I was only too happy to accept. Besides, I was a rotten drummer."

Stewart went on to enjoy success as a writer, penning several Rough Guide volumes, and has recently published a memoir entitled DRIVING OVER LEMONS.

The remaining quartet drafted a friend named John Silver to take Stewart's place behind the drum kit. Silver arrived in time for the group's first album sessions. After Genesis' lack of success as a pop singles act, King had decided to have them make a concept album. Playing on the group's name, King suggested a Biblical theme, FROM GENESIS TO REVELATION.

"He very decently said 'Well, okay, this hasn't worked, I'll let you do your own thing,' as it were," Phillips recalls. "So he let us do this album, which was kind of much more visionary. The songs weren't particularly commercial. They didn't really have build-ups to the choruses. They weren't aimed specifically at the singles market. He just basically let us do our own thing, up to a point. That was great. There wasn't much compromise on that."

However, King didn't entirely leave the group to their own devices. "We had to demo," Phillips points out. "I mean, he knew what he was getting." So, in the spring of 1968, Genesis recorded another batch of demos at Regent Sound A, songs that were candidates for the album. Some of these demos, such as *Am I Very Wrong?* and *One Day*, impressed King enough to be properly recorded for the LP. Others, such as *The Magic Of Time* and *Humanity*, did not make the cut. These versions of *One Day* and *The Magic Of Time* did appear eventually, on the ARCHIVE box set.

stereo
F 22909
DECCA

GENESIS
FROM GENESIS TO REVELATION
Where the sour turn to sweet - In the beginning -
Fireside song - The serpent - Am I very wrong? -
In the wilderness - The conqueror - In hiding -
One day - Window - In Limbo - Silent sun - A place
to call my own.
SKL 4990

The FROM GENESIS TO REVELATION concept was King's idea, and he picked the songs that were to be included. Some of these were written especially for the occasion, others were adapted from the group's existing repertoire. *Patricia* became *In Hiding*, and *She Is Beautiful* became *The Serpent*. Given King's apparent preference for radio-friendly pop songs, it's curious that he would encourage such an ambitious venture. Perhaps it was an attempt on his part to accommodate the young group's "progressive" tendencies, while still keeping the individual songs short and catchy. And — given the success of such concept albums the Who's TOMMY and the Moody Blues' DAYS OF FUTURE PASSED — the idea was certainly not lacking in commercial potential.

FROM GENESIS TO REVELATION was made during a marathon session on September 4, 1968, at Regent B Studio, London. Starting at 9 a.m., the band worked through until midnight, with King overseeing. They hadn't played live at this point, and their approach in the studio reflected this. According to King's preference, the arrangements tended to be fairly simple, based around acoustic guitar and piano. Banks was keen to play the organ, but King discouraged this.

"Really, it was pretty much a schoolboy outing," says Phillips of the session, which was done on two four-track tape machines.

Although the band already had a certain amount of dynamic energy, it was undermined somewhat by the string arrangements that King chose to overdub without the group's involvement. The group had been impressed by Arthur Greenslade's string arrangement on the first single, but were disappointed by the arrangements added to the album tracks.

> "There were some disagreements about the production, and the way it turned out," says Phillips. "I hated what happened to it in the end. (The original tracks) sounded rough and naive, but as the process went on, it all got reduced and they added these strings. It was done behind our backs — we knew nothing about it. To be fair, we were at school, but we were presented with a fait accompli. And I was very distressed. It wasn't just a personal thing. I mean, all our friends who had heard the original tapes said, 'How could you have let them do this?' "

> "You've probably heard the version of In The Wilderness that's on the (ARCHIVE) box set. In full stereo, it sounds quite powerful but what happened was, on the album, in order to get the strings on, they reduced the backing track to mono and put it on one side of the stereo, so it all sounded very weak. And the strings weren't full strings, they weren't rich and warm. It was kind of these high, wheeling, thin strings. So you've got Peter in the center of the stereo image and the strings on the right. We felt it was a complete disaster. It was a belated attempt by Jonathan King to make it more commercial. I mean, I guess, to be fair, he felt forced into it, because we hadn't come up with a sound that was irresistibly commercial and complete. But I just felt it made it worse, and all our friends said, 'What have you let them do?' "

> "I was shocked and a little upset when I heard it," said John Silver many years later in an interview with Record Collector. "Because when you are playing on something, all you are really listening to is how far forward you are in the mixes, so I was somewhat amazed at the overpowering element of Arthur Greenslade and the gang. Nevertheless it was a real thrill when Peter sent me the album. But if Jonathan King said 'stand this way' or 'do it that way', we were in no position to argue. I do remember he said he wanted a Charlie Watts feel for a lot of the drumming, so I worked hard on that."

Surprisingly, given the brevity of the recording period, the session spawned several out-takes: Build Me A Mountain, The Image Blown Out, Visions of Angels and The Magic of Time. All of these, except for Visions Of Angels, eventually found their way onto the ARCHIVE box set.

Visions Of Angels would see the light of day on the band's second album, TRESPASS, in a considerably longer version than the one recorded for FROM GENESIS TO REVELATION. Phillips describes the first attempt at doing the song:

> "Terrible. I felt it was ghastly. I mean, if it wasn't good enough to have gone on the first album, then it must have been seriously bad! (The first recording) was very twee. It was a big disappointment, because it was regarded as one of the potential star tracks of the album. And it was a screw-up, didn't make it at all. But it was a nice song, and it worked well on TRESPASS."

Phillips is glad that the original take of *Visions of Angels* wasn't included on the ARCHIVE box set, which it was at one point being considered for. He feels that putting out the earlier, inferior version might tarnish the song's image. "I think it's okay people hearing things that they never have heard a better version of. But to hear a song which they know and like in a really grim form . . ."

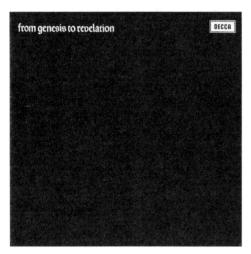

In March 1969, Decca released FROM GENESIS TO REVELATION. The label had told the group and King that, since there was already an American group calling itself Genesis, they'd have to find a new name. They refused, but a compromise was reached. Actually, it was a compromise in the sense that Spinal Tap's none-more-black *Smell The Glove* cover was a compromise. The group's name did not appear on the sleeve, except as part of the title, FROM GENESIS TO REVELATION. (The idea being that the group would be billed as "Revelation" in America.) To further confuse matters, the American group called Genesis named their album *In The Beginning*, which was the title of one of the songs on FROM GENESIS TO REVELATION.

With its somber, hymn book-style cover, and no artist credit, FROM GENESIS TO REVELATION was filed in the Religious section of many record shops. Needless to say, the album didn't reach its intended audience, and only sold about 650 copies. ("And we knew virtually everyone that bought them," says Phillips.) This figure would be boosted considerably by the numerous reissues that appeared after Genesis became successful.

Although the original release has inevitably become a prized collector's item, the music it contained is still easily obtainable. Since the mid-70's, FROM GENESIS TO REVELATION has appeared countless times on vinyl and CD, with most versions adding the four Decca

JAPANESE RELEASE OF FROM GENESIS TO REVELATION LP

single sides to the line-up. (More recent versions have added early demos and / or interviews with Jonathan King.)

"Now we are the band without a name, but we have a record and we want to give it to you, name or not," read the insert that was packaged with the original LP. "It was a hard sound to get together, conceived over a period of months, with rainbows of music color filtering through the glass partition on to the sliding faders and echo knobs, searching for the pot of gold . . . Thoughts of a very young group looking shortly back and far forward, over the grey mountains of time shrouded in the mist of harmony. We hope you will find no one to compare it with, not because we don't want to be compared, but because there are better things to do. We hope you won't find it pretentious or humorless because it was intended to be neither. It was intended to be just very pleasant. Melodic, unusual, containing what is natural and genuine . . . Listen and cast your mind into the sound spectrum. Hear what you hear, smile and enjoy, from the beginning to the end, from Genesis to Revelation."

"I felt the album was a pretty terrible version of a lot of the songs we were doing," Tony Banks told *Trouser Press* in 1982. "One or two stand up. I think *Silent Sun* works; *In the Wilderness* is probably the best song on the album. *The Serpent* was really good when we used to play it, but the version on the album was terrible — and that applies to a few of the others. *One Day* is another song which was really nice when we used to play it, but didn't sound good on the album. There were nice things on it, but not exceptional."

Although largely ignored, the album did earn a decent review in the underground London paper *International Times*, which called FROM GENESIS TO REVELATION "a beautiful, entirely valid musical exercise." The reviewer lamented the fact that Decca had given the album virtually no publicity. A rare ad for the album proclaimed, "Revelation is the giving of knowledge to man. Genesis is the source of new knowledge.") Former Anon singer Richard MacPhail was in London at the time and happened to pick up the *International Times* which included the Genesis review. He immediately phoned Peter Gabriel and read him the review. Before long, MacPhail would once again find himself working with former bandmates Phillips and Rutherford, although not in a performing capacity.

On June 27, 1969, the album version of *Where The Sour Turns To Sweet* was released as a single, backed with *In Hiding*. This third Decca single did little to improve the group's standing and it proved to be their last release for the label. The label did consider issuing a remixed version of *In The Beginning* as a single, but it never materialized, although acetates have surfaced. Clearly, Genesis was not a priority for Decca. It's indicative of the band's relationship with the label that, whenever they showed up to see their A&R man, the receptionist would tell him that a group called the Janitors was here to see him!

Chapter 3: A Voyage Into The Dark

The members of Genesis did little to promote their first album. By the time FROM GENESIS TO REVELATION came out, Tony Banks was studying Physics at Sussex University, uncertain about his future with the group. Although he had no access to a piano while at university, he wrote songs on his acoustic guitar, including what became the *Guaranteed Eternal Sanctuary Man* section of *Supper's Ready* and the music for two songs that would appear years later on A TRICK OF THE TAIL.

Peter Gabriel was equally unsure about continuing with the group. He had been offered a place at the London School of Film Technique and was very tempted to take it. Even after he chose music as his career focus, Gabriel retained his interest in film. For a number of years, he would attempt to make a film version of Genesis' album THE LAMB LIES DOWN ON BROADWAY. Although that project wouldn't reach fruition, Gabriel eventually found success writing music for films, including BIRDY and THE LAST TEMPTATION OF CHRIST.

By the summer of 1969, Phillips and Rutherford had decided to "turn pro," and there was a period of uncertainty while Banks and Gabriel vacillated about whether or not they would join them again. In the meantime, Ant and Mike spent many hours together with their 12-string guitars, developing the gentle acoustic sound that would play a big part in the next stage of Genesis' development. As an affirmation of his desire to continue, Mike Rutherford bought himself a Gibson bass and a Marshall cabinet. During the next year or so, Rutherford would develop into an accomplished bassist, his skill on the instrument being an important factor in the sound Genesis would develop of the next few years.

> "Anthony and Mike wanted to go professional; Peter and I didn't," Tony recalled in an interview with *Trouser Press*. "We were both bound to do other things: I was at the university and Peter wanted to go to film school. We said we would help them out for the summer until they found new members. At the end of that summer (1968) I found I was really getting into it and maybe wanted to stay. One

day I'd persuade Peter to stay, and the next he'd persuade me. We couldn't really decide because it was quite a commitment."

By the end of the summer, Gabriel and Banks had decided to give Genesis another chance, and the group began writing new material. One of the first pieces developed in this era was an acoustic epic called *The Movement*, which included bits that would later be recycled into songs such as *Stagnation* and *Get 'Em Out By Friday*. *The Movement* has variously been described as lasting either twenty or forty-five minutes — it's probable that it was different lengths at different stages in its development. (While preparing the ARCHIVE box set, the group looked — without success — for a version of *The Movement* that had been recorded at John Silver's house in Oxford.) Genesis also revised existing material, expanding the unreleased *Visions Of Angels*, and working an instrumental passage from FROM GENESIS TO REVELATION into a new song called *Twilight Alehouse*.

Having parted ways with Jonathan King, the members of Genesis were free to write for themselves, rather than tailoring their work to someone else's expectations. Their new musical direction could only be pursued in isolation. The input of anyone who was looking to sell more than 650 copies of a record would only have hindered their development during this transitional phase.

> "We went our own separate ways," says Phillips of the split with King. "And then the group was forced, slightly reluctantly, into going on the road and thereby, through a lot of grief and hard work, sort of found its truly original voice. The other way hadn't worked. Everyone wanted to be composers, you see, and just write, or just be a studio band. But it didn't work. So it was either give up or try and turn ourselves into a playing band. It was a voyage into the dark, really."

On August 20, 1969, the group made their first post-Decca recordings. A demo session at Regent B Studio in London produced takes of *Family* (which later became known as *Dusk*), *White Mountain*, *Going Out To Get You* and *Pacidy*. (With the exception of *White Mountain*, these versions all subsequently appeared on the ARCHIVE box set.) Part of the reason for doing this tape was to help everyone decide if it was worth continuing on. The demo tape was flatly rejected by every agent and label the group played it to. It's indicative of the Genesis spirit that this complete lack of interest only reinforced their dedication to stay the course.

All except John Silver, that is. Not long after the new demo tape was completed, the drummer left the band to go to university in America. He obviously had a special place in the hearts of Ant and Mike because they wrote a song in his honour, a gorgeous acoustic number entitled *The Silver Song*.

> "Mike and I wrote it together for John Silver when he left," says Phillips. "Genesis never did it, but Phil Collins did a single version of it with Mike and myself at the end of 1973. It was going to be released as a single, but that never happened." *The Silver Song* was finally released — in demo form — on the CD reissue of Phillips' PRIVATE PARTS & PIECES album. "It wasn't actually done as an album track," he recalls. "It was actually done as a kind of song demo, in a slightly

more country style. The song is slightly out-of-character with normal stuff that we ever wrote. It was a slightly kind of laid-back country-style song."

John Silver's place behind the kit was taken by John Mayhew. With the new drummer in tow, Genesis set about becoming a real, working band — as opposed to a group of school friends who wrote songs and recorded them. In order to make this transition, to turn "pro," they would have to start performing live. Not only was a rigorous performance schedule necessary to sharpen their musical chops, it was necessary for a more practical reason. They were now without a record deal and without Jonathan King's patronage. For the time being, live gigs were their only potential source of income.

In September, the group spent a couple of weeks rehearsing their new material at Send Barns. In the middle of this time, Phillips and Rutherford decided to demo some of the acoustic material they had been writing together.

> "We did stacks and stacks of two-12-strings recordings," Ant recalls. "Because we had a feeling that, once we hit the cottage and went on the road, that we would sort of lose sight of all that stuff. And indeed it turned out to be the case. There are a number of things on it that I would say are of some interest to Genesis fans, because it's stuff that sounds quite similar to stuff that ended up on the later songs."

Titles recorded by Mike and Ant that weekend included *Farewell, The Silver Song, Queen Bettine, What Is The Meaning?, The Geese And The Ghost, F Sharp* and *F Sharp 2. F Sharp* was essentially an early instrumental version of *The Musical Box*, comprising several of the key sections that would be utilized in that song. The title referred to the guitar tuning Mike and Ant used on this number. Such unusual tunings were integral to the distinctive two-12-string-guitars sound they were developing.

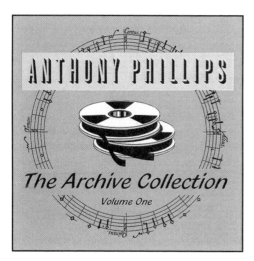

Mike and Ant's demos of *F Sharp, F Sharp 2* and *The Geese And The Ghost* were released in 1998 on Phillips' excellent CD THE ARCHIVE COLLECTION (on the Blueprint label). *What Is The Meaning?* and *Farewell* were included on a limited edition bonus EP included with early pressings of the album. THE ARCHIVE COLLECTION provides plenty of insight into Ant's contribution to Genesis. It also provides an introduction to some of his later solo material.

In September 1969, Genesis landed a gig, of sorts. The occasion was a teenager's birthday party at the home of a Mrs. Balme, for which they were paid £25. A somewhat inauspicious venue, considering that the band had already released a major label album and three singles, yet this was a time of rebirth for Genesis. "At that stage, we hadn't really rehearsed," says Phillips. "Nobody really listened to us, to be honest."

In those days, Genesis' repertoire included songs from their first album (*The Serpent, In Limbo, Window, In Hiding, One Day, In The Beginning and The Conqueror*), a few that would end up on TRESPASS (*Visions Of Angels, White Mountain* and *Dusk*) and others that would not be released at all (*Black Sheep, Going Out To Get You, Eastern Magic Boogie, Build Me A Mountain, Digby, Masochistic Man, Grandma, Sitting On Top Of The World, Nice, Pacidy, Babies, Let Us Now Make Love, Little Leaf, Epic, Think Again* and *Key To Love*).

Over the summer of 1969, the group had been staying at the houses of various band members' parents, but a more stable arrangement was needed. In November, they moved into a cottage owned by Richard MacPhail's parents, in the woods in Dorking. Richard became their roadie and the unofficial sixth member. The group stayed at the cottage all winter. "Getting it together in the country" was a common practice among British bands of the early 70's and it was just what Genesis needed. They spent the winter days writing new material and rehearsing, often spending ten or eleven hours a day honing their increasingly complex new songs. They stayed in the MacPhails' cottage until April 1970, the isolation allowing them to develop a sound that was less susceptible to outside influences. From this point on, there would be no more compromises, no more trying to sound like the Bee Gees.

The new Genesis sound was an ambitious mixture of electric and acoustic music. Pastoral acoustic 12-string guitar sequences segued into heavy electric sequences and back again. There was a compelling epic quality to their best work, taking the listener on a musical journey. In those days, the group was at its best when it could stretch out.

> "Procol Harum had started doing things like that," Tony Banks recalled. "Which showed us a longer form could be an interesting thing to try, but using acoustic instruments as well as electric stuff."

In contrast to other artists of the period, Genesis' lengthy musical workouts were never improvisational. Every note was worked out and planned at the rehearsal stage and, despite the length of the songs, Genesis rarely lapsed into self-indulgence. They had tried writing short, catchy pop songs but, even with Jonathan King's commercial instincts to guide them, the charts did not beckon. If they couldn't get arrested with radio-friendly pop songs, they might as well forget about being commercial and follow their instincts. They did, but it wasn't easy.

> "It was a bit too intense," says Anthony Phillips of the winter spent at the cottage. "It was very secluded. We didn't really live proper lives, and therein lay the seed of some of the later troubles, mainly for me. But it was a very fertile period. The group went from a rough acoustic sort of combo, if you like, into a proper live band, with quite an original style, quite a tight unit. There was a lot of hard work."

> "We just used to get up and play all day, basically. We virtually never went out

— never went out to the pub, never did anything, really. It was wonderful countryside, but we never even went out for any walks. We were very, very determined."

By this point, Genesis had already established a collective songwriting approach that was — at least in theory — democratic. Each member would present their material to the 'committee,' who would deem it worthy or unworthy of inclusion in their repertoire. Often, the decision had as much to do with personality as anything else. Banks in particular seemed to be good at getting his ideas across, but Gabriel and Phillips also managed to get much of their material in.

In November 1969, the group did their first real public performances. Their unofficial manager at the time was Marcus Bicknell.

"They had just left Charterhouse and they were rehearsing *The Knife* and everything for the first Charisma album," he recalls. "THE FROM GENESIS TO REVELATION album had done nothing and they wanted to get on the road. So it was me that gave them their first gigs, because I was an agent. Then I left the agency and took over managing them, but it was really just driving the bread van, which was their gig wagon. Some of the gigs were for a fiver (five pounds) and some of them were for £20, but at least it got them going."

"The repertoire was FROM GENESIS TO REVELATION," Bicknell says of the band's early gigs. "From time to time they would be very, very daring and try one of the new ones, in particular *The Knife*, which was pretty proficient by the time they were doing some of the slightly bigger gigs, like supporting name bands at Uxbridge Technical College and Leicester Poly and Ewell Technical College. But they were very underground, and even the college kids found Genesis difficult to understand early on. You know, they couldn't dance to it or shake their heads around like they could to Blodwyn Pig or Black Sabbath, which was who they were supporting. So they were kind of tentative. I wouldn't say timid, but they were tentative about their music and how it would go down. But, even though they were totally lacking in confidence, they were absolutely intent that it was the right thing. Peter in particular was expressing something which was alien to a lot of bands and certainly to the audiences. He wasn't dressing up much, but he was certainly beginning to be nice and weird onstage."

Mrs. Balme's house notwithstanding, Genesis' first real gig was in November at Brunel University, Uxbridge. It was the first of many Genesis gigs in which the band's confidence was shaken by technical trouble, in this case Ant's guitar. "My guitar went wildly out of tune," Phillips recalls of that show. "It was pretty terrifying, actually. But they seemed to quite like us."

"When we first went on the road, it was a very gentle little thing," says Phillips. "We used to actually swap guitars. Guitars used to be passed over the stage. Tony Banks used to play my Stratocaster through his Leslie organ speaker. These sort of things stopped very quickly, because it wasn't practical. We started off with *In The Beginning* and a lot of acoustic stuff. But it went pretty quickly, because nobody would listen. The tech gigs at the weekend, obviously everyone just basically wanted to have a few pints and have a good time. A kind of intense acoustic group wasn't really what they wanted to listen to. So those songs had to go ..."

"We did a lot of acoustic concerts back in 1969 with three guitars and a piano," Gabriel explained. "It was considered a very trendy thing to do. We played a lot of pubs, but our music was so quiet that if forty people were ordering drinks and talking, they'd drown us out."

"The stuff with more power started to come in," Phillips continues. "We started writing heavier stuff. *The Knife* was actually written before, but there were a fair few new things that came in. Once we were really established on the road, there wasn't an enormous amount of time to write new stuff, because it was quite complex. Within a couple of months of starting, our set was pretty much established. We started with something powerful. We did *Dusk* and *White Mountain*, and we used to end with *Visions Of Angels, Twilight Alehouse* and *The Knife*."

The band did their second public gig at Twickenham Technical College. They received £50 for their performance — a good sum of money in those days. Other gigs from this era were played at such venues as the Kingston Hotel in London, Worley Social Club in Birmingham and the Cheadle Hulme Youth Club in Manchester.

"We picked up gigs here and there," says Phillips. "There were good ones and bad ones, but the reputation gradually grew." Before long, the band ditched their trusty bread van and began using an old taxi to get from gig to gig. "Lots of irate old ladies were very angry when we failed to stop for them," recalled Peter Gabriel, years later.

One of the more successful shows from this period was a performance at Eel Pie Island, Twickenham. "For our first gig there we had a fee of five pounds," Mike Rutherford told *Beat Instrumental* years later. "But, because we went down so well and (the promoter) liked us, he gave us seven pounds."

When the band weren't gigging, they were ensconced in the cottage, working on the new songs.

"It was a very exotic place," says Bicknell. "Whenever they weren't rehearsing, they'd be listening to other bands. I remember them spending hours with (a certain Crosby, Stills, Nash and Young track). They played the track over and over again and were modeling something they were doing on that sound. It was a great creative period."

During this period, the group was also heavily influenced by King Crimson's debut album IN THE COURT OF THE CRIMSON KING.

Genesis' first major achievement of 1970 was a radio session, for the BBC's *Night Ride* program. Since FROM GENESIS TO REVELATION had gotten little exposure, the chance to have their music heard on the radio was a great opportunity. It was also a chance to showcase some of the new songs they had been writing. On January 22, the group assembled at the Beeb's Maida Vale Studio 4, with producer Alec Reid. There they recorded *The Shepherd, Let Us Now Make Love, Stagnation, Looking For Someone, Dusk* and *Pacidy*.

"We were just writing and writing then, with very little to work towards," recalled Mike Rutherford. "And suddenly that first session appeared, and we had a goal to work towards." *The Shepherd* was particularly noteworthy for featuring Tony Banks as lead singer on some sections — a role he would not reprise until his solo album THE FUGITIVE twelve years later.

Banks was not especially happy with the first BBC session.

> "I remember the sessions being very hurried," he commented. "And musically we would have preferred to have spent more time getting it right. We weren't that happy with the end result, but we look back with affection."

Producer Alec Reid was certainly impressed with the group's first radio session, stating, "I rate this group very highly." Others at the Beeb agreed, noting the group's "intriguing tone colors" and giving them an enthusiastic "pass." The session was broadcast on April 1 and, unlike many vintage BBC sessions, the tape has survived, allowing several of these recordings to appear on the ARCHIVE box set.

Shortly before the NIGHT RIDE session, Genesis were asked to provide music for a BBC documentary about a painter named Mick Jackson. With producer Paul Samwell-Smith, they recorded about fifteen minutes' worth of music, in four sections: *Provacation* (similar to *Looking For Someone*), *Frustration* (a vocal number, which later became *Anyway*), *Manipulation* (featuring elements of *The Musical Box*) and *Resignation* (AKA *Peace*). Although the documentary wasn't finished, the group were pleased with the tape and asked Samwell-Smith to produce them. Samwell-Smith wasn't interested in producing the group, but he did recruit Gabriel to play flute on a Cat Stevens track he was producing, Katmandu.

Through January and February, Genesis gigged regularly in the Greater London area, appearing at such venues as:

° Ewell Technical College (on a bill with Atomic Rooster and Nick Drake)

° Eel Pie Island

° Queen Mary College

° Brunel University

° Twickenham Technical College

° Kingston Hotel

- ° Hurlington Tennis Club
- ° Revolution and the Blaises Club
- ° Essex University in Colcester

They made their first appearance at London's legendary Marquee club on February 4th, 1970, and were back again on the 19th.

There was a definite strategy behind the band's set lists during this era. They'd start off quietly, with four or five acoustic numbers, then add more dynamics with *White Mountain*, *Stagnation* and *Looking For Someone*, before building to the electric climax of *The Knife*, a powerful number about a revolutionary leader. The new material was growing stronger with each performance, and the FROM GENESIS TO REVELATION numbers were soon gone from the set.

On March 1, 1970, Genesis opened for Mott The Hoople at the Farx Club, Southall, Middlesex. Later that month, they opened for David Bowie at the Roundhouse. (A brief clip of the Roundhouse performance was played by Peter Gabriel during a late 70's radio interview.)

Towards the end of March, the group landed a regular Tuesday night slot at Upstairs at Ronnie Scott's in London. A producer named John Anthony caught one of the Ronnie Scott's gigs and was very impressed. At the time, Anthony was a staff producer for Charisma Records. He came back to Ronnie Scott's the following week, accompanied by Tony Stratton-Smith.

Stratton-Smith — "Strat" to friends — owned Charisma Records. A former journalist and manager (whose stable of clients included Beryl Marsden and Creation), Stratton-Smith had started Charisma in 1969 to provide a more daring alternative to the major labels. Initial signings included, not surprisingly, Strat's management clients the Nice and Van Der Graaf Generator. Other acts were soon added to the roster, a diverse assortment including Monty Python's Flying Circus, Clifford T. Ward, Rare Bird, Emerson, Lake & Palmer, String Driven Thing, Rick Wakeman and Lindisfarne. But the label's greatest success was to come from the group and solo efforts of Genesis.

Once Tony Stratton-Smith took an interest in Genesis, the band was on its way to the proverbial big time. It wouldn't be a particularly quick or easy journey, but the group had found a label willing to invest the necessary time and effort in them. Within a couple of weeks of that Ronnie Scott's gig, Strat signed them to Charisma.

Stratton-Smith was particularly taken with Gabriel's stage presence. "He has a touch of evil about him when he gets onstage. He almost reminds me of Jagger at times," he commented. However, it was only onstage that Gabriel became extroverted. Offstage he was shy and very 'normal.' Sonja Kristina of the group Curved Air remarked (in a 1970 *Melody Maker* "Blind Date" column) that Gabriel was "surprisingly inconspicuous offstage, but on it he is really good. He comes to life as soon as he walks on. He's like an actor — when he gets onstage he can really do things."

> "They started picking up some reviews and people were realizing that they had some value," says Marcus Bicknell. "It was at that stage that they began to think that I had run my course with them. I can remember a long evening at the country club in Hempstead with Banks and Rutherford. At least they had the honesty to express their doubts, to express the need to get a heavyweight manager and a big record company. Then Tony Stratton-Smith of Charisma made the record offer and he said, 'Here's the record deal and oh, by the way, I'll manage them as well.'"

On April 11, Genesis opened for Deep Purple at the DeMontfort Hall in Leicester and, two days later, the band played for the first time at Friar's, Aylesbury. Over the next few years, Friar's would become one of their favorite venues, and its owner, David Stopps would prove to be an invaluable Genesis supporter. Even at this first appearance, the audience reaction brought the group out for three encores. Although he only paid them £10 for this first appearance, Stopps immediately saw the group's potential and upped their fee to £30 for their second appearance. His support and belief in the band was crucial at this stage in their career. Genesis' second Friars appearance, on June 15, drew an even bigger audience than the first, justifying David Stopps' 300% increase in their fee.

Chapter 4: Going Out To Get You

Genesis spent much of June and July 1970, at Trident Studios in London, recording their second LP. They were well prepared when they arrived at the studio, having rehearsed extensively at the Gin Mill Club in Surrey. The sessions for what would become the TRESPASS album were produced by John Anthony and engineered by Robin Cable. The tape operator was a young man named David Hentschel, who would eventually play a much more significant role in the group's recording career.

TRESPASS was a big step forward for Genesis. Charisma spent a considerable amount of money to book the band into Trident, which was one of the best studios in London at the time. A couple of years earlier, the Beatles had recorded some of the WHITE ALBUM there, and Genesis were excited to be recording in the same studio that the Fabs had used. Whereas FROM GENESIS TO REVELATION had been made very quickly on two four-track machines, the group now had sixteen tracks (and considerably more time) at their disposal. They made the most of this by overdubbing layers of 12-string guitars, sometimes six at a time, creating rich, atmospheric tracks. With hindsight, though, the band felt that they did too many overdubs, and that Gabriel's vocals sometimes tended to get buried in the mix. Although they weren't completely happy with the production of TRESPASS, they got along well with John Anthony and chose to work with him again on their next album. "John Anthony was very amusing, and just good fun, really," says Anthony Phillips.

Certainly the relationship between the band and John Anthony was quite different from the one they'd had with Jonathan King.

> "We look on him as another member of the band," said Gabriel of Anthony in a 1970 interview with *Melody Maker*, "rather than the one with all the power, the one who dictates what we want and what we don't want. The group did all the arrangements and we considered the type of sound we wanted before we went into the studio."

> "John Anthony was producing Rare Bird, who were on Charisma, and also doing Van der Graaf Generator," recalled Banks in *Trouser Press*. "So he was almost the Charisma house producer. Even then we all had quite a strong say in the production."

Phillips remembers the TRESPASS sessions as being "much, much more professional" than the sessions for the first album.

> "I mean, we knew what we were doing, you know? I wouldn't say we were quite

hardened pros, but we'd been on the road a long time. It was a little bit daunting going into a huge studio like Trident. I remember having big arguments with the engineer — who was a very established engineer called Robin Cable — about how to record my 12-string. I think we had the confidence of being on the road for a long time and knowing our sound, having a sound, and we wanted it to be that way. I insisted on my 12-string being recorded in what he thought was a really weird way. I'll always remember him turning to me and saying, 'That doesn't sound like a 12-string.' And I just said, 'Well, it does. It's what I want it to sound like.' Because so many people had 12-strings that sounded like a kind of washboard, where all you heard was the plectrum noise. And I wanted every note to be heard as a note and to be sort of sparkling."

"There were one or two difficulties, but it was a much, much more professional thing. I don't remember the sessions as being particularly inspiring, but I remember it being very professional and pretty exciting, hearing the sound on these huge speakers. It was great to hear it being properly recorded."

Banks played piano, and used a Hammond organ on several tracks, including *The Knife*. Onstage, *The Knife* had been a much longer piece, sometimes stretching out to nineteen or twenty minutes. "We cut out a whole section to make the album version of *The Knife*," Banks recalled. Freed from Jonathan King's anti-organ stance, Banks used the instrument more and more, making it one of the most important parts of the Genesis sound. Even earlier numbers like *Going Out To Get You* were re-worked onstage, with organ replacing the piano. For the closing number on TRESPASS, it was a toss-up between *The Knife* and *Going Out To Get You*, both of which were stage favorites. The group opted for the former, possibly intending to save the latter for a single release. (A version of *Going Out* was recorded as a possible single at one point.)

Anthony Phillips didn't feel that TRESPASS was necessarily representative of the band's best material at the time. He felt it included the songs in their repertoire that worked best onstage, while leaving off some other good songs that just didn't work as well live.

"I think the one regret that we perhaps all had was that, when we came to do the album, there wasn't time to go back to any of those other quieter numbers," he says. "We just really reproduced our live set on the album. There were some other very good songs that just didn't make it on the road, given that it was those sort of hit-'em-hard gigs. *Let Us Now Make Love* is one of them."

That song was one of the highlights of Genesis' early gigs. Among those who praised it highly was Nick Drake, with whom they shared the bill a few times. The only available recording of Genesis performing the song is the radio session version on the ARCHIVE box set, which Phillips regards as "a very poor version. It was a BBC recording and we weren't really up for it. It's a pretty awful performance really." Nonetheless, the song was a classic early Genesis number and, with no other released version to compare it to, the BBC recording sounds superb. Tony Banks has said that *Let Us Now Make Love* would have been recorded for TRESPASS if the group hadn't planned on holding it back for a single.

Another of the songs Genesis didn't record for TRESPASS was *Twilight Alehouse*, which they recorded several years later, circa FOXTROT. By the time they recorded it, Banks said, "it was played out." Other stage songs that didn't make it onto TRESPASS included *The Shepherd, Pacidy, Grandma* (said to be similar in style to *Happy The Man*), *Little Leaf, Digby, Stranger, I've Been Travelling All Night Long* and *Jamaican Longboat*.

Phillips comments on some of the acoustic numbers feeling that they . . .

> "kind of lost it, really. I think, in a way, they were sort of battered, they were beaten into submission by the road. I think the love went out of them, in a way, and when it came up to the album, it was too much of an effort to get them back again. Time deemed that we had to stick to the tried and tested stuff that we'd been signed for. I mean Charisma had come along and heard this stuff and that's what they were signing us for."

Banks, too, has expressed regret that more of the early acoustic material wasn't recorded.

As was the policy during the Gabriel years, the songs on TRESPASS were group-written, yet often one or two members were the main writers of a particular number. *The Knife* was largely written by Peter and Tony, but evolved with group input, while *White Mountain* featured lyrics by Tony.

"*Visions Of Angels* was basically my song," says Phillips, "with, obviously, strong additions from the others." That song, *Dusk* and *Let Us Now Make Love* are good indicators of Ant's contribution to the group's sound. Much of the early Genesis style grew from the gently cascading sound that Phillips and Rutherford coaxed from their 12-string guitars.

> "I mean, obviously I was involved in parts of the writing of *The Knife* and some of the heavier stuff," Phillips points out. "So it wouldn't be right to say I was only responsible for the gentle acoustic things. It's difficult to say who wrote what, but if I had to distill it, I'd say, 'Well, Mike and I started the two-12-strings thing, really.' That was very much the sum of two parts."

The album was generally well received. Writing in *Sounds*, Jerry Gilbert called it . . .

> "an extremely picturesque album where the lyrics are highlighted in the foreground of some fat, melodic chords. Liberal use of keyboards and twelve-string guitars captures the mood of the stories admirably. Every structure and every scene has been meticulously threaded together . . ."

Although by no means a huge hit, TRESPASS ended up selling about ten times as many copies as FROM GENESIS TO REVELATION. As well as the improvements on the musical front, the record boasted a much more compelling sleeve design. The striking cover artwork was done by Paul Whitehead, who had met the group through John Anthony. Whitehead also did cover art for Van Der Graaf Generator, another group Anthony was producing at the time. Anthony had taken Whitehead to see a Genesis gig at Ronnie Scott's. "I knew something was going on," Whitehead recalls. "I knew it was different."

"We spent quite a lot of time together, so the cover kind of evolved as part of the album," he says. "I knew what they were all about, I'd hear them chatting over breakfast . . . You could tell from the songs, really, where they were going."

Peter, Mike, Tony, Ant and John would play Whitehead the songs as they rehearsed them, bringing him into the creative process from the beginning.

"And then I would say, 'Hey, you know what? I think a pen and ink thing would be good for this'," he recalls. "And they said 'That sounds nice — what kind of thing are you thinking of?' So then I'd go and get some books, and I'd show them styles — 'You can do it like this or like that . . .' And they'd say, 'Oh yeah, something like that would be great.' And then we came up with the idea of making (the *Trespass* cover) very pastoral, you know, and then that hint of violence with the knife."

To the band's amazement, Whitehead slashed his own picture with a razor blade, then inserted a dagger that was rented from a prop house and photographed the defaced image. "They thought I was crazy!" he remembers. "They didn't believe I was going to do it, but I just took out this razor blade and, with one slash, it was done."

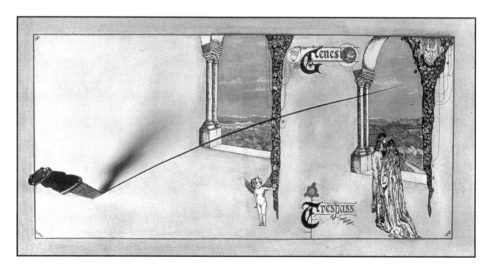

The Knife was released as a single in Britain, split into two parts for the A-side and B-side. Not surprisingly, it didn't chart. But hit singles were not really important during this stage of the group's career. The market had changed a lot towards the end of the 60's, with many record buyers more geared towards albums rather than singles. This was perfect for Genesis, whose music could only be properly absorbed over the course of an album or a gig.

Just as things were finally starting to come together, Genesis suffered a near-fatal blow. During the TRESPASS sessions, Anthony Phillips told the others that he was leaving the group.

Before the TRESPASS sessions, the guitarist had "already been quite ill, actually," he explains:

"The band had had to stop, because I'd had pneumonia. I just got completely washed out of the whole thing. My health was really a bit of a mess, to be honest. I went right downhill. I was almost forced into deciding. The band was off the road for three weeks. And I think, by the time I came back in and tried to make a go of it, my heart had just gone out of it, really. And it was extremely unfair on the band to expect them to kind of put up with this. I mean, we'd just signed this deal with Charisma. I just couldn't handle the pace, to be honest."

"There was quite a lot of tension in the group," Phillips continues. "I think it didn't help that we all lived in the same place. I mean, eventually you realize it is a job, and you must get away from it, however much you love it. But at that stage we worked too many hours, living it. I mean, artistic work has to be very controlled, in terms of the amount of hours you do. You blow a fuse if you over-cook it. And not only did we over-cook it, but we were all living in the same place and never getting away from it. Looking back on it, it looks almost inevitable that things were going to go wrong given that. It's a very unhealthy way to approach things. I'm surprised more didn't go wrong. There were quite a few arguments, but I'm surprised that nobody killed each other, really. I mean, it was all very polite."

Although he's not credited on the album, guitarist Kim Shaheen says he added some guitar parts during the TRESPASS sessions, after Phillips quit. Although his memories of the era are sketchy, he probably played on *Stagnation* and possibly other tracks, although he's not sure if his contributions were included in the final mix.

"I don't know for sure what, if anything was used," Shaheen says. "I fixed some parts that were needed to connect sections together. I don't know how much you know about the recording process, but the vocals are usually put on last, so I didn't always get to hear a vocal track — particularly if it hadn't been recorded yet. So as to tracks I've done, I don't always know what, which, and if I made the final mix."

It's likely that Shaheen was being tried out as a possible replacement for Phillips. "They didn't say Ant had officially quit," he recalls. "They just figured if they needed someone to replace him on guitar anyway it was better sooner than later."

After his departure, Anthony Phillips expanded his musical horizons, studying piano and classical guitar, and teaching music. He would still collaborate with Mike Rutherford, when the latter's increasingly busy schedule permitted. Although it would take several years for a solo album to appear, Ant was always working on his music. In the summer of 1970, he was already recording solo demos of songs like *God If I Saw Her Now, In Memoriam A.D.* and *Queen Bettine*. Sometimes, he'd take an unused Genesis idea and rework it into a new composition.

"There was one on my PRIVATE PARTS & PIECES 3 called *Old Wives Tale,* which was a Genesis song called *Little Leaf.* I think I'd stick my neck out here and say it was almost exclusively mine. There was a little bit of input from the others in the band version, but I just went back to my original version of it and changed it to a guitar duet. It was called *Little Leaf* on the road, and it's a good illustration of the type of song that we started off by doing."

"I did a piano version of *Let Us Now Make Love* on one of my PRIVATE PARTS AND PIECES series in the mid-80's. Because it was mainly my song, there was no problem. When it came to releasing the Genesis version, with all the lyrics and stuff on top, which had more input from everyone else, it got a bit complicated and we had to revert to it being a group composition."

Another early Genesis number, *Pacidy,* was re-worked into a Phillips solo track called *Field Of Eternity.*

Anthony Phillips' decision to pursue formal musical training brings up an interesting point about Genesis. Although the group's music was very complex and bore classical influences, Tony Banks was the only member with a strong formal background in music.

"I can't read music and I have absolutely no idea about chord sequences, chord structures or progressions," Mike Rutherford revealed in 1977. "But I think this actually helps me."

Certainly, Rutherford's more intuitive skills have provided a counterpoint to Banks' more technically correct approach. Mike's compositional input was seemingly as complex as Tony's, but the two approached their work from a very different perspective.

Phillips' departure was a huge loss to the band. He had been a seemingly indispensable part of the group's infrastructure and replacing him seemed like an impossible task. He had contributed a lot to the band's sound, in particular the interplay of his and Mike Rutherford's 12-string guitars.

"Once Anthony left, I didn't think the group would carry on," Banks told *Trouser Press.* "I was quite surprised when Mike and Peter said they wanted to continue. I said, 'OK, I'll stay — but I really think we should change the drummer. John Mayhew just wasn't right, didn't fit in. Everything he played was taught to him by the rest of us and I don't think his heart was in it. The drums definitely seemed weak to me."

Tellingly, although the records credited the composer as "Genesis," all the songs from the pre-Phil Collins era are registered as Banks / Phillips / Gabriel / Rutherford compositions. Clearly, before Collins joined, the drummer was not a part of the group-writing process, or at least wasn't regarded as such.

"They knew that they needed a good drummer, you know, a good sort of driving drummer," says Paul Whitehead. "Peter, Tony and Mike were pretty tight — they were pretty certain of what they wanted to do. And I think Peter, more than anybody, was pushing them ahead all the time. And he was the one that said, 'We need a good drummer.' "

In August 1970, an ad was placed in *Melody Maker*. It read, "Tony Stratton Smith requires drummer sensitive to acoustic music, and acoustic twelve-string guitarist." A few likely drummers were invited out to Mike Rutherford's parents' house in Surrey, to try their hand at some of the group's material, including *Twilight Alehouse, The Knife* and *Stagnation*. The last drummer to audition that day was Phil Collins.

A former child actor, Collins' early career included a stint in a West End production of the musical *Oliver!* (as the Artful Dodger) and an appearance in a film called CALAMITY THE COW. Although he'd been playing drums since the age of five, Phil's recording debut was with a group called Flaming Youth, whose live repertoire included a fifteen-minute version of *Norwegian Wood*. The group had also released an album, entitled ARK 2, a concept piece which, according to a *Melody Maker* write-up, dealt with "the escape from burning earth by the last space ship."

Phil initially spoke with Mike Rutherford on the phone. The young drummer mentioned that he'd worked with George Harrison, which no doubt helped him get an audition. Collins neglected to mention that the extent of his work with Harrison was a conga part on the *All Things Must Pass* sessions that wasn't included in the final mix.

Since Genesis were looking for a guitarist as well as a drummer, Phil brought his pal Ronnie Caryl along to the audition. Caryl had played with Phil in Flaming Youth and the Freehold, and was a good friend. As Ronnie's car pulled up at the Rutherfords' country house, the duo were impressed by the picturesque setting and by the sight of Michael Rutherford showing up clad in his dressing gown and slippers!

> "It was a lovely day," Phil told *Drums And Drumming* many years later. "The grand piano was pushed out onto the patio, and there was a big umbrella for the drum kit to set up underneath. I was a little early, as always, and they said, 'Go have a swim while we've got a couple of guys in front of you.' So while I was swimming I heard the other guys auditioning, and by the time I got to play I kind of knew everything. I didn't know the songs when I started swimming, but I did by the time I finished. I went in there and made it look a little hard, so it looked like I hadn't been cheating."

The group hired Collins for ten pounds a week salary and, on August 24, the new lineup reconvened at the Maltings in Farnham, to begin rehearsals. They initially tried working with Ronnie Caryl but, before long, it was clear that he wasn't the guitarist they were looking for. Although Ronnie didn't last with Genesis, he did play one or two gigs with them as a fill-in guitarist. He eventually ended up playing with Phil again — as rhythm guitarist on Collins' 1997 DANCE INTO THE LIGHT tour.

Ronnie Caryl didn't really like Genesis' music and this fact made it difficult for him to adapt to their style. Apparently, Collins wasn't too thrilled by the music either, initially regarding Genesis as a "poor man's Yes." (Collins was a big Yes fan at the time.) But Phil was skilled enough to adapt to the music and learnt to like it, especially as he began to bring his own sound and style to the Genesis sound. Among other things, Collins brought more of a jazz influence into the mix.

For the next couple of months, they rehearsed at the Maltings as a four piece. *The Musical Box* was developed during those rehearsals, although much of the music had been written during the Phillips era. The next few gigs were played as a quartet, with Banks playing the lead guitar lines on an electric piano run through a fuzzbox! Unreleased songs from this era included a song called *Wooden Mask* (later recorded as a potential single) and an instrumental called *Moss*.

On October 4, Collins made his debut with Genesis at the Marquee. Two days later, the rhythmically-reinforced group appeared at the British Legion Hall in Princes Risborough. Put on by David Stopps, this was one of Genesis' few gigs as a foursome. The group was beset by the technical difficulties that plagued them during their early years. During a half-hour delay, Gabriel filled time by chanting into the microphone, his voice drenched in echo. Both Banks and Rutherford improved as players during this period, as they stretched themselves to fill the void left by Anthony Phillips. But, despite their best efforts to compensate, it was a void that could only be filled by another guitarist.

Chapter 5: Looking For Someone

In October 1970, Genesis made another attempt to replace Anthony Phillips. David Stopps of Friar's suggested Mick Barnard, who had previously played with a group called Farm and a blues band called Smoky Rice. "Farm was a local band in Princes Risborough," says Barnard. "Dave (Stopps) was getting gigs for us, he was basically looking after us."

After Stopps mentioned that Genesis was looking for a guitarist, Barnard went to see them perform.

"I went and checked out the guitarist that was sitting in prior to me joining, Ronnie Caryl, over at Cambridge Corn Exchange," he recalls. "I thought, 'At least I can do as well as he can.' And, a few months later, Steve Hackett said the same thing about me! "

"Genesis came and played at Princes Risborough, at the British Legion Hall, and I went down with Dave to meet them," Barnard continues. "Phil Collins had just joined at that point. They were very good, I was very impressed. I couldn't believe how dynamic they were. I mean certainly they weren't doing their full repertoire, because they were in a learning stage with Phil. I went down in my little Mini to Mike Rutherford's father's house. And I played some stuff to them and they played some stuff to me. Mike was the first one I played guitar to and he persuaded me to come in. Then, basically, it was a case of, 'Here's the album,

TRESPASS. Go away and learn it.' I didn't think it was going to last, but I thought, I'll get in, have a go and then get out again. But I didn't realize it would be quite as quick as it was."

MICK BARNARD

Barnard gave up an apprenticeship, in a lab testing flight simulators, in order to commit himself to Genesis.

"I was still learning guitar at the time, basically, and it was quite a struggle," he says. "Some of the numbers that they were doing I found quite difficult. They had a specific technique and that was a lot of open string playing. There were a lot of open chords, with sort of single notes to make the chords up and things like that. It was designed for 12-string guitar. I think they really wanted a 12-string guitarist, which I definitely wasn't going to do." (Barnard played a Gibson acoustic 6-string with Genesis.) "I must admit, I had my reservations, because they were very regimented. You just couldn't move(outside the arrangement). There was no movement at all."

Steve Hackett — Barnard's successor — agrees with this assessment.

"We, as a band, tended to be obsessed with the idea of the form of the song," he says. "Everything was written, everything was crafted. Even the solos were worked out."

With the exception of *The Musical Box*, for which he wrote his own lead guitar parts, Barnard was told to simply copy Anthony Phillips' guitar parts on existing numbers like *Stagnation* and *The Knife*.

"Phil Collins and I got on quite well when I used to go off on a tangent playing some blues licks and things," says Barnard. "But they soon pulled me back! They seemed so dedicated. They'd come straight out of school, they'd never done any work, as such. And they had it all given to them on a plate, except of course Phil Collins. He did come up the normal way."

This was a transitional phase for Genesis, their sound was still developing and growing more powerful. "With the addition of Phil and Mick it's made me more rhythm conscious," Gabriel explained in a *Melody Maker* interview.

During Barnard's brief tenure, Genesis debuted *The Musical Box*, a number that had its roots in the Phillips era and would become a staple of their live set. Although parts of the song had been written by Phillips and Rutherford in 1969, *The Musical Box* came together while Barnard was with Genesis. Yet there exists no recording of him playing on it.

> "I never did record with them," he says. "We used to practice in North London in a practice room. We used to meet down there. Occasionally we'd meet at somebody's house to go through some numbers."

Although Barnard's tenure with Genesis lasted only a few months, they were busy months. Charisma released TRESPASS in October and it was important that the band got out on the road to support it. Genesis played several gigs a week, at venues like Club Liscard in Walasey, Friars, the Resurrection Club in Barnet, the Marquee, the Farx Club in Southall, the Gin Mill in Godalming (near Charterhouse), Victoria Road Hall in Chelmsford and even a Christmas dance at Aylesbury Grammar School.

On November 13, 1970, the group played at Rutherford College, at the University of Canterbury for a £40 fee. They played one sixty minute set on that occasion. In those days, depending on the venue, the group would do two 45-minute sets, or one 60-minute set.

STRATTON SMITH MUSIC LIMITED		ARTISTE GENESIS w/e 27/11/		DATE	
DATE	VENUE	ARRIVAL TIMES	PAYMENT	HOTEL	OTHER INFOR
Friday 20th P.T.O. for Thurs Hotel.	Harriot Watt, University, Edinborough.	Equipment: 6.39pm Artistes: A representive On stage: from the Agency will advise you spot	£60. C.O..	St. Margarets Hotel, 32/34 Murrayfield, West Edinborough. Tel No. 1170	27/6 each per night.
Saturday 21st	Lido Ballroom, Hallock, 18 miles from Edinborough	Equipment: t.b.a. Artistes: by rep. On Stage: from agency mins spot	£60. C.O.N.	Just off Edinborough-Glasgow road, Registered in Peter's name. Tel No.	
Sunday 22nd	Kinema Ballroom Dunfermline, 18 miles from Edinburgh.	Equipment: t.b.a. Artistes: by Rep. On Stage: mins spot	£60 C.O.N.	Tel No.	
Monday 23rd FREE		Equipment: Artistes: On stage: mins spot		Tel No.	
Tuesday 24th FREE		Equipment: Artistes: On stage: mins spot		Tel No.	
Wednesday 25th	Hermitage B/R Hitchin, Hertfordshire,	Equipment: 6.30pm Artistes: On stage 2x45's mins spots	50% of G.B.R. C.O.N.	Tel No.	
Thursday 26th	Dead End, Talbot Road, Blackpool.	Equipment: 6.30pm Artistes: On stage 2x45's mins spot	£40. C.O.N.	Tel No.	
Friday 27th	Nevilles Cross, College, Durham City, Northumberland	Equipment: 6.30pm Artistes: On Stage 2x45's mins spot	£70. cheque from T.K.A.		

A "GIG LIST", GIVEN TO MEMBERS OF GENESIS IN LATE 1970. LISTS THE BANDS UPCOMING ENGAGEMENTS, WITH DETAILS OF SET LENGTH, NUMBER OF SETS TO BE PLAYED, FEES, ETC.

The following day — more than two years after *The Silent Sun* failed to get them on *Top Of The Pops* — Genesis made their television debut. They appeared on a BBC 2 program called *Disco 2*, performing *The Knife*. Actually, Peter Gabriel was the only one who was actually performing — the other four were all miming to the backing track from the record! The afternoon taping, at the BBC's TV Center in Wood Lane, was later described by Gabriel as "fairly disastrous." The group appeared in front of a blue screen, with battle scenes added to underscore the song's theme. Mick Barnard remembers the show's producer, Steve Turner, becoming upset when Gabriel started swinging his microphone around, as he was prone to do during *The Knife*. "Don't do that!" shouted the producer, "That microphone's expensive!"

> "I was very nervous on that occasion," Gabriel told *Melody Maker* in reference to his TV debut. "I don't want to do TV again for a long time. I'm not just ... a performing animal being put through his tricks, how the (BBC) sound engineer saw it. I think the BBC has a condescending attitude to pop and pop musicians."

That evening, after the afternoon BBC taping, the group played two 45-minute sets at Watford Technical College. A few days later, they headed north for a three-date tour of Scotland. For £60 a night, they played at Harriot Watt University, Edinburgh on November 20, the Lido Ballroom, Ballock on the 21st, and the Kinema Ballroom, Dunfermline on the 22nd.

> "I think we were trying out some of the new stuff then," Barnard recalls. "Certainly things like *The Musical Box* I was well into."

Although he wasn't a 12-string player, Barnard worked hard at developing a lead guitar sound for the band.

> "I was trying to get a fuzz guitar sound that would actually penetrate the rest of the band," he explains. "I was having quite a lot of difficulty because as soon as you got the fuzz it went to very quiet, you couldn't get the dynamics there. So I used an old compressor and cranked it up really to the point of distortion and it was brilliant. And I used that through most of the tour."

After the Scottish jaunt, Genesis returned to England for more gigs:

o The Heritage Ballroom, Hitchin on November 25,
o The Dead End, Blackpool on the 26th,
o Neville's Cross College, Durham on the 27th,
o Imperial College, London on the 28th,
o The Farx Club, Southall on the 29th (Farx was one of Genesis' favorites)
o Letchworth Youth Club on the 30th
o Worcester College on December 4.

By this point, Genesis were being paid anywhere from £30 to £75 per gig.

Barnard's stint with Genesis only lasted a few months, and he quotes:

"I kept asking, 'Well, am I in the band or not?' And they really didn't make a commitment to me. So, in the end, I said, 'Well, what's happening?' I was getting more and more frustrated, because they only wanted the guitarist to play what they said he could play. It got to the point where they were trying out this other guitarist, Steve Hackett, but I didn't know about it. I realized that they were holding back for some reason or another."

Barnard's last show with Genesis was at High Wycombe Town Hall in January 1971. "My old band, Farm, were actually supporting," he recalls.

"They'd got a new guitarist and they were supporting us. And that was the last gig I played. They called me out to the van afterwards and said, 'We've got a new guitarist.' "

"I think I was a fill-in, basically. The fact that I didn't want to do 12-string was a thing for them. I could see the potential there and I thought, 'Well, surely I can bring some freeness into the band' — exactly what Phil Collins eventually went out and did on his own. Not as rigid. Peter Gabriel was very nice to me, him and Phil Collins I got on with. And I got on with Mike Rutherford. But Tony Banks, I couldn't ever get on with him. I was having real problems with him. Peter was very conscious of what he had done as far as me and Steve Hackett, and he was very apologetic, but I didn't get much out of the others, except for Mike Rutherford."

The feeling among the other members of Genesis was that Barnard was at the stage they had been at a year earlier. "He just wasn't good enough," said Tony Banks. "So we had to change him." At this point, the group may have been wondering whether they'd ever find anyone to take Anthony Phillips' place. The task of finding a replacement had fallen to Mike Rutherford, but it was decided that Banks and Gabriel should join in the search.

One December day, Gabriel was perusing the latest *Melody Maker* when a classified ad caught his eye: "Guitarist / writer seeks receptive minds determined to strive beyond existing stagnant musical forms." The short ad was Steve Hackett's latest bid to find some kindred musical spirits, something he'd been attempting without success for the previous few years. In his own words, Steve was "a young egotist, very much a would-be, waiting in the wings, having tried for five years to either form my own outfit or get into others."

Like the Charterhouse contingent, Hackett's musical style drew not only from pop and rock, but also from classical music.

"In about 1965, I heard a Segovia record," he remembers. "I'd only been playing guitar for about a year at that point and I realized, 'Boy, I've got a long way to go before I can manage this stuff.' It was not just the left-handed technique, with chords, but so much was going on with the right hand as well. And really that kind of style had nothing to do with rock at that point. Rock players were really 'plectrum players.' The idea of using the fingers of your right hand was something that took me many years to get together. I resisted it, initially. In a way, I wanted to fit in with everybody else's style. And then I found that I couldn't really do that. So I started developing a style despite myself, in a way."

Like most of Genesis, Steve had no formal musical training.

"Listening to those records was training enough," he explains, "And watching people. You can learn a lot by watching people. And exploring chords — I'm not even sure that you need training to be able to do that. I guess the more you delve into music, you more you find odd harmonies that seem to appeal to you. I was constructing chords and I thought 'That's not a real chord.' And then I would listen to a bit more Bach and I would discover that chord was indeed in use, and many hundreds of years ago. Just by listening, you can teach yourself an awful lot."

> **IMAGINATIVE   GUITARIST/**
> **writer   seeks   involvement   with**
> **receptive   musicians,   determined**
> **to strive beyond existing stagnant**
> **music forms. — Steve 730 2445.**

Peter Gabriel was intrigued by Hackett's ad.

"There was something in the wording of it that made me curious," he recalled in the Genesis *History* video. "A lot of the other guitarists we were coming across were into notes and flash and all that stuff. Steve was into atmospheres, and that's what attracted us."

Gabriel called Hackett, gave him a rundown of the group's history, and invited him to their free Christmas show at the Lyceum. But Steve's first taste of Genesis came in the listening booth of a record store, where he and his brother John gave TRESPASS a spin. Gabriel had advised him that *Stagnation* was particularly representative of what the band was about.

On December 28, at the Lyceum, Steve Hackett saw Genesis for the first time. It's safe to say that he was impressed by the audience reaction that night. Genesis' performance got them a standing ovation from the thousand fans who turned out. Still, Hackett was underwhelmed by certain aspects of the show.

"I thought that the presentation was pretty ramshackle, to be honest," he recalls. "And I remember thinking, 'I wonder if I could do as well as this?' I thought, 'There's room for improvement here. These guys are definitely not better than I am, so I think we can do business.' "

Tony and Peter went up to see Steve at his parents' flat. There Steve and his brother John put on a performance for them, rather than doing an run-of-the-mill audition. John played the flute, which inevitably gave the performance a feel akin to what Genesis were doing. And, unlike Mick Barnard, Steve was very much into the 12-string guitar at the time. Banks and Gabriel were suitably impressed and soon, with the approval of Collins and Rutherford, Steve was in.

"I was very concerned with the way the stage show looked," he says of his first impressions of Genesis. "I was keen that the band professionalize itself as much as possible. I wanted the band to get a Mellotron and have its own light show, so that we could control both dimensions much more closely. I wanted it to have the width and depth of an orchestra, and the control over the environment, in the same way that a theatre can be controlled. Musically, I think I brought an air of experimentation to it."

What impressed Genesis most was Steve's ability creating atmospheres and unusual sounds. "I'm very interested in the amount of sounds that are at your disposal with one instrument," he explained to *Guitar Player* in 1976. "All the different things you can put a guitar through to make it sound like a piano or a harp or a voice."

"We've got very little ambition in terms of instrumental techniques," Gabriel had told *Sounds* in late 1970. "We are more interested in having available textures of sound."

"Steve's strength was as a lead player with a great sound and quite weird stuff going on," Mike Rutherford recalled many years later during an interview with Intermusic.com. "It wasn't until later that Steve got hot for the acoustic and classical guitar. At that stage he was quite like Robert Fripp. We became less acoustic because of him and took me somewhere else with the electric guitar which was good."

Both Phil and Steve found the interaction between the members of Genesis markedly different from the other groups they had played in. In other bands, the players were all "mates" and expressed themselves well to each other. The members of Genesis were more like colleagues than friends and tended to be very reserved, due in no small part to their public school background. Steve has said that he would've liked to have gotten closer to Tony, for example, but felt that he would come up against a wall of reserve.

At his first gig with the band, at City University in January 1971, Hackett found himself confronted with the type of technical problem that frequently dogged Genesis in their early days.

"I was sharing a fuzz box with Tony Banks and that had been fine," he recalls. "I'd been using his Marshall Super Fuzz, which was fine for rehearsals. And then Richard MacPhail, who used to mix sound for us and do equipment in those days, handed me a new fuzz box on the night of the gig. It was a Shaftsbury Duo-Fuzz — a fuzz box which in time I came to love and adore and use in a fairly controlled manner. But that night I'd not used it before, and the thing just started feeding back like crazy. There was no way I could get the thing under control, which totally threw me, because I was trying to remember a zillion guitar parts. So, for that first gig, I played dreadfully. Most of the time, all I managed to do was feed back horrendously, so you probably couldn't hear the bum notes that I was playing. At least I hope not."

Adding to the chaos was Phil Collins' inebriated state. Phil was playing perfect drum fills — three inches to the left of every drum! Thankfully, Steve was too was too preoccupied with his uncontrollable feedback to notice Phil falling off his drumkit.

"I was too busy with my own misery to be aware of that," says Steve of Phil's performance. "All I knew was that I was trying to cope with my own problems. I must have died about a thousand deaths that night. It was my worst ever stage experience, and I've had a few."

When Steve unplugged his Gibson Melody Maker guitar at the end of the show, he feared he had just played his first and last gig with Genesis.

"I immediately assumed, after the gig, that I hadn't cut it at all and that the band was destined to find another guitarist. I thought, 'Maybe turning professional isn't as easy as I thought!'"

There *was* a huge argument backstage after the gig but, to Steve's surprise, none of the anger was directed at him. "Luckily, no one steamed into me," he recalls.

CONCERT AD FOR "CHARISMA PACKAGE TOUR".

With Steve on board, Genesis resumed their relentless pace of gigging. From late January to mid-February, 1971, they took part in the "Charisma Package Tour." Sharing a bill with fellow Charisma acts Lindisfarne and Van Der Graaf Generator (Genesis went on first), they played:

o The Lyceum in London
o Birmingham Town Hall
o Colston Hall in Bristol
o Sheffield City Hall
o St. George's Hall in Bradford
o The Manchester Free Trade Hall
o Newcastle City Hall
o The Dome in Brighton
o The Winter Gardens, Bournemouth.

In between, they slotted in a few other gigs, playing at Aylesbury City Hall and opening for Johnny Winter at Watford Town Hall.

The band's April 9th appearance at the Lyceum drew a very positive review from Chris Welch in *Melody Maker*. Welch called their performance "absorbing and entertaining," and noted that Genesis had "improved greatly on their early days." On May 6, with Steve

Hackett integrating into the group more and more, the new lineup made their first appearance at the Marquee.

On May 10, Genesis recorded a session for BBC radio's Bob Harris Show. With Pete Dauncey producing and Adrian Revill engineering, they recorded two songs at Studio T1, Transcription Service, Kensington House, Shepherd's Bush. For the occasion, they selected *Stagnation*, a favorite from the TRESPASS LP, and a new number, *The Musical Box*. This session was broadcast on May 31, giving many listeners their first taste of the new Genesis lineup. This recording of *The Musical Box* is of interest, since it's a longer arrangement than the one that appears on the NURSERY CRYME album.

"It's possible that the May 1971 date was a pre-album session," Phil Collins said of this BBC session. "As *Musical Box* was written in Farnham Maltings during my first rehearsal, it could have been the first studio session by the band with me on drums. Probably the most historical fact of these sessions was the fact that (influential British disc jockey) John Peel almost liked us then! "

A CONCERT POSTER FOR A GENESIS SHOW AT CITY HALL IN NEWCASTLE.

On June 19, Genesis returned to Friars. By this time, David Stopps had re-opened Friars in its new location at the Aylesbury Borough Assembly Hall. The performance drew a typically fervent reaction from the local crowd, inspiring Gabriel to add another dimension to his performance. At the climax of *The Knife*, the singer moved to the back of the stage and took a "Harold The Barrel"-style running jump into the crowd. As much as they adored him, the fans weren't quite ready to have Gabriel land on them, and they parted like the Red Sea. Peter crash landed on the floor and broke his ankle.

On June 26, Genesis made their first appearance at the Reading Festival. They were paid £100 for their performance on the second day of the festival. Gabriel was most likely using a crutch, following the Friars incident, although some reports suggest he made at least one concert appearance in a wheelchair. The London *Times* reported that undercover cops disguised as Hippies put a slight damper on the festival. "More than 50 pop music enthusiasts, including girls, were arrested by detectives with long hair and dressed in jeans," reported the paper. "Those found with suspicious substances were detained."

Still undeterred by his broken ankle, Gabriel appeared with Genesis at Friars' sister club in Bedford on July 2. With his leg in plaster and a broom for a crutch, this gig may be regarded as one of Gabriel's first costumed appearances, although it was probably not intended that way. This was followed on the 9th by a show at the Marquee.

Live performances were kept to a minimum over the summer. During July and August, with Gabriel still recuperating from his accident, the band rehearsed for their next LP. The rehearsals took place at Luxford House in Crowborough, Surrey, owned by Tony Stratton-Smith. By this point, Genesis' sound was bolstered by Steve Hackett's more aggressive guitar style and by their newly-purchased Mellotron, a keyboard that incorporated tape loops to recreate the sound of choir, flutes or a string section. As they worked on new material, the new line-up grew into a strong songwriting unit.

> "It was really a songwriters' collective," says Hackett. "When I joined the band, everybody was encouraged to write. They'd been writing for longer than I had. At that point, I was learning the craft of writing."

One of the techniques the band was fond of in those days was to have two or three guitars playing different chords simultaneously. This approach grew from Ant and Mike's collaborations of two years earlier. "We deliberately used to put note clusters together so that it produced a third chord," Steve explains. Sometimes the group expanded this effect by using three guitars. In the early days, Tony Banks played acoustic guitar alongside Steve and Mike on a number of songs, including *Happy The Man, Harlequin* and *Stagnation*, as well as parts of *The Musical Box* and *Supper's Ready*.

> "I sometimes found that, at times, if I was a writer, that exerted no more control than if I just remained a player," Hackett points out. "So I found that, at times, to let other people write and to work through it as a player, sometimes produced stronger guitar parts in a way. But I did write quite a lot of stuff for the band."

AN EARLY GENESIS PHOTO, FROM THE LEFT: COLLINS, RUTHERFORD, HACKETT, GABRIEL AND BANKS.

Genesis was — in theory, at least — a democracy. But certain group members tended to side with each other when there were decisions to be made. As Peter Gabriel told author Ray Coleman in the latter's Phil Collins biography, "Mike drifted into Tony's camp; Steve drifted into mine . . . with Phil sitting in the middle." Gabriel has said that Collins' tendency to be non-confrontational was a source of some frustration to him, that he felt that Phil was more in tune with his ideas, but wouldn't provide strong enough support.

Chapter 6: Play Me My Song

Genesis spent August 1971 recording the NURSERY CRYME LP at Trident Studios. Produced by John Anthony, the sessions were a turning point for the group, their first real recordings without Anthony Phillips and the first with Collins and Hackett.

"It was the third album for the band of old boys, shall we say," recalls Steve Hackett. "For myself and Phil Collins, it was a rather different experience. For the guys that had known each other as a five-piece, since God-knows-when, they found it disappointing that Anthony Phillips wasn't with them. They'd known him for years and they'd grown up together and had their own language. And it was early days for me as a writer, so I didn't quite know what was expected of me. I found it quite difficult writing with a team. You never really knew what was going to strike a chord or not."

The album was engineered by David Hentschel, who had been a tape operator for TRESPASS and would eventually become Genesis' producer. Hentschel has fond memories of the NURSERY CRYME sessions.

"It was a very exciting time, not least because everyone involved was overflowing with the enthusiasm of youth," he says. "Phil and Steve had just joined the band, which provided a huge boost. Also, at that time, there was great enthusiasm in the record business for making those kind of records. Over the years, even by the time we were doing the later albums, it has become harder and harder to approach an album solely from an artistic point of view, which we had the luxury of doing in those early heady days, when record companies were run by people who loved music. This obviously freed up all the creative spirits and allowed us all to focus on the music rather than worrying about radio formats, marketing, singles and so forth. Peter's influence obviously was a major force as well. His abilities brought a unique flavor to the band. Not to say the band was better either with him or without him. That's a subjective question."

Tony Banks has often said that, to him, NURSERY CRYME didn't feel like much of an improvement over TRESPASS. "I think it was perhaps a disappointment to the original three," says Hackett. "But, because it was my first professional album, I decided to put everything into it that I possibly could."

The opening number on the album was *The Musical Box*, which featured lyrics by Gabriel. He has said he imagined the song taking place in a big old house where he spent time as a child. The lyrics told a typically twisted Gabriel tale which begins with two children, Cynthia Jane and Henry, playing croquet. For reasons perhaps known only to Gabriel, Cynthia Jane beheads Henry with her croquet mallet, only to have him reappear as a spirit which emerges from his beloved musical box. The song reaches its peak as Henry, whose spirit form is aging a lifetime in a matter of minutes, tries to express his physical desires for his playmate, calling out, "Why don't you touch me, touch me, touch me . . . Now! Now! Now! Now! Now!" A spectacular climax, in more ways than one — especially when the song was performed live, with Gabriel in his "old man" mask, frantically thrusting his pelvis in time with the music.

Musically, *The Musical Box* originated from Anthony Phillips' days with the group and Tony Banks has said that Phillips probably should have had a co-writing credit. Mick Barnard also contributed, at least to the arrangement, as did Steve Hackett. In fact, Banks has said that Barnard wrote all the lead guitar parts. "I think Steve literally took what I did and put it onto the album," says Barnard. However, if one compares the NURSERY CRYME version to the later version on GENESIS LIVE, it's clear that Hackett put more and more of his own ideas into the song over the next couple of years. Certainly the guitar leads that Steve had devised by the GENESIS LIVE performance had a lot more impact, so his contribution shouldn't be underestimated.

As multitrack recording technology grew from two to four to eight, sixteen, twenty four tracks and beyond, many bands would increasingly record musical elements separately. In the 70's, it became common to start a track by recording a rhythm track of just drums, or drums and bass. Genesis music — at least during those early days — was too complex to be recorded in such a fashion. There were stops and starts, passages with no drums, changes in rhythm and tempo, and so on. To get a song like *The Musical Box* down on tape, it was necessary not only for most of the band to play together, but to record the song in several sections.

"We recorded *The Musical Box* in three different sections," Hackett recalls. "The first bit, which was acoustic, was one section. The second bit, where the drums come in, was another. And then where it goes down to one guitar for the 'She's a lady' section. I remember triple-tracking the guitar solo at the end, so that it was a three-part harmony. Although the mix, which was done in one go, only showed two parts. There's a missing part, a third harmony."

Another key Hackett contribution was the high-pitched guitar figure that appeared during the "Play me my song . . ." section. This was something that was added after the rest of the track had been completed.

"We came to the end of the recording of *The Musical Box* and I suddenly realized that no one had really made a satisfactory sound of a musical box," says Steve. "So I stuck in a little phrase, which was a guitar recorded at half-speed and then sped up to its original speed, which made a little tinkly phrase, where you could imagine a ballerina on top of a musical box doing a pirouette. I liked very much being involved with the detail of a song. I was learning a lot."

"I'd imagined that, because it was a democracy, that people would immediately applaud you for each good idea that you put forward," Steve says. "In fact, it was just a case of, 'Well, just get on with it and do it.' I was not writing as much as the other guys were, because I hadn't really learned the craft of songwriting. And I think, as a team, they were very self-sufficient."

Even before Hackett and Gabriel eventually left the group, Phil Collins, Mike Rutherford and Tony Banks seemed to form the musical core of Genesis. The three seemed to have an intuitive musical communication with each other, and material often grew from their jam sessions.

"It seemed as if they were self-sufficient in a way, with the rest of us chipping in," observes Hackett of the trio who would survive the departure of their lead vocalist and lead guitarist. "A lot of the keyboard parts that Tony came up with . . . I think Mike used to have this kind of unspoken alliance with Tony, which meant that Phil would join in. So I think that Tony's ideas were usually probably given precedence over anybody else's at that stage."

"It always appeared to me that Tony and Mike were the two driving forces in the studio," says Paul Whitehead. "They were the ones that would lay down the initial track, with Phil, and then all the other things were kind of like extras on top of that. And then Peter would come in and add his vocals, which was a whole other dimension."

Steve Hackett was less comfortable with the group writing situation, preferring to hone his ideas in isolation, before presenting them to the band. "Sometimes it was quite difficult to write eyeball-to-eyeball in the rehearsal room," he says. "I prefer to have a rough idea of what I'm going to do, if I'm working with a band, and then go away and hone it down and work on it."

Steve's first major compositional contribution to Genesis was *For Absent Friends*, a short song he wrote with Phil Collins.

"I seem to recall that the first thing that anybody liked was a little song called *For Absent Friends*," Steve remembers. "Which I sat down to write with Phil Collins. I already had the song and I didn't have a lyric. We wrote the lyrics together. A song about two old ladies. In a way, it was two Eleanor Rigbies instead of one. Two bereaved old ladies lamenting the loss of their husbands."

Apart from *The Musical Box*, the other highlight of NURSERY CRYME was its epic closing track, *The Fountain Of Salmacis*. This expansive piece grew from a musical idea Tony wrote during his university stint. It came to life when he played the grandiose chords on the Mellotron that Genesis had purchased from King Crimson. Steve Hackett had been eager for Genesis to acquire a Mellotron and the instrument took the group to a new level. With its tape loops of sampled string, brass and choral sounds, the keyboard added a powerful dimension to the Genesis sound. Lyrically, *The Fountain Of Salmacis* told the tale of Hermaphroditus and his encounter with a water-nymph named Salmacis. Not your typical rock and roll subject matter.

All the members of Genesis contributed to the lyrics in those early days, even though many assumed that they were all by Gabriel. Both *Seven Stones* and *Harlequin* featured lyrics penned by Tony, while *For Absent Friends* sported a Hackett-Collins lyric.

One of the best short songs was *Harold The Barrel*, a compelling little piece of black comedy about an unusual restaurateur on the run from the police. Although often overlooked, the humor in Genesis' songs was very important to Gabriel, who felt that tracks like *Harold* and *Willow Farm* followed the tradition of British absurdist humor

(Gabriel was a fan of Charisma labelmates Monty Python). Gabriel's onstage announcements and stories were further proof of Genesis' comic tendencies.

The cover art was once again rendered by Paul Whitehead, who was involved from the earliest stages of the songwriting process.

"I used to socialize with Peter," Whitehead recalls. "Every now and then he'd give me lyrics and say, 'I wrote this — what do you think?' And I'd look at it and say, 'Oh yeah — what's the music like?' And he'd say, 'Well, I don't know yet!' He's always been very into his lyrics, you know. He spends more time on his lyrics than he does on his music."

"A lot of the time, I was in the studio when they actually cut the song or added the vocals," Whitehead says. "It was all part of the process."

The focus of the TRESPASS cover illustration was inspired by the album's musical centerpiece, *The Knife*. On NURSERY CRYME, the musical centerpiece was *The Musical Box*, and it was this song that inspired the album cover painting.

"I'd heard them doing it acoustically, rehearsing it," Whitehead remembers. "And then they went down to the house in Crowborough, with all their instruments, and rehearsed it there. So I got the idea of what it was about. And then I saw Peter developing his kind of act to go with it. I just said, 'Hey, this is a strong song.' And we talked about what the song was about. It was obviously Victorian, so I said, 'Why don't we do something like *Alice In Wonderland*-type, dark, Gothic Victorian?' And once again I went away and got a whole bunch of books and came back with ideas of styles of paintings. And I think it was Mike who particularly liked a Dali picture that I showed them. It was very green-ish, yellow-ish, green-ish. And he said, 'That's the kind of feel.' "

"So that just got me started, you know, and I came back with sketches and showed them the basic layout and everyone went, 'Yeah, great, go for it.' When we'd decided to go with that, I suggested that we make the inside of the album like a Victorian photo album, with each song having its own little illustration. And the whole thing all tied together, I thought it was great."

Whitehead was very aware of the way the group changed after Hackett and Collins joined.

"I think they brought a level of professionalism, you know?" he says. "When Phil joined, he'd been in bands already, and he had the talk, you know? He had the sort of 'band talk.' He knew all the angles — he's been around the block, in other words. He definitely brought a level of professionalism to the whole thing, like regular rehearsals, sort of a discipline. I think he brought a new kind of ambition to the band, as well. Steve was a little quieter, but he was very businesslike and hard working. He was very meticulous in the studio, you know. He would insist on doing another take and another take."

After the recording of NURSERY CRYME was finished, the new Genesis hit the road again. The Civic Centre in Gravesend, The Temple in London, Kensington Town Hall, Preston Public Hall, Newcastle City Hall and other venues hosted a preview of the new album during September and October.

The group's sets from this period typically consisted of: *Happy The Man*, *Stagnation*, *The Fountain Of Salmacis*, *Twilight Alehouse*, *The Musical Box*, *The Return Of The Giant Hogweed* and *The Knife*. Sometimes they would include *Harlequin* or the single-that-never-was *Going Out To Get You*.

By this point, a particularly entertaining element had been added to Genesis' live show. In the early days, the unusual tunings favored by Mike Rutherford and Anthony Phillips caused delays between numbers while they re-tuned their guitars. Eventually, Gabriel began to tell stories between numbers, both as a way of filling the awkward tuning periods and also to illustrate the meaning of the songs. *The Musical Box* was a perfect example. While the guitarists adjusted their pegs to achieve the *F Sharp* tuning, Gabriel regaled the audience with the bizarre tale of Henry and Cynthia Jane.

Charisma released NURSERY CRYME in November. Although the new line-up was very strong, the sales of the album weren't really any improvement on those of TRESPASS. Tony Banks has said he found the album to be surprisingly similar to its predecessor, given that there were two new members. Some of the band's fans did notice a substantial difference between TRESPASS and NURSERY CRYME, and suspected that Genesis had experienced a few chemically induced revelations.

"People are convinced that we moved from ordinary dope to acid from TRESPASS to NURSERY CRYME," an amused Michael Rutherford revealed to *Zig Zag*. Gabriel assured the magazine's readers that "a small glass of milk is the most potent thing I do."

Considering the bizarre musical soundscapes they presented onstage, many who met the Gabriel-era group were surprised to discover how down-to-earth and normal they were offstage.

Across the Atlantic, NURSERY CRYME was released by Buddah Records and eventually got a review in *Rolling Stone*. Reviewer Richard Cromelin felt that the band's potential was severely hampered by the record's ...

> "godawful production ... a murky, distant stew that at best bubbles quietly when what is desperately needed are the explosions of drums and guitars, the screaming of the organ, the abrasive rasp of vocal chords."

Certainly, the LP's sound was on the muddy side, but the 'Definitive Edition' remastered CD release of NURSERY CRYME presents a much clearer version of the album.

> *Rolling Stone* called Genesis a "new contender for the coveted British weirdo-rock championship" and concluded that "It's definitely a type of music that skulks down back alleys far from the beaten path, but if Genesis learn how to gear things up to explosion level and manage to develop their ideas a bit more thoroughly, they could be the ones to successfully repopulate those forgotten passageways."

Genesis plugged away through November and December of 1971, playing all over Britain:

o The Marquee in London,
o Watford Technical College,
o The Chez Club in Leytonstone,
o The Lawns Centre in Cottingham,
o Hobbit's Garden in Wimbledon (with support acts Gravy Train and Roxy Music)
o Lynn Technical College,
o Teeside Polytechnic in Middlesborough,
o Culham College in Abingdon,
o Cranbrook School,
o The Windrush Club in High Wycombe,
o The Big Brother in Greenford,
o Weymouth Grammar School
o The South Parade Pier in Portsmouth.

On the first day of 1972, Genesis played at the Dagenham Roundhouse in London. Eight days later, the quintet loaded their instruments into the BBC's Studio T1, Kensington House, Shepherd's Bush for a John Peel session. Produced by John Muir, the session comprised four songs from NURSERY CRYME: *Return Of The Giant Hogweed, Harold The Barrel, The Fountain Of Salmacis* and *Harlequin*. This session was broadcast January 28.

At the end of 1971, while Genesis were promoting NURSERY CRYME, they received some unexpected news: TRESPASS had just reached No. 1 in Belgium, belatedly becoming the first Genesis record to chart anywhere in the world. Naturally, the band headed over to continental Europe to make the most of their Belgian success. Their first appearance was at the Charleroi Festival near Brussels on January 16, 1972. Their set for this legendary gig included *Happy The Man, Stagnation, The Fountain Of Salmacis, Twilight Alehouse, The Musical Box* and *The Return Of The Giant Hogweed.* They also appeared on Belgian television, performing *The Fountain Of Salmacis, Twilight Alehouse, The Musical Box* and *The Return Of The Giant Hogweed.*

In the 1990's, a live recording of this first Belgian visit surfaced and has appeared on a number of bootlegs. Aside from the brief snippet of *Twilight Alehouse* from a Phillips-era performance at London's Roundhouse, this is the earliest live recording of Genesis in circulation. It includes *Happy The Man, Stagnation, The Light* (a ten minute number that evolved into *Lilywhite Lilith*), *Twilight Alehouse, The Musical Box, The Knife* and *Going Out to Get You.*

For the rest of January and throughout February, Genesis gigged all over Britain: Southampton, Bristol, Luton, High Wycombe, Brighton, Exeter, Glasgow, York, Newcastle, Sheffield, Manchester and Leicester. The highlight of this stint on the road was the February 9 show at the Rainbow Theatre in London.

On March 2, the BBC recorded a Genesis performance at the Paris Cinema on Lower Regent Street, London. Nine days later, the Beeb broadcast three songs from that performance: *The Fountain Of Salmacis, The Musical Box* and *The Return Of The Giant Hogweed.*

On March 4, Genesis played at Watford Technical College, a gig notable for a rare live performance of *Harlequin*. Otherwise, the group played their standard material of the era.

On March 11, Genesis returned to Friars, Aylesbury, which the group regarded as their "spiritual home" in those days.

Another European triumph had occurred in March, when NURSERY CRYME had reached No. 4 in Italy. Genesis consolidated their Italian success with their first tour of the country, starting at the Palasport in Belluna on April 6. The next day, it was off to Treviso, to play at the Apollo 2000 Club.

An April 8 date at the Dancing Paradiso in Trieste was cancelled at the last minute, so the next appearance turned out to be the Lem Club, Verona on April 9. Genesis played both an afternoon and an evening show at this venue, their set starting with *Happy The Man*, and including such other period favorites as *Stagnation, The Knife* and *Going Out To Get You*. They also played a new number called *Bye Bye Johnny*, which Gabriel dedicated to the people of Trieste, who hadn't been able to see them. By the time it was released, on the FOXTROT LP, *Bye Bye Johnny* would be re-titled *Can-Utility And The Coastliners*.

On April 11, the group played the Palasport in Pesaro and the following day they played at another Palasport, this one in Reggio Emilia. During the afternoon rehearsal for this show, the music for *Watcher Of The Skies* came together for the first time in all its glory. Steve Hackett feels that the recorded version of *Watcher* didn't match the power of that afternoon's rehearsal. Hackett also remembers that evening's gig as one of their most powerful shows ever.

A typical set from this tour included *Happy The Man, Stagnation, The Fountain Of Salmacis, Twilight Alehouse, The Musical Box, The Return Of The Giant Hogweed, The Knife* and *Going Out To Get You.*

On April 19, Genesis did two shows at the Teatro Mostra Mediterraneo in Naples. Sitting on the roof of a building in Naples, Tony and Mike wrote the lyrics for *Watcher Of The Skies*, for which the group had already rehearsed the music. Banks and Rutherford read a lot of science fiction in those days and the view from that Italian rooftop inspired a lyric about an alien who visits Earth to find it devoid of all lifeforms.

Singles were certainly not the strong suit of the Gabriel-fronted Genesis, but that didn't stop them from trying.

> "It was the long and fairly fruitless search for a hit single in those days," says Steve Hackett. "Whenever we went away and recorded anything that was intended to be a potential single, everyone at the record company despised it."

In early 1972, the group recorded the stage favorite *Happy The Man* for a single release. In those days, *Happy The Man* was the group's regular set opener. In a holdover from the Phillips era, the show would begin with Banks, Rutherford and Hackett all playing acoustic 12-string guitars together. Tony has observed that part of the reason for having *Happy The Man* in their sets was to appeal to fans of folky outfits like Lindisfarne (who Genesis often shared a bill with in those days). Indeed, the song's release as a single may have been an attempt to win over some of the British record-buying public, who were driving Lindisfarne records such as FOG ON THE TYNE up the UK charts.

Happy The Man grew from a riff of Mike's, with further musical input from Tony on guitar. "*Happy The Man* was a song that was already written before I joined the band," points out Steve Hackett.

The sessions for *Happy The Man* took place at a new studio called The Manor, owned by Richard Branson's fledgling Virgin Records label.

> "They gave us a free day there," recalls Hackett. "They were touting for business. And Peter Gabriel introduced me to a guy called Richard Branson, who I'd never heard of, who drove a clapped-out old car. I remember he drove us to the station afterwards and he just looked like a student, you know. I assumed he must have been one of the guys hanging around, little realizing that he was the guy who owned the whole thing. Obviously that hippie disguise was a disarming device."

AS THROUGH EMERALD CITY, BOOTLEG LP

Unfortunately, the length of time and amount of money spent on recording this track caused a rift between John Anthony and Charisma, and the label fired him. *Happy The Man* came out in May 1972, backed with *Seven Stones* from NURSERY CRYME. At the time, it seemed to be Genesis best shot at a hit single, a short, catchy number, more easily digestible than most of their other material. Despite that fact, and a Charisma ad campaign touting it as "A new single from one of the truly great groups," it failed to make the charts. Charisma gave the single another chance in October, reissuing it in a yellow picture sleeve at around the same time the FOXTROT LP appeared. *Happy The Man* wasn't included on FOXTROT, however, and was only available as a single, until the release of the ARCHIVE box set twenty-six years later. It did, however, appear on a bootleg LP called AS THROUGH EMERALD CITY.

Another candidate for single release was *Going Out To Get You*, which had been in the group's repertoire since 1970. A studio version was recorded, but wasn't released and the tape is long since lost. A demo recording from 1970 eventually surfaced on the ARCHIVE box but, since the live performances from the 71-72 era are quite different, it's possible that the single version would have born little resemblance to the demo. By 1972, the song had become longer, heavier and more dynamic, driven by organ rather than piano. All that survives of the later arrangement are a few live bootleg recordings.

Another lost track from this era was *Wooden Mask*, which was recorded as a possible single.

> "No one has got a copy of the tape," Steve Hackett says. "Tony and myself had some affection for it. It was one of those things that was intended potentially as a single. It had a bit of a vibe. It wasn't terribly well-produced, it wasn't really finished, but it had something."

Chapter 7: This Planet's Soil

On May 28, 1972, Genesis appeared at the Great Western Express festival in Lincoln. Although their appearance on the third day of the festival was not very well received, this show was notable for opening with one of the first public performances of *Watcher Of The Skies*. *Watcher* quickly usurped *Happy The Man* as the group's regular set-opener, adding a dramatic new dimension to their performances. The days of starting with quiet acoustic numbers were over, and that wasn't the only change: Shortly before the Lincoln performance, Gabriel decided to shave off a triangular portion of his hair, giving him a peculiar appearance, accentuated by eyeliner and an Egyptian-style necklace.

ITALIAN "HAPPY THE MAN" SINGLE

"The shaved head is a very cheap way of getting myself in the papers," Peter said. It was only the beginning of a trend that would simultaneously boost the band's popularity and drive a wedge between the singer and the musicians over the next three years. The visual aspect of Genesis grew quickly during this era, with *Watcher Of The Skies* providing a stunning opening: an ultra violet light bathed the stage, revealing a white gauze curtain, dry ice ("when it wasn't such a cliché," Banks pointed out) and Gabriel with his shaved head and makeup. Genesis spent June on the road, playing shows in Leeds, Cambridge, Wellingborough, Swansea, Durham, Felixstowe and Slough.

BRITISH "HAPPY THE MAN" SINGLE

Despite the improvements in terms of both music and visuals, the members of Genesis were growing somewhat despondent over their progress. Fearing that they might give up, David Stopps put on a "Genesis Convention" at Watford Town Hall towards the end of June. "Home Counties Genesis Freaks Unite!" said the ad Stopps took out to promote the show. This performance earned Genesis a good review in *Melody Maker*, which was very important at this stage in their career. In those days, any mention in the music press — even an ad for a gig — gave the group credibility in the eyes of club owners and promoters.

A typical show from this era comprised *Watcher Of The Skies, Can-Utility And The Coastliners, Happy The Man, The Fountain Of Salmacis, Get 'Em Out By Friday, Twilight Alehouse, The Musical Box, The Return Of The Giant Hogweed* and *The Knife. Harold The Barrel* and *Seven Stones* were also performed on occasion.

On August 11, Genesis made a memorable appearance at the Reading Festival. For this occasion they altered their set list, opening with *The Knife* and closing with *The Return Of*

THESE TWO ADS WERE PROMOTING GENESIS GIGS
DURING THE MONTH OF JUNE 1972.

The Giant Hogweed. Sharing a bill with acts like Mungo Jerry, Nazareth and Curved Air, Genesis made quite an impression on the festival crowd. Although they weren't the only "progressive" band on the scene, there was no one quite like Genesis in terms of mixing epic songs with surreal humor and a dramatic stage presentation. Bands like Yes and ELP focused more on flashy musicianship, extended solo pieces, etc. Hackett, Banks, Rutherford and Collins provided those elements in Genesis, but Gabriel's presence took it all to another level. Even the drum solo, the scourge of those who loathed prog-rock, was rendered with a touch of theatrical genius. A favorite bootleg track from this period is Phil's "One-Handed Drum Solo," on which Collins' single-handed technique is hilariously accompanied by a typically deadpan Gabriel commentary.

During this period, Genesis rented a rehearsal room in the basement of Una Billing's School of Dancing in Shepherd's Bush, London. It was there that they wrote much of the material for the FOXTROT album, piecing together numbers like *Get 'Em Out By Friday* and *Can-Utility And The Coastliners*, to the sound of dancing feet from the floor above.

In August, Genesis returned to the studio to start work on a new album. However, after a few weeks of generally unproductive sessions, they put the project aside to embark on another tour of Italy. On September 2 they returned to Friars, Aylesbury, playing many of the songs that would soon appear on their next LP. After the Friars date, it was back to the studio to work on their next album, FOXTROT. Although the credits read "Produced by David Hitchcock and Genesis; engineered by John Burns," it was a little more complicated than that.

After John Anthony was let go, Charisma had hired Bob Potter to produce Genesis, with Bob Johnston engineering. The producer wasn't fond of Genesis' music (something which he apparently didn't try to hide) and felt that *Watcher Of The Skies* would work better without its trademark Mellotron intro. Potter only lasted about a week.

"For some reason, I was the only one who got on with him," says Steve Hackett. "He didn't actually like the band's music very much. There was a day when we were recording something and he felt it was taking too long and Mike decided to change the strings on his bass guitar or 12-string. And (Potter) said to me, 'I can't stand much more of this. Is there anything you want to do?' I said, 'Well,

I've got this unaccompanied guitar piece I'd like to do.' "The piece in question was *Horizons*. "It must've taken me about four takes to do it," recalls Steve of what would become one of his signature pieces. "I was doing it on a Yamaha acoustic, which was really designed as a strumming guitar and not as a classical guitar. But I felt he did a nice job of producing that. We did a rough mix where he stuck it through a Leslie cabinet, to give it a sort of rolling feel, and put some reverb on it. And suddenly my guitar sounded professional. Afterwards he said, 'Look, I'm going to jack this in. The only thing I've liked that we've done is that guitar piece that you and I did when no one else was around.' "

After Potter, Island Studios engineer Tony Platt came on board, but he didn't fare much better than his predecessor. Platt was soon gone, replaced by producer Dave Hitchcock and engineer John Burns.

Burns was certainly more of a kindred spirit than Potter or Platt, or even Hitchcock, and became actively involved in the album's production.

"We'd already recorded the guitars that formed the backing track for the beginning of *Supper's Ready* — all these 12-strings, three of us playing 12-strings — myself, Mike and Tony," Steve recalls. "But, because it had been a bit of a drag with Bob Potter, when we played it to John Burns we were kind of saying, 'We don't know if this right' or whatever. But John was very good. He said, 'No, I think this sounds very good. I don't get a bad vibe off this.' He was very positive and he was just what the band needed."

"In fact," Steve explains, "Although John was the engineer and, officially, Dave was the producer, John actually took on a lot more of the producing role. He went on to share production credits with us on one or two albums after that. I liked very much working with John, someone who was gung-ho positive. That's what we needed. We needed someone to shake us out of the doldrums at that point."

One of the highlights of FOXTROT was the opening track, *Watcher Of The Skies*. A favorite from the band's live shows, it was chosen as the potential single from the album and an abbreviated version was recorded. For the single version, the song's dramatic Mellotron introduction was dropped. Steve Hackett says,

"For me, the high point of *Watcher Of The Skies*, as well as the lyric, is the atmosphere that's built at the beginning through the Mellotron, where the rhythm crescendos out of the Mellotron adagio. It's almost as if the Mellotron introduction is a spacecraft coming in to land and the earthy rhythm section comes up to meet it. To me, it's a depiction of two separate worlds meeting. To leave the intro off — because it was considered to be too long for a single — defeated the whole object of the song. So the song didn't soar, it didn't take off." Even without the intro, the track didn't exactly sound like a pop hit. "You couldn't dance to it," says Steve. "You couldn't tap your foot to it. We decided to loop the stuff at the end. They weren't really choruses as such — in those days we didn't really write chorus-based music. We looped up the harmony vocal and I did sort of an apology for a backwards guitar solo. Once again, an early attempt by Genesis to write a hit single failed dismally! "

Another concert favorite that appeared on FOXTROT was *Can-Utility and the Coastliners*. In a Virgin online chat many years later, Tony Banks recalled the song's creation:

"In those days we very much used to pool ideas that we had around and, in the case of *Can-Utility*, (we used) more of Steve's bits, particularly the first part of the song. Another part of *Can-Utility* emerged as a jam, like a lot of Genesis things we don't just put it in an order and arrange things. It varies, some songs stuck more with one person and others very much grew out of improvisation."

As usual, the songwriting duties were divided among the group members. *Time Table* featured lyrics by Tony, while *Horizons* was composed by Steve alone. *Get 'Em Out By Friday* featured lyrics by Peter, the music having evolved from a Banks riff. Tony was apparently on the verge of abandoning the riff until Phil reworked the rhythm. Although Collins didn't write much in those early days, he was already proving himself to be an invaluable asset to the songwriting team. Phil's more instinctive approach to playing was the perfect foil to the more cerebral approach of Tony Banks.

Get 'Em Out By Friday was a cutting piece of social commentary. Gabriel's lyrics told of a family being evicted from their house by ruthless property developers in the year 2012, and a plan to place a "four foot restriction on humanoid height" in order to cram twice as many tenants into the same space. "With land in your hand you'll be happy on earth," concludes Gabriel. "Then invest in the Church for your heaven."

The lyrics to *Supper's Ready* were the brainchild of Gabriel, who also wrote the music to the *Willow Farm* segment, originally penned by him as a separate song. Since the *Willow Farm* lyrics were already done, Gabriel used them as a starting point from which the rest of the *Supper's Ready* lyrics grew. Divided into several individual sections, this song was an epic, twenty-minute tale of good versus evil.

A handout given to audience members in 1972 attempted to clarify the story of *Supper's Ready* through each of its sections:

Lover's Leap — In which two lovers are lost in each other's eyes, and found again transformed in the bodies of another male and female.

The Guaranteed Eternal Sanctuary Man — The lovers come across a town dominated by two characters; one a benevolent farmer and the other the head of a highly disciplined scientific religion. The latter likes to be known as *The Guaranteed Eternal Sanctuary Man* and claims to contain a secret new ingredient capable of fighting fire. This is a falsehood, an untruth, a whopper and a taradiddle, or to put it in clearer terms; a lie. Ikhnaton and Its-a-con and their band of merry men — Who the lovers see clad in greys and purples, awaiting to be summoned out of the ground. At the G.E.S.M's command they put forth from the bowels of the earth, to attack all those without an up-to-date 'Eternal Life License,' which were obtainable at the head office of the G.E.S.M's religion.

56

How Dare I Be So Beautiful? — In which our intrepid heroes investigate the aftermath of the battle and discover a solitary figure, obsessed by his own image. They witness an unusual transmutation, and are pulled into their own reflections in the water.

Willow Farm — Climbing out of the pool, they are once again in a different existence. They're right in the middle of a myriad of bright colors, filled with all manner of objects, plants, animals and humans. Life flows freely and everything is mindlessly busy. At random, a whistle blows and every single thing is instantly changed into another.

Apocalypse in 9/8 (Co-starring the delicious talents of wild geese) — At one whistle the lovers become seeds in the soil, where they recognize other seeds to be people from the world in which they had originated. While they wait for spring, they are returned to their old world to see Apocalypse of St. John in full progress. The seven trumpeters cause a sensation, the fox keeps throwing sixes, and Pythagoras (a Greek extra) is deliriously happy as he manages to put exactly the right amount of milk and honey on his corn flakes.

As sure as eggs is eggs (aching men's feet) — Above all else an egg is an egg. And did those feet . . . . making ends meet.

Apocalypse in 9/8 grew from a Banks / Collins / Rutherford jam. Its title suggests, this number was in an unusual time signature and became even more rhythmically complex when Genesis played it live. Years later, in an interview with *Modern Drummer*, Phil Collins explained how he could deliver such odd rhythms so deftly.

> "I think it comes from being a singer. When I learn a section of music that's in an odd meter, I don't count it. I sing the pattern in my head. You can get more inside the feel of a pattern if you think of it as just music."

During the FOXTROT sessions, Genesis finally got around to recording the stage favorite *Twilight Alehouse*, which had been around since the Anthony Phillips era. However, it wasn't included on FOXTROT and remained unreleased until late 1973, when it showed up as a flexi-disc single, released first with *Zig-Zag* magazine and then through the group's fan club. It also appeared as the B-side of *I Know What I Like*, in early 1974. (A remixed version of *Twilight Alehouse* appeared many years later on the ARCHIVE box set.) Credited as composed by "Genesis" upon its release during the Hackett / Collins era, the song is registered with BMI as having been composed by Banks, Phillips, Gabriel and Rutherford.

With five writers contributing material, the group members inevitably came up with more material than Genesis could accommodate. One instrumental section that didn't end up on FOXTROT was a piece in 3/4 time, written by Mike Rutherford. The band rehearsed it but never used it and Steve Hackett eventually incorporated it into *Shadow Of The Hierophant* on his first solo album.

FOXTROT was the Gabriel-Hackett-Banks-Collins-Rutherford line-up's most unified effort. The tensions of the SELLING ENGLAND BY THE POUND / LAMB LIES DOWN ON BROADWAY era hadn't surfaced yet and the quintet were able to fully exploit their respective strengths.

The press reaction to the album was generally favorable.

> "There are occasions when the overall sound does lack the required vitality and other occasions where Genesis are trying just that little bit too hard," wrote Jerry Gilbert in *Sounds*. "But these moments are sporadic indeed, and by and large the album is a showcase for the genius of this young experimental band, which manifests itself in numerous different ways."

As on the two previous albums, Paul Whitehead worked closely with Genesis on the cover artwork for FOXTROT. The cover painting was largely inspired by *Supper's Ready*.

> "The song was about the Apocalypse," Whitehead recalls. "I suggested that we try to come up with an original way of showing the four horsemen of the Apocalypse. And it grew from that basic idea, then became a little more whimsical. It was kind of a follow-on from *Nursery Cryme*, because *Nursery Cryme* was about croquet, which is an English upper class sport. So the next one, logically, was fox hunting, another English upper crust sport, which actually some of Genesis' families indulged in, which was kind of funny. But it was very symbolic of the upper classes in England, so it was fair game, you know? It was a little satire there."

The image of the woman with the fox head was inspired by the American slang referring to an attractive woman as a "fox." Whitehead heard the term from friends who had visited America, as well as in Jimi Hendrix's *Foxy Lady*, and painted his own interpretation of it as part of the FOXTROT cover. This in turn inspired the first of Gabriel's onstage costumes, which drew a great deal of attention from the press. FOXTROT turned out to be Whitehead's last cover for Genesis. He lost touch with the band after moving to America, where he still resides.

September 25 brought another John Peel session, at Studio T1, Kensington House, Shepherd's Bush. Although the legendary DJ reportedly never liked Genesis, Peel did feature sessions by them on a couple of occasions. Produced by John Walters, the session consisted of *Watcher Of The Skies*, *Twilight Alehouse* and *Get 'Em Out By Friday*. It's interesing to note the inclusion of *Twilight Alehouse* on this session. It's possible that it was still being considered as a contender for FOXTROT at that point. This session was broadcast on November 7 and has since appeared on a number of bootlegs.

SOUNDS DECIDED THEY WOULD PUT GABRIEL ON THEIR COVER IN JAN, 1973.

Another landmark gig from this era was the September 28 show at the National Stadium in Dublin. At this show, Peter wore a fox head mask, completing the ensemble with his wife Jill's red dress. The idea of recreating this image from Paul Whitehead's FOXTROT cover art came from Charisma promotion man Paul Conroy. What started out as merely a gimmick to promote the new LP would soon evolve into a regular part of Genesis' stage shows, with other masks and costumes being added.

Gabriel didn't tell the other group members beforehand, so they were as surprised as the audience when a fox in drag wandered onstage halfway through *The Musical Box*. The crowd was shocked and Gabriel — with a new feeling of authority and stage presence — thought to himself, "I must be onto something here."

DOUBLE LP PAIRING OF NURSERY CRYME AND FOXTROT.

A photo of Gabriel in the dress and fox head soon appeared on the front of *Melody Maker*. After that credibility boost, Genesis' fee doubled, going from £300 to £600 per show.

Although it would appear as an American 45, Charisma decided not to release the re-recorded *Watcher Of The Skies* as a single in Britain. No U.K. single would be extracted from FOXTROT, although Steve Hackett had suggested the *Willow Farm* section of *Supper's Ready* as a likely candidate. The others rejected this suggestion, but the idea had merit. Gabriel's quirky little ditty could certainly have fared no worse than the other Genesis singles of the era. *Willow Farm* did show up on an American single, as the flip side of *Watcher Of The Skies*. (*The Watcher*

Of The Skies / Willow Farm 45 was also released in several other countries, including Italy, Germany and New Zealand.)

Charisma released FOXTROT in October 1972. Despite the producer troubles that bogged down its recording, the finished album was their best sounding record to date. It was also their best seller, with the group's costume-enhanced live performances winning over new fans every week. The press was starting to give the group plenty of coverage and Charisma were very happy with the group they took a chance on. FOXTROT was the first Genesis record to chart in Britain, peaking at No. 12. *Sounds* hailed the album as "the Genesis that we've seen all too often on stage and been longing for on record."

During October and November, the group gigged extensively throughout Britain. In November, they added *Supper's Ready* to their live set. Although it became a highlight of their set for years to come, it took some time to get up to speed. The song really came into its own a few months later, when Gabriel began illustrating its characters with masks and costumes.

AD FOR GENESIS AND CAPABILITY BROWN.

A November 18 date at London's Imperial College included *Watcher Of The Skies, The Musical Box, Get 'Em Out By Friday, Supper's Ready, The Return Of The Giant Hogweed* and *The Knife.* The support act was String Driven Thing, who would shortly be opening for Genesis on the other side of the Atlantic.

During the second week of December, both groups jetted across the Atlantic for Genesis' American concert debut. They played two shows, the first being a warm-up gig at Brandeis University, near Boston, on December 11. This unannounced appearance didn't exactly psyche the group up for a Stateside conquest. "We played to a completely disinterested group of people," recalls Steve Hackett. "Nobody, but nobody, was interested. It was dismal, absolutely awful."

Then it was on to the Big Apple for a show at the prestigious Philharmonic Hall, a benefit for the Cerebral Palsy Foundation. Unfortunately, Leonard Bernstein insisted on rehearsing his orchestra that afternoon, and Genesis were not given an opportunity to have a soundcheck. A soundcheck is a necessity at the best of times, but to a group in Genesis' position, it was especially important. As if the lack of a soundcheck wasn't enough cause for concern, the band's legendary technical difficulties once again reared their head. Steve Hackett, who had the flu, lent his amplifier to the guitarist from String Driven Thing. Hackett watched from the wings as his amp blew up during their set.

Philharmonic Hall
LINCOLN CENTER

Wednesday Evening, December 13, 1972 at 8:00 and 11:00

WNEW-FM in association with
CHARISMA RECORDS

present

A CHRISTMAS CONCERT
for the benefit of the

CEREBRAL PALSY FOUNDATION

STARRING

Genesis

AND INTRODUCING

String Driven
Thing

Sound by Bob Heil
Produced by Dominic Sicilia
Charisma Records is part of The Buddah Group

A CHRISTMAS CONCERT AT THE LINCOLN
CENTER'S PHILHARMONIC HALL IN NEW YORK
CITY ON DECEMBER 13, 1972.

"So this was my big New York debut and I was bundle of nerves with a temperature of 104," he recalls. Thirty seconds before the band was due to go on, Steve was informed that his amp was working, but probably wouldn't last for the whole show. "It wasn't easy," he says. "New York always seemed to be a challenge."

Despite the technical setbacks, Genesis went down very well with the New York audience. They opened with a great *Watcher Of The Skies*, Gabriel appeared in the fox head and dress for the closing section of *The Musical Box* and they played *Supper's Ready*. It's safe to say that the crowd had never quite seen nor heard the likes of Genesis before.

"Genesis is a quintet that blends perversely fashionable theatrics with complex, often ingeneous arrangements," wrote John Rockwell in the *New York Times*. "The visual focus is Peter Gabriel, the lead singer, who center-parts his hair to the crown of his head, changes costumes frequently (from clinging pants suits to dresses and back again) and is clearly working hard to project an androgynous demonism. He succeeds, especially when helped by fireflash and smoke bombs set off on the beat at the climax of the act."

"Mr. Gabriel sings well enough, but musically Genesis is most notable for its hammering, heavy obstinatos and luxurious organ playing. Occasionally things get mired in pretension, or lose their rhythmic grip. But the climax worked, and climaxes are what rock is all about."

Genesis' early American shows were a challenge for the band. Musically and lyrically, they were trying to convey very complex ideas and, for audiences accustomed to more straight-ahead rock and roll, Genesis took some time to digest.

"It's quite a problem when you come face to face with an audience that doesn't like you, a crowd that wants you to play loud and play rock," Tony Banks told the *NME*. "In those situations, it's easy to get the feeling that you're trying to educate the people which is obviously all wrong. I can now understand why so many English bands break up after American tours. You're in England, secure and doing well then once in the States it feels like you're getting nowhere. That situation can be quite a bring-down, smashed egos and all."

61

A TOUR POSTER FOR GENESIS WITH STRING DRIVEN THING OPENING THE SHOW.

January was spent touring Europe and, in February, Genesis returned to Britain. Their February 9 show at London's Rainbow Theatre was a groundbreaking performance, at which many of Gabriel's classic masks were debuted. The fox head and dress had been a bit of a gimmick, but Gabriel loved the response he received, so he devised costumes that would actually help illustrate the lyrics of Genesis' more obscure numbers. So the fox was out, replaced by an "old man" mask to signify the prematurely-aged Henry on the last part of *The Musical Box*. *Supper's Ready* came to life with a flower mask to illustrate "Narcissus" (in *How Dare I Be So Beautiful*) and a scary-looking red box mask for *Apocalypse In 9/8*. At the end of *Supper's Ready*, Gabriel pulled off his black cape to reveal a white suit, to symbolize the triumph of good over evil. At some performances Gabriel even "flew" during the number, but nixed this idea after getting tangled in the wires while dangling several feet above the stage.

"When we first started doing *Supper's Ready* onstage it didn't go down very well, until Peter started wearing a few costumes to demonstrate the characters," Tony Banks said several years later. "Suddenly, it became the strong point of the act."

CANADIAN COMPILATION PRESENTING GENESIS.

The flower mask became one of the most recognizable Gabriel costumes of the period, and graced the cover of a rare Canadian compilation called PRESENTING GENESIS.

Although he had described his shaved head as a gimmick to get in the papers, Gabriel defended the new costumes and masks he was using as an integral part of the performance.

"There are people who believe that the costumes, props, and slides we use are crutches to hold up crippled music," he said. "But if the visual images are conceived at the time of writing, and you don't use those visuals, then you're not allowing the audience to listen to the song in the full strength of which it was created. And that's what we're after, to give the listener as much in a song as we get from it. Visuals are only rubbish unless they are integrated with the continuity of the music."

"I remember we were playing the same set before the days of Pete going glam-rock and it didn't always grab the attention of an audience that might be there to see two or three other bands," said Steve Hackett in the Virgin online chat. "When you were sharing stages like that as we were with Lindisfarne who were headlining and were immensely more popular than we were, we needed that extra edge I think that Pete gave it."

The visually-enhanced Genesis show traveled to:

- o The Dome, Brighton on February 10,
- o Plymouth's Guild Hall on the 12th,
- o Exeter University on the 14th,
- o Green's Playhouse Glasgow 16th
- o Sheffield City Hall on the 17th,
- o Birmingham Town Hall on the 18th,
- o Oxford, York, Newcastle and Lancaster.

Later in their career, Genesis would be criticized for limiting their British tours to a handful of arena shows but, in these early days, fans all around the country could see the relatively unknown combo in their local clubs and theatres. After years of relentlessly touring small venues, Genesis could be forgiven for taking it a little easier.

The band's February 24 performance at the Free Trade Hall in Manchester was recorded for the American radio program *The King Biscuit Hour*. The recording of *Return Of The Giant Hogweed* on GENESIS LIVE is from this concert. The following day's gig at the DeMontfort Hall in Leicester, also recorded for *King Biscuit*. That evening's performances of *Watcher Of The Skies, Get Em Out By Friday, The Musical Box* and *The Knife* would all eventually appear on the album GENESIS LIVE.

In March, the group returned to North America, playing in Quebec City, Rochester, Miami, New York City (at Carnegie Hall this time), Pittsburgh, Cleveland and Philadelphia. Although far from being a household name, Genesis was cultivating a devoted fan base in Canada and the United States. However, not everyone was prepared to move forward. Richard MacPhail, who had known them since Charterhouse and had been their road manager in the leanest years, left. As the group grew bigger, MacPhail became disillusioned with the business side of the music business. His departure was noted on the back cover of GENESIS LIVE, in such a way that some fans assumed he had died! He is, in fact, still alive, gainfully employed as an environmental consultant. Richard recently shared his Genesis memories in an essay included with the ARCHIVE box set.

Chapter 8: I Know What I Like

In the spring of 1973, Genesis took some time off from gigging, to write and rehearse material for their next long player, SELLING ENGLAND BY THE POUND. After the success of FOXTROT, Charisma gave the group two months to write and rehearse new songs. If anything, the luxurious (by their standards) length of time they were given made things more difficult. Used to working to tight deadlines, the extra time let them endlessly re-work ideas, sometimes going round in circles. This album was, in Rutherford's words, "bloody hard to write." It was a depressing time for the group, probably the beginning of the negative feelings that would remain until Gabriel's departure. However, there were enough magic moments and inspired jam sessions to produce such enduring compositions as *I Know What I Like (In Your Wardrobe)*, *The Cinema Show* and *Firth Of Fifth*.

"I approached it from a player's point of view," says Steve Hackett of the writing process for SELLING ENGLAND. "I thought, 'I'm not gonna try and compete with the others with regards to songs.' My domestic life was in chaos at the time (Hackett's first marriage had just ended), so I didn't really try and write songs. I thought, 'I'll just give the band riffs and that way they can reject them or incorporate them.' And this seemed to pay off. It meant that someone else could be the Poet Laureate, somebody else could do their thing. I didn't want to stand in anyone's way or steal their thunder."

"Obviously we're out of the public's attention," Tony Banks told the *NME* during a break in the rehearsals. "But we come back that much stronger; some bands seem afraid to take time off; they feel they have to capitalize on their popularity. What we've been doing is running through many different musical ideas. That's what takes up most of our time. The rest of the time is spent putting everything together, making it flow. We try to file all these little musical ideas into a giant catalogue in our heads. And quite often we'll find room for old passages — after all, joining on any two sequences is possible."

With work on the next Genesis album progressing slowly, Charisma were eager to get some new product out, to capitalize on the band's newfound success. The label suggested releasing some of the live recordings that had been made for the KING BISCUIT show in February. The KING BISCUIT recordings were very impressive, capturing on tape the power of the group's live show.

Although Genesis didn't want to release a live album at that stage, Charisma proposed releasing one in Germany only. Reluctantly, the band agreed. After the go-ahead had been given, the label explained that a Germany-only release might cause problems with imports coming into Britain, so it would be better if the album could just be released worldwide. It was also explained that the record would be a budget release, which would get a wider distribution than a full-price release. The group gave in, and Charisma released GENESIS LIVE in July 1973. The album's budget price and wider distribution helped boost the record's sales and it reached No. 9 in Britain. It was also the first Genesis record to chart in America, albeit at a peak position of No. 105.

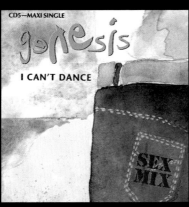

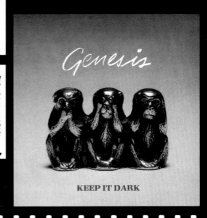

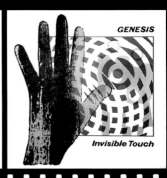

SELLING ENGLAND BY THE POUND

CIRCUS

NO. 106 · GREAT BRITAIN · 35p · #48241 MARCH 1975/$1.00

MARK FARNER IN EXCLUSIVE: Confessions Of A Hard Rocker

GENESIS— WILL AMERICA SWALLOW 'THE LAMB'?

JONI MITCHELL— CAN 'MILES OF AISLES' KNOCK CARLY & CAROLE OFF THE THRONE?

RINGO— MIXING DOWN 'GOODNIGHT VIENNA' WITH RICHARD PERRY

THE GUESS WHO BATTLE OBSCURITY WITH 'FLAVOURS'

KISS— WHY THE BIG BANDS HATE THEM

NEKTAR LAUNCH A GERMAN ROCK SIDESHOW WITH 'DOWN TO EARTH'

THE KINKS'

LANCE LOUD On The Death

GENESIS

ROMA - 17 MAGGIO '87
STADIO FLAMINIO

MILANO - 19 MAGGIO '87
STADIO SAN SIRO

AFFICHE WHO
POSTER BOWIE

Best
96

LES SHOWS DE
GENESIS

INTERVIEWS
PATTI SMITH
ROD STEWART

**LES STONES
EN FRANCE**
TOUT
SUR LES
FESTIVALS
LE
ROCK
D'ICI

mensuel·5F·5FS·50FB·Canada $1

GENESIS — A TRICK OF THE ACTION

PRESENTING GENESIS

KNEBWORTH

THE STORY OF
GENESIS

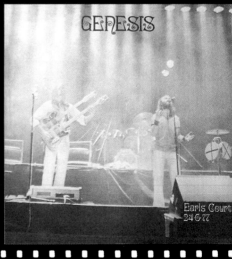

GENESIS

Earls Court
24·6·77

Face Value · Phil Collins

Steve Hackett

peter gabriel

PLAYS LIVE

ANTHONY PHILLIPS

The Archive Collection

Volume One

TONY BANKS
The Fugitive

Voyage of the Acolyte

Steve Hackett

CHESTER THOMPSON

GENESIS REVISITED
STEVE HACKETT

A CURIOUS FEELING
TONY BANKS

Twenty-six years later, GENESIS LIVE remains an excellent representation of the classic line-up's dynamic stage shows. It's the least polished of the five live Genesis albums, but the most powerful. Its only flaw is the omission of Gabriel's stories, although his dry humor is briefly evident before *The Musical Box*.

"Up until then, we never actually felt that we sounded as good live as we did on record," said Phil Collins. "In fact it was just the opposite — we always sounded more gutsy on stage than we did on record."

It's possible that GENESIS LIVE may at some point have been planned as a double album. There exists a test pressing of a two-record version, featuring the following line-up:

Side 1: *Watcher Of The Skies / The Musical Box*
Side 2: *Get 'Em Out By Friday*
Side 3: *Supper's Ready*
Side 4: *The Return Of The Giant Hogweed / The Knife*

ITALIAN VERSION OF THE GENESIS LIVE ALBUM.

Whether this was ever intended for release is open to speculation. However the idea of a double album would seemingly have gone against the intention of making GENESIS LIVE a budget-priced release.

"When you're working on new material it's quite difficult getting excited about old material," Steve Hackett told the *NME*. "Our best number, *Supper's Ready*, isn't on the live album as we couldn't very well release two albums with identical sides. Some tracks on the album are better than the studio recordings especially *Return of the Giant Hogweed* and *Musical Box*. Aside from occasional flaws in the playing, the sound is very good."

In August, the band returned to Island Studios, ready to record their new batch of songs. Having found a sympathetic ear in John Burns, they retained his services as co-producer on the new album, with Rhett Davies serving as engineer.

SIDE 4 OF THE DUTCH TEST PRESSING OF GENESIS LIVE.

The album's title, SELLING ENGLAND BY THE POUND, came from the lyrics of the opening track, *Dancing With The Moonlit Knight*. (Actually, Gabriel had taken the phrase "selling England by the pound" phrase from the British Labour Party manifesto of the time.) Musically, this number combined several Gabriel piano pieces with a Hackett guitar figure, and lyrics by Gabriel. At one point during the *Selling England* sessions, the group reportedly considered linking *Moonlit Knight* and *Cinema Show* together as one long piece.

A particularly noteworthy feature of *Moonlit Knight* was Hackett's nimble lead guitar work.

"I'd invented this thing called 'tapping'," he remembers. "Which I'd used briefly on *The Musical Box*. I decided to put it to full use on the solo for *Dancing With The Moonlit Knight*. It was very fast guitar playing, which was only made possible through tapping. It was ideas like that that seemed to fire people up. I played that to Phil and he said, 'Well, if you do that, I can do this.' And suddenly we were all steaming along at a million miles an hour and the thing took flight."

I KNOW WHAT I LIKE SINGLE.

I Know What I Like (In Your Wardrobe) was based on a guitar riff that Steve had come up with a year or two earlier. When he and Phil had jammed on it during the FOXTROT sessions, some of the others dismissed it as "too Beatle-esque." But Steve's riff refused to go away, and Genesis started jamming on it again during the writing period for SELLING ENGLAND. The band would jam on the hypnotic riff for hours and, one day, when Banks added fuzz electric piano and organ, a song began to take shape. The two keyboards were just a little out of tune with each other, which created a great effect, while Gabriel made strange noises into his microphone. Banks came up with the melody for the chorus and Gabriel penned the lyrics, inspired by the Betty Swanwick painting that ended up gracing the album sleeve.

"I think we probably felt at the time that it had single potential," said Tony. "But we also accepted we had very little idea about singles and we never aimed for them anyhow."

GENESIS

SELLING ENGLAND BY THE POUND

SELLING ENGLAND BY THE POUND, 1973

"We used to joke about it as our hit single," said Steve. "Everyone used to say, 'Oh, pass the hit single please, will you.' We sat around and Pete and Phil jammed a vocal which developed from something on the guitar, and it was transformed from something which sounded a little too much like the Beatles to something which sounded a lot like Genesis."

Firth Of Fifth was mostly written mostly by Tony Banks. The song was initially attempted for FOXTROT, but didn't gel with the band. It was successfully revised for SELLING ENGLAND, and went on to become a Genesis classic and a staple of their live sets for many years to come. Interestingly, Banks has said that he doesn't like the songs lyrics, which he himself wrote, at least in part. He told Hugh Fielder that it was "one of the worst set of lyrics I've been involved with ... I really don't think it has anything going for it." Musically, however, the track had plenty going for it, including Tony's glorious solo piano intro and some haunting lead guitar work from Steve.

TWILIGHT ALEHOUSE, B-SIDE TO THE BRITISH *I KNOW WHAT I LIKE* SINGLE, 1973.

"*Firth Of Fifth* was more sort of my bits really," recalled Banks during a Virgin online chat in the late 90's. "Then we would arrange it as a group and the idea was to give it a group character so that one person didn't dominate and you let everybody play their instruments and you tried things out. Like for example you mentioned before the feeling in *Firth Of Fifth*. I originally conceived it as a piano thing and we just tried it one time, I played the Mellotron and Steve played it on guitar. It sounded fantastic and we obviously had to use that and it gave another dimension to the song."

Written by Mike and Phil, *More Fool Me* was a precursor to the post-Gabriel Genesis sound. A simple acoustic love ballad, the track featured Phil on lead vocals and featured a lyrical directness that anticipated his later solo work.

The Battle Of Epping Forest was inspired by a newspaper story about rival gangs from London's East End. It featured Peter singing his own lyrics and melody over a backing track penned in part by Tony. The consensus among the band members seems to be that the main battle in this number is the battle between the complex backing track and the tricky vocal line, each of which seems in danger of overwhelming the other. The song anticipated the streetwise storytelling of THE LAMB LIES DOWN ON BROADWAY, but there was too much happening at once.

> "We all had a part of our own and none of us would shift on our own parts," said Tony Banks during the Virgin online chat. ""It worked really well in places and (was) lyrically very interesting, but there's so much going on that many parts get lost in the depth."

> "*The Battle of Epping Forest* just has too many words per minute," Phil told writer Hugh Fielder. "If we had worked on the lyrics beforehand, or if there'd been a melody to start with, we could have said, 'Hang on, we'll take a breather here.' As it is, you end up having to take the record off to have a burst of oxygen before you can listen to the next track!"

Gabriel has admitted that he got "carried away" with the lyrics to *Epping Forest*, and that they didn't really fit with the music. As on THE LAMB LIES DOWN ON BROADWAY, Gabriel insisted on writing the lyrics himself, since he felt that he was a better lyricist than the others in the band. But, as on THE LAMB, Gabriel took so long finishing the words that the other four had already recorded the instrumental backing tracks before the lyrics were done. Therefore there was no way to change the music to better accommodate Gabriel's lyrics.

Many years later, during the Virgin online chat, Banks offered the following assessment of *Epping Forest*:

> "At the time of SELLING ENGLAND BY THE POUND we were actually a little bit dry of ideas. We had six weeks of rehearsal and we ended up playing that song every day and it got more and more elaborate, we added more and more bits and expanded on it. Everybody had a part and everybody's part on its own was good enough to be the top line of the song and none of us would give an inch. Then when we finally finished this thing we had to put vocal on it and of course the vocals were really good as well. The trouble is there is so much going on in that song, I find it a very uncomfortable song actually. I find the rhythm of the middle section very uncomfortable, Steve at the time said we should not have done it that way and I'm absolutely with him on that."

Steve wrote the instrumental *After The Ordeal* mostly on his own, but Mike contributed the ending section. Apparently, neither Gabriel nor Banks felt this should have been included on the LP. Tony has said that his dislike of the track came at least in part from his dissatisfaction with his own playing, although Banks was never exactly a champion of Hackett's compositional contributions to Genesis. The track made it onto the album through a loophole of band politics. Neither Gabriel nor Banks wanted it on, but Gabriel didn't want the last section of *Cinema Show* included either, which weakened his position.

THIS *CINEMA SHOW* BOOTLEG FEATURES LIVE PREFORMANCES FROM 1973 AND 1977.

One of the album's most enduring numbers was the penultimate track, *The Cinema Show*. Musically, the first part of the song was penned by Mike Rutherford, beautifully reminiscent of the kind of 12-string pieces he used to devise with Anthony Phillips. The latter parts of the song grew from jamming between Collins, Banks and Rutherford.

The trio jammed on a Rutherford riff in 7/8 time, with Banks experimenting with chord changes. Rutherford played rhythm guitar, but only strummed the bottom strings of his guitar, giving Banks greater freedom to play different keyboard chords. They developed a number of different sections, then assembled them in a cohesive order, a technique similar to the one the trio would use in their songwriting efforts in the 80's.

Banks and Rutherford penned the lyrics for *The Cinema Show*, inspired by T.S. Eliot's 'The Waste Land'. The idea of using the names "Romeo" and "Juliet" was Gabriel's, although the singer was not particularly fond of the results. "Pete didn't like the lyric at all," Tony Banks told Hugh Fielder. "He felt that we were out of our depth. But I think he was wrong." Gabriel also disliked the last section of the song and felt that it shouldn't be included. In terms of band politics (since the other four all liked the end of *Cinema Show*), this weakened his position on *After The Ordeal*, allowing that track to be included. The closing number, *Aisle Of Plenty*, was essentially a reprise of *Dancing With The Moonlit Knight*, with Peter singing his own lyrics (and quoting supermarket prices) over Steve's guitar figure.

During this period, Peter showed the band a song he was working on, called *Deja Vu*. The song wasn't finished and the group didn't record it, but it clearly made an impression on Steve Hackett. More than twenty years later, Steve — with Peter's co-operation — finished the song for inclusion on his GENESIS REVISITED album, with vocals by Paul Carrack. "It always seemed like it was going to be a nice one," Hackett says. "It was a little idea that had something."

Hackett has vivid memories of another promising number from the SELLING ENGLAND era that was never finished.

> "There were a couple of chords that Tony used to play — something that I thought was going to become the natural successor to *Watcher Of The Skies*. It used the same Mellotron sound — brass and strings mixed, with the accordion playing the bass on the left hand manual. It was something that sounded really great to my ears, but we never managed to develop it into anything. We

approached it in the same way as *Watcher Of The Skies*, trying to put a jerky rhythm underneath it. In fact, we should have abandoned that and just let it go for what it was."

Although the others have expressed dissatisfaction with the album, SELLING ENGLAND has always been a favorite of Steve's.

"I felt there was a vast improvement in the level of musicianship on SELLING ENGLAND BY THE POUND," he says. "We used to take jams and refine them and put them into sections, lots of sections of lots of jams. We would play endlessly over the same riffs together, so that whoever was soloing could get a chance to hone his bit down. Sometimes I would use a tape that Phil had made. He used to like to record rehearsals."

Although Tony Stratton-Smith had been unwavering in his support of Genesis, he was a little disappointed with SELLING ENGLAND BY THE POUND, feeling that too much of the album was instrumental. The fact that he didn't attempt to tamper with the band's choice of material says a lot about their relationship with Charisma and Strat. Although the label let the band indulge themselves in areas that seemed to be less 'commercial,' their faith was ultimately rewarded. For all its lengthy instrumental workouts, SELLING ENGLAND also included that which Genesis had previously been incapable of producing — a hit single. In early 1974, *I Know What I Like* climbed to No. 21 in the British charts, with the FOXTROT-era recording of *Twilight Alehouse* on its flipside.

During this period, Mike Rutherford renewed his partnership with Anthony Phillips. The duo recorded the unreleased single *Silver Song* with Phil Collins, and worked on material that would eventually surface on Phillips' 1977 album THE GEESE AND THE GHOST. The initial plan was to release *Silver Song* as a Phil Collins solo single backed by *Only Your Love*, another number recorded at the same sessions. Sadly both were shelved and fans have only heard them as lo-fi bootleg tracks.

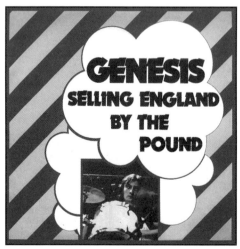

THIS VERSION OF THE SELLING ENGLAND BY THE POUND LP WAS RELEASED IN PORTUGAL.

"I have a feeling that they might well put Phil's version on the next Genesis box set, if they do one," Phillips speculates. "Even then, in late 73, his vocal was fantastic, brilliant, and his drumming. The whole thing was done in a rush, A-side and B-side, recorded and mixed all in a day, because it was in the middle of a tour. And it sounded like it."

In October, SELLING ENGLAND BY THE POUND was released and Genesis took their new songs out on the road. The British tour in support of the album was supposed to open at the Apollo Theatre

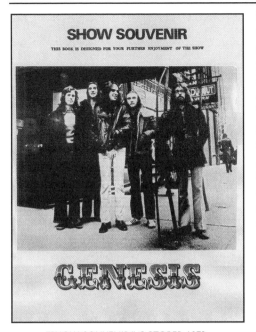

"SHOW SOUVENIR," OCTOBER 1973.

A 1973 CONCERT PROGRAM.

in Glasgow on October 5, but the show was cancelled at the last minute — with the audience already seated — due to technical problems. Instead, the tour began at the Opera House in Manchester on the 6th, moving to Oxford's New Theatre the next day. Glaswegian fans returned to the Apollo for the rescheduled dates on the 8th and 9th. After Glasgow, Genesis played the Gaumont in Southampton, the Winter Gardens in Bournemouth, the Dome in Brighton, Colston Hall in Bristol and the DeMontfort Hall in Leicester.

The live recordings on the third disc of the ARCHIVE box set were made at the band's October 20 appearance at the Rainbow Theatre in London. Along with the new songs on the SELLING ENGLAND tour, there were new stories and new costumes. After removing the traditional batwings of the opening *Watcher Of The Skies*, Gabriel reappeared in a new, unfamiliar guise, the helmet and shield of "Britannia." *Battle Of Epping Forest!!* ventured an eager audience member. "Wrong," countered a deadpan Gabriel, before setting the scene for *Dancing With The Moonlit Knight*.

They played the soon-to-be-hit single *I Know What I Like*, followed by *Firth of Fifth, More Fool Me, Supper's Ready, The Battle Of Epping Forest* and *Cinema Show*. *Epping Forest* proved to be a difficult live number for Gabriel, who performed it with a stocking pulled over his head and was frequently out of breath as he delivered the word-packed lyrics. After the Rainbow, the show moved on to Liverpool's Empire Theatre, Sheffield City Hall, Newcastle City Hall and the Hippodrome in Birmingham.

In November, Britannia and company took their new songs to North America, playing to appreciative crowds in Buffalo, Quebec City, Toronto, Montreal, New York City, Columbus, Cleveland, Ann Arbour and

Miami. The New York performance, at the Felt Forum, was reviewed in the *New York Times* by Ian Dove, who stated,

> "Genesis runs the full spectrum, employing back projection, mime costume changes and a little spectacle. Not that Genesis's music needs any window dressing to disguise any inadequacies: it is not rock perhaps, but stories and ideas, decked out in costume and gesture, tied together strongly by the music. Genesis appears to be poised at the brink of a real American career."

A typical set from this era comprised *Watcher Of The Skies, Firth Of Fifth, The Musical Box, Dancing With The Moonlit Knight, The Cinema Show, I Know What I Like, Supper's Ready, Horizons, More Fool Me, The Battle Of Epping Forest* and *The Knife*.

In December, Genesis made an appearance on the popular American TV show *Midnight Special*. The group performed their current Stateside single *Watcher Of The Skies*, but the record still managed to evade the American singles charts. Chart-toppers like Charlie Rich's *The Most Beautiful Girl* and Steve Miller's *The Joker* had little to fear from the English quintet's sci-fi ditty. Still, Genesis were slowly winning over an American following. They played six successful shows during a three-night stand at the Roxy in Los Angeles, on December 17, 18 and 19, 1973. "Genesis' show is the most perfectly realized piece of rock theater yet to come along," said *Los Angeles Times* writer Richard Cromelin of the Roxy gigs.

A GENESIS EUROPEAN TOUR POSTER.

After a three week break over Christmas, it was back to work. From January 18-22, 1974, the band played a five-night stand at the Theatre Royal, Drury Lane in London, a prestigious venue was not normally associated with rock groups. The London *Times* observed that "never before has a rock group taken over the house for a week." But Genesis were hardly your run-of-the-mill rock combo. Their lofty musical aspirations and theatrical presentation made them a perfect choice for such a venue. It was a prestigious event and helped solidify the group's rapidly growing reputation.

There followed a trek through Europe, with stops in Brussels, Dusseldorf, Offenbach and Winterthur, Switzerland during the last days of January. In early February, they returned to the Palasports of Italy, regaling their devoted fans with newer numbers like *Firth Of Fifth, Dancing With The Moonlit Knight* and *The Cinema Show*.

Notably absent from most of the concerts was Tony's gorgeous piano intro to *Firth Of Fifth*.

"I used to play it on an RMI piano," he explained during the Virgin online chat. "We played it one time at Drury Lane, we just didn't finish it actually, I ran out of notes and threw my hands up in the air in despair and we started the song without it. I think the feeling was actually more that the show slowed down at that point, it didn't seem appropriate. At certain kinds of venues at a certain kind of period it was right but once the song was known and people had heard the solo a few times to keep playing it seemed a little bit unnecessary."

As March began, so did another North American tour, their most extensive to date. For the first time ever, the citizens of Baltimore, Fort Wayne, Kansas City and Phoenix got a taste of this very English ensemble.

The group's Santa Monica show won them another rave review from the *Los Angeles Times*' Richard Cromelin, who wrote:

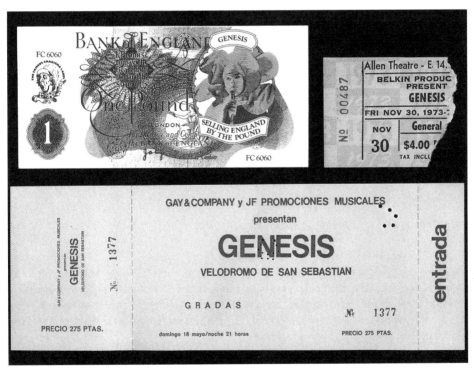

A COUPLE OF CONCERT TICKETS AND A PROMOTIONAL POUND NOTE BEARING THE LIKENESS OF PETER GABRIEL.

"It's the array of archetypal characters who roam through the lengthy *Supper's Ready* that cling most tenaciously. The moment at which the apocalyptic war ends in a blinding explosion and Gabriel emerges through the smoke as a silver-suited Christ-like figure (or is it just a rock 'n' roll star?) is completely breathtaking and makes all the tentative, dead-end steps theatrical rock has taken worth the trouble."

The tour lasted more than two months and took in most major cities in the States and Canada. Audiences in Montreal seemed to have a particular affinity for Genesis' progressive sound, and the April 20 and 21 dates at the University Sports Center went over particularly well. To the delight of the audience, Gabriel told his stories in French at these shows. The typical set list for these shows was: *Watcher Of The Skies, Dancing With The Moonlit Knight, Cinema Show, I Know What I Like, Firth Of Fifth, The Musical Box*, a Steve Hackett solo performance of *Horizons, The Battle Of Epping Forest* and *Supper's Ready*.

Chapter 9: The Light Dies Down

HEADLEY GRANGE, HAMPSHIRE

In June 1974, Genesis began the writing and rehearsal period for their next album. The plan was to write, rehearse and record at Headley Grange, Hampshire, where other groups — notably Led Zeppelin — had found inspiration. The group was eager to record in a more natural setting, to capture a vibe closer to their rehearsal sessions. Phil Collins, who diligently recorded all the group's rehearsals, was especially keen on this idea. "Whenever I tape a rehearsal it always seems to have more feeling than when the final LP comes out after it's been mixed and remixed in the studio," he told *Melody Maker*. It was a notion that predicted the more spontaneous recording approach of later albums like ABACAB.

Since their earliest recording sessions, Genesis had been very aware of how the initial energy of a new song can dissipate through the process of rehearsing, recording and mixing. Even back in 1970, Gabriel had lamented (in a *Sounds* piece) that, "we can't always recapture the goodness of a song when it's first organized. It's very difficult to get the circumstances and the set-up to recreate the sound; for instance when you create a sound in a rehearsal room you get a really exciting moment when things haven't got a shape." But, with looming deadlines and Gabriel's slow progress with the lyrics, the "planned spontaneity" fell by the wayside.

Several ideas had been discussed for a concept album, including an adaptation of the book *The Little Prince*. Although Mike Rutherford was particularly fond of this idea, Gabriel felt it was "too twee . . . I thought we needed to base the story around a contemporary figure, rather than a fantasy creation." The quintet eventually agreed upon an idea of Gabriel's, to be called THE LAMB LIES DOWN ON BROADWAY. Gabriel's story of Rael, a streetwise Puerto Rican youth in New York City, was a bizarre, somewhat obscure parable.

"THE LAMB was intended to be like a *Pilgrim's Progress*," Gabriel told author Spencer Bright, "An adventure through which one gets a better understanding of self — the transformation theme. I was trying to give it a street slant, and that was before punk happened. I felt an energy in that direction, and it seemed that prancing around in fairyland was rapidly becoming obsolete."

Perhaps Gabriel simply felt that Genesis was rapidly becoming obsolete. Shortly after rehearsals for the new record began, the singer was briefly estranged from the rest of the group, while pursuing a possible film project. In the early days of Genesis, he had been considering a film career, so he was naturally tempted when director William Friedkin expressed interest in having him write a screenplay. Also, Peter's first child was born that July, giving him all the more reason to re-evaluate his priorities. Staying at home to work on a screenplay would certainly give him a lot more time to spend with his wife and new daughter.

"He left before we started THE LAMB," recalls Steve Hackett. "He was going to work with William Friedkin, the guy who directed *The Exorcist*. He wanted Peter to write a screenplay for him, as far as I know. So he left, and we were thinking about other singers for the band, but luckily, a few days later, he changed his mind, or Friedkin went off the boil, or whatever it was. He rejoined the band. He said, 'I'm gonna rejoin the band for one album and I'm gonna tour it. I'm not gonna let you down.'"

"It turned into a double album," says Hackett. "I'm not quite sure why. I think it was because we were all traumatized by Peter's departure, and no one really wanted him to leave. Reading between the lines, the subtext was that everyone felt that the longer we stretched everything out, the less likely he was to leave. So the album became very long, the touring became very long. We ran out of time at Headley Grange, so we didn't get to record there. And that was a shame, because we all liked the drum sound on the Zeppelin album, in particular *Kashmir*, which I gather was recorded using the stairwell. The place had a haunted house vibe. I used to hear weird scratching sounds at night."

The four musicians spent their days writing the music, with Gabriel sequestered in another room, toiling over the lyrics. Although other band members had previously written song lyrics on each album, Gabriel insisted on writing all the words for THE LAMB himself. The story was very much his baby and he strongly felt that the lyrics should all be his. The others reluctantly agreed, although time constraints eventually caused Gabriel to let Rutherford and Banks do the lyrics for one number, *The Light Dies Down On Broadway*. The fact that Gabriel insisted on writing all the lyrics, but then couldn't complete them on schedule, only worsened his increasingly strained relationship with the other four. In some cases, Gabriel wrote the music as well as the lyrics. He wrote all of *Counting Out Time* on his own and most of *The Chamber Of 32 Doors*.

In July, the quintet ran out of time at Headley Grange and had to find another place to park the mobile recording studio. In August, they relocated to a farmhouse in Glosspant, Wales. Using the Island Mobile Studio, they spent two weeks there, laying down the backing tracks for the album. Once again, John Burns co-produced with the band, and David Hutchins engineered.

In spite of the tension that surrounded the project, there were many inspired musical moments. *The Waiting Room* (AKA "Evil Jam") came out of a spooky late night session, during which the band switched off all the lights and coaxed strange sounds from their instruments. While Steve and Tony drew eerie noises from guitar and synthesizer, Peter blew his oboe reeds and layered his flute with the looped sound of an Echoplex unit. Amidst the dark, disturbing sounds, there came a sudden burst of thunder and rain, and the quintet shuddered at the thought that their "Evil Jam" had conjured up some higher power.

Tony Banks has said that *The Grand Parade Of Lifeless Packaging* was one of his favorite tracks on THE LAMB, although he felt that it was under-developed. *Lilywhite Lilith* was essentially a rewrite of *The Light*, and *Anyway* was also recycled from an earlier idea, some of its music having been featured the BBC documentary Genesis scored in 1970.

The backing tracks for THE LAMB were done in a couple of weeks but, a month after the music was finished, Gabriel was still working on the lyrics. To make matters worse, Gabriel then came back to the others asking them to write more music to fit in with the lyrics he was writing. And, when he finally finished and recorded his vocals, Gabriel sang over passages that the others had assumed were instrumental, which only worsened an already tense situation. To Steve Hackett, it was as though he had done a painting and then watched someone else come in and paint all over his work. The vocals were recorded at Island Studios in London, with the band mixing the record in shifts to meet the November release date.

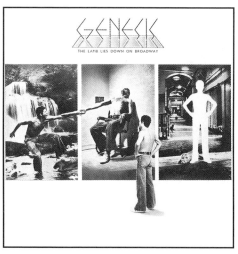

THE LAMB LIES DOWN ON BROADWAY, 1974.

When THE LAMB LIES DOWN ON BROADWAY came out in November 1974, it baffled many listeners. Even coming from a long-established group of chart-toppers it would have been a risky proposition, but for Genesis, it was a huge gamble. The LAMB was difficult to fathom, and the Gabriel-penned story included in the gatefold sleeve didn't really make it much clearer.

The consensus, after the fact, was that it was a mistake to put THE LAMB out as a double LP. Phil Collins suggested that THE LAMB ought to have been a single disc. "The trouble was it was a double," he told the *NME* after Gabriel's departure. "That album should have been a single and our *next* could've been a double." At one point, the band even toyed with the idea of releasing THE LAMB as two single LP's, a few months apart. This would have given them more time to finish it and would probably have made the whole thing a little easier to digest.

From Gabriel's point of view, THE LAMB was very accessible.

"The album seems clearer in my head than a lot of what we've done before," he told *Creem*. "We look upon it as being comprised of much shorter units than before. I would like best to see THE LAMB as a film, because that would clarify the imagery further than a performance or the record. A film is the easiest medium by which to build another reality. The point of Rael being earthy and aggressive is that he provides an accessible response to these fantasy situations. Rael seemed a good starting point because he's surrounded by all this speed and aggression which New York has more of than any other city."

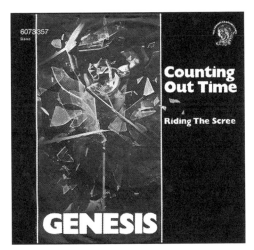

The album was preceded in the U.K. by the single *Counting Out Time*. Musically, the song was simple and catchy — about as close as Genesis got to pop in those days. Only the lyrics (chorus: "Erogenous zones, I love you . . .") hinted at what was to come on the sprawling double concept LP. Steve Hackett's propensity for unusual guitar sounds was particularly evident on his solo on *Counting Out Time*. Although many listeners assumed it to be a kazoo or a keyboard or a voice, the solo was in fact conjured up by Hackett's new High Fly guitar synthesizer.

As if the double LP wasn't already overwhelming fans with new material, Genesis' subsequent tour dates consisted of THE LAMB LIES DOWN ON BROADWAY performed in its entirety. Those who came to hear anything pre-*Lamb* had to wait until the end of the show, when the group performed *Watcher Of The Skies* and *The Musical Box* (or, on occasion, *The Knife*). In fact, since THE LAMB wasn't even released until a few dates into the American tour, many fans were treated to almost an entire show of songs they'd never heard before.

The British tour, planned to coincide with the album's release, had to be re-scheduled, so the Americans were the first to get a taste of THE LAMB show. The tour was originally to have started on October 29 in Britain, but was pushed back due to delays on the album, not to mention a injury incurred by Steve Hackett, who had severed a tendon and a nerve in this thumb.

"With this new stage show, we've left a lot of things looser than we ever have before," Hackett told *Creem*. "We're taking a chance that our spontaneous improvisations will create something we haven't had much of as yet. I think we're playing THE LAMB even better live now than we did on record."

"There are about six improvised sections, but one — *The Waiting Room* — is about ten minutes long," Tony told *Melody Maker*. "Some nights it's great, some nights it's awful, which is nice, really, because it means there's a challenge to it."

THIS 80'S EUROPEAN REISSUE OF THE LAMB WAS CLEARLY DESIGNED TO CAPITALIZE ON PHIL'S SOLO SUCCESS.

Indeed, the idea of improvising onstage was new to Genesis, who had previously mapped out every note of their performance, right down to the guitar solos.

THE LAMB show featured as its backdrop three screens, onto which 3,000 slides were projected in the course of the concert. It was an extravagant presentation for an up-and-coming band and probably pushed Genesis deeper into debt. As the notes in THE LAMB tour program explained, "Not a terribly wealthy band, Genesis continually feed profits back into the stage show."

Despite the increasingly elaborate staging, it appeared that the band's priorities hadn't changed too much since the Charterhouse days. "To this day," stated the program, "the band insist that they are primarily songwriters who play at being musicians and only later play at being presenters." It was this distinction that made them different from groups like Yes or ELP, whose musicianship often seemed like showing off, or Kiss and Alice Cooper, whose costumes seemed like a gimmick rather than an aid to the songs.

1974 PROGRAM

The tour began on November 20, at the Auditorium Theatre in Chicago. That day is still clear in Steve Hackett's mind. Although the tour had been delayed due to his injury, Steve's hand still hadn't fully recovered.

"That day I had a very weakened left hand," he recalls of the day THE LAMB lay down in Chicago. "I went to a hospital and had electric shock treatment on my hand, to set it working. I swear the guy who was giving me the so-called physical therapy was a sado-masochist, who was turning the juice up much too high and getting off on it. I swear. And then I had a shot in my tooth. I had bitten on a pretzel the night before and a filling had come out. And then, in the evening, I had to remember almost two hours of music that I'd never played before."

78

It was a challenging show, played to an audience who had yet to hear the double album.

"You had an audience who were coming along to listen to old favorites," Steve explains, "Who were not exactly thrilled to see this English band playing a concept album based on the idea of a New Yorker who hails from Puerto Rico. It was one of those days when life throws everything at you."

Once the show started, Genesis threw everything at their audience. In concert, THE LAMB was a multimedia extravaganza. The show opened with Tony Banks' piano intro, as images of "early morning Manhattan" filled the screens at the back of the stage. Gabriel soon appeared, almost unrecognizable at first, in his Rael gear: short hair, make-up, leather jacket and jeans. It was a far cry from his Britannia and Narcissus guises, just as the music contrasted sharply with Genesis' earlier work.

GABRIEL MAKING AN APPEARENCE IN HIS SLIPPERMAN COSTUME.

For *The Arrival / Colony Of Slippermen* sequence Gabriel, disguised by his hideous Slipperman costume, emerged from a long plastic tunnel. Although the costume was visually striking, it rendered Gabriel's vocals somewhat inaudible (a problem that would have to be addressed for the release of the live LAMB recording twenty-three years later). During *It*, an onstage explosion was followed by the appearance of two Peter Gabriels onstage. A clever bit of visual trickery, and few in the audience could determine which Rael was real and which was the dummy.

American audiences soon got to know THE LAMB and it became Genesis' highest charting album there yet, reaching No. 41. Back home in Britain, it peaked at No. 10, a few spots lower than SELLING ENGLAND BY THE POUND.

In late November, the band arrived in Cleveland for a two-night stand at the Allen Theater. From the outside, the tour appeared to be going well, but Peter Gabriel was not a happy man. After just a handful of dates, Gabriel had realized that this tour had to be his last with Genesis. Although he had left and come back before THE LAMB, there was still hope that he would decide to stay on with the group. But, in Cleveland, the singer became acutely aware that it was over. He went to Tony Smith's hotel room and told the manager that he was leaving. Smith urged him to reconsider, but this time there would be no talking Gabriel out of his decision. It had been weighing heavily on his mind and he needed to let his feelings be known. The fact that Gabriel decided to tell the group's manager first, rather than his bandmates says a lot about the situation in Genesis, and about Gabriel's relationship with the others at that time. (Interestingly, when Phil Collins decided to jump ship two decades later, he also told Tony Smith before he told Banks and Rutherford.)

Gabriel didn't tell the other band members until a few days later, when the tour rolled into Montreal. Understandably, they resisted his decision, which seemed to be chucking away all that they had worked so hard to achieve. It wasn't just that Gabriel wanted out of Genesis, but also that he wanted the opportunity to work on other projects, outside the group. Like Steve Hackett two-and-a-half years later, Gabriel felt that if he were to stay in Genesis, he would have little chance to pursue other projects. The aborted Friedkin project had been a missed opportunity and Gabriel didn't want to miss the next one.

Also, Gabriel had been writing on the piano more and more and wanted to play the parts he was writing himself. In Genesis, this wouldn't have been possible, Tony Banks being particularly territorial about his keyboard duties. Once, when Banks was absent from a recording session, Gabriel had fired up one of his keyboards and recorded a part. Reportedly, Tony was none too pleased to discover this upon his return the next day. And Gabriel, like Phil Collins, was not a formally trained keyboard player and would likely have written parts that were not "technically" right, and that a formal player like Banks might have tried to "correct."

In addition, the more successful Genesis became, the less freedom Gabriel seemed to have. As he later put it in *Solsbury Hill*, he felt like he was trapped in "the machinery."

> "There was all this big time stuff happening," he recalled in the *History* video. "Long tours being planned way in the future. I just felt I was getting to be part of the machine . . . I didn't feel free."

The others certainly didn't want Peter to leave. In part, this was for financial reasons.

> "When I left, we still hadn't made any money, even though everyone assumed we were millionaires," Gabriel said years later. "We'd accumulated huge debts, which was one of the reasons why I had a lot of pressure to stay in the band at that point."

The tour continued through Canada and the United States through until late December: Columbus, Detroit, Pittsburgh, Baltimore, Richmond, Philadelphia, New York City, Providence, Montreal, Albany, Waterbury, Toronto, Rochester, Buffalo . . . The New York gig, at the Academy of Music, garnered another positive review from the *New York Times*, in which Ian Dove observed that "Peter Gabriel, who has previously been given to dressing on stage as Merlin the Magician, appeared this time in 'punk' street clothes — leather jacket, T-shirt and jeans — to fit the story."

"As usual, Genesis was occasionally profound, sometimes bombastic, now and then overblown and with music to match all these moods — not to mention the non-abstract slides the group projects along with the story. For all the high-seriousness, Mr. Gabriel has always been able to inject some esoteric humor into the show. There were only flashes of it on Friday — maybe being a lamb on Broadway does that."

1975 BRITISH TOUR PROGRAM.

After a two week break for Christmas, the epic tour resumed on January 10, 1975, at the West Palm Beach Convention Hall in Florida. From there, Rael and company traveled to Lakeland, Atlanta, New Orleans, Houston, Dallas, Oklahoma City, San Diego and Berkeley.

On January 24, Genesis' performance at the Shrine Auditorium in Los Angeles was captured on multi-track tape. Two tape machines were set up in tandem, so that nothing would be missed when each machine ran out of tape. In spite of this, the tape apparently ran out during the last LAMB number, *It*. After a considerable amount of tinkering, this performance would be released on the Genesis Archive box set. In the intervening years, fans would have to make do with lo-fi bootlegs such as SWELLED AND SPENT.

In the *Los Angeles Times*, Richard Cromelin gave the band another glowing review.

"The moments of bombastic spectacle are fewer and are more judiciously utilized than in last year's concert (though when they do come along the impact is startling)," Cromelin said of THE LAMB show at the Shrine. "But the relationship of sound and visuals and the sustaining of continuity and energy provide even more satisfaction than would constant but disconnected pieces of stagery."

After the Shrine gig, the North American LAMB trek was completed with dates in San Diego, Phoenix, Vancouver, Grand Rapids and Chicago. On February 19, the Lamb arrived in Europe, debuting at the Ekeberghallen in Oslo. Then it was Copenhagen, Hanover, Berlin, Amsterdam, Cambrai, Colmar, Dijon, St. Etienne, Paris, Cascais, Portugal, Barcelona, Madrid and Annecy.

The March 25 show in Turin was marred by a police confrontation with fans. "The police fired tear gas tonight at young people trying to get into a 'rock' concert by the British group Genesis at the Turin sports palace," reported the London *Times*. "Several police and rioters were injured." But the tour kept on going, with shows in Bern, Saarbrucken, Ludwigshafen, Stuttgart, Frankfurt, Munich, Kiel, Dusseldorf, Dortmund, Hamburg, Rotterdam and Brussels.

Although the four musicians insisted on keeping news of Gabriel's departure under wraps, their own unhappiness was evident in an interview with *Zig Zag*, conducted during THE LAMB tour.

> "We're trying to stress a group thing and it is difficult," said Tony Banks. "Much of the publicity rests on Peter, but we want to be known as a five man band rather than a backing group for a singer."

But what really seemed to irk Mike, Steve, Phil and Tony was the assumption that Gabriel wrote most or all of the band's material.

Britain's first taste of the new show came with the April 14 and 15 dates at Empire Pool, Wembley. As an indication of the band's growing stature, one of the Wembley shows was covered in the London *Times*, a publication that didn't include a lot of pop music coverage. Michael Wale reported that "the screen could have been tauter, as at times it gave the images a scratched effect. Often, I found Gabriel's words indistinct because I was too near the amplifiers." On the whole, though, Wale praised the show, adding that Genesis' success proved "that British youth is ready to grapple with music much more complicated than that provided by the Bay City Rollers."

Considering the overall length of THE LAMB tour, the British leg was fairly brief. After Wembley, Genesis stopped in Southampton for a performance the Gaumont on April 16. Then they played three shows at Liverpool's Empire Theatre on the 17, 18 and 19. From there it was on to Edinburgh, Newcastle, Manchester, Bristol and the Birmingham Hippodrome.

Then it was back to the continent for the last stretch of dates with Gabriel. It had been a trying few months and THE LAMB tour was taking a physical toll on Genesis. Steve Hackett recalls that, by the end of the trek, Genesis were ...

> "Dead tired. We were all green, we were like death warmed up. We were losing our singer. We were in debt to the tune of £220,000. It was a depressing period, although we had enthusiastic audiences by then. THE LAMB was becoming a hit."

Gabriel was reluctant to do a second European tour but agreed, in part because it would help the group pay off more of their debts. He undoubtedly felt guilty about leaving Genesis just as they were starting to "make it." They soldiered on, hauling their slides, screens, costumes and instruments with them, through Kiel, Wiesbaden, Reims, San Sebastian, Paris, Cambrai, Colmar and Dijon. The names still sound exotic but, to the road weary members of Genesis, they must have seemed a little less exciting than they had in 1972.

The date and location of Gabriel's last performance with Genesis is still the subject of debate among fans. Some sources indicate that the tour wound up on May 27, at the Palais des Sports in St. Etienne, France. However Phil Collins has stated that Gabriel's last gig with the group was in Besancon, France. One thing is certain: Gabriel acknowledged his last show in a typically cryptic manner. Although the audience didn't realize the significance at the time, Gabriel marked the occasion by playing *The Last Post* on his oboe.

Years later, in the mid-80's, Gabriel was able to look back on his Genesis years with some fondness, and acknowledge the group's influence on his solo work.

"Among the musical elements that are still present in my work would be the exploration of chord sequences and progressions that are not rock and roll standards," he told *Musician*. "We may have taken that too far in Genesis, because we would never go near something like a 'C, Am, F, G' sequence which, oddly enough, was the basis of *Solsbury Hill*, but it was sometimes very interesting. I've also retained a little bit of our folk and hymn influences. I now see Genesis as a lot of fun and a healthy part of my growing up. Certain periods of my time with the band were great. The Italian tours, for instance, are a fond memory. They were chaotic, crazy, but really exciting."

Chapter 10: Right Out Of The Machinery

After Peter Gabriel's departure, the remaining members of Genesis took a few weeks off to write new material and reassess the situation. "We very nearly decided not to carry on," said Tony Banks.

Voyage of the Acolyte
Steve Hackett

Steve Hackett used the brief hiatus to make his mark as a solo artist. During June and July 1975, he assembled VOYAGE OF THE ACOLYTE, the first solo album by a Genesis member. Inevitably, the album included some musical ideas that had been passed over by Genesis. *A Tower Struck Down* was a more developed version of a piece that Steve had offered to the group, while *Shadow Of The Hierophant* grew from an idea Mike Rutherford had been working on.

"There was something that Mike had," Steve recalls, "which is the end passage of *Shadow Of The Hierophant*, which I always liked. Genesis rehearsed it, but didn't end up putting it on an album. I remember saying to Mike, 'Look, how do you feel about this?' He said, 'I don't think it's going to go on an album at this point, so why don't we use it?"

Rutherford also played on ACOLYTE, as did Phil Collins. As well as playing drums, Collins sang lead on one number, *Star Of Sirius*.

"It was a very exciting time for me," Steve recalls. "It was marvelous to feel that I could complete a whole album by myself. I was very excited hearing all this music that I'd strung together."

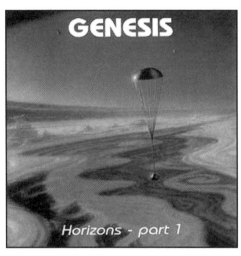

HORIZONS BOOTLEG

Record buyers in the U.K. were also impressed and the LP reached No. 26 in November 1975. In America, the record reached No. 191 in May of 1976 — not bad considering that Genesis had only started to crack the U.S. charts two years earlier. The British success of Steve's album came just as Genesis were back in the studio starting work on their first post-Gabriel effort. The remaining members took heart in the fact that fans were interested in Genesis music that didn't involve Peter Gabriel. Though no one realized it at the time, *Star Of Sirius* — with its Phil Collins vocal — was indicative of the way Genesis would sound on their next album.

Despite the success of VOYAGE OF THE ACOLYTE, no one really knew how the post-Gabriel Genesis would be received. In the wake of Gabriel's departure, even Phil Collins was considering other options. He began playing with Brand X, which provided an outlet for his love of jazz fusion. For Phil, Brand X was a reaction against the music constraints of Genesis. During THE LAMB era, Phil had been heavily into the Mahavishnu Orchestra and longed to break free from Genesis' rigidity. In Genesis, "the arrangement was king," as Hackett put it. Once a song had been arranged, there was no room to stretch out and improvise. So Brand X became Phil's musical "mistress," he has said, while Genesis was the "staid wife" who undoubtedly felt somewhat alienated by the drummer's musical philandering.

In a 1976 interview with *Melody Maker*, the workaholic drummer explained his reasons for playing with Brand X. "In between tours, the other guys in Genesis can sit at home, writing, but I prefer to be out playing. For instance, when they were writing (A TRICK OF THE TAIL), I was rehearsing with Brand X." At that time, Brand X comprised Collins (drums), John Goodsall (guitar), Percy Jones (bass), Robin Lumley (keyboards) and Geoff Seopardi (percussion).

In spite of doubts about the viability of a Gabriel-less Genesis, the remaining four decided to get back together and see what happened. The ability to withstand the departure of a key member has proven to be a recurring trait of Genesis. It has always seemed that the entity of Genesis was strong enough to ride out the loss of any one of its components.

During July and August, the four-piece Genesis wrote and rehearsed material for their first album without Peter Gabriel. Steve Hackett was absent for the first four days, finishing off his solo album. The fact that Gabriel's departure had not been made public was certainly to the group's advantage. Without the knowledge of the fans or the press, they made up their minds to continue, unhindered (for the time being) by any outside judgements about what Genesis should be. The first stages of work on a new album were conducted in a kind of splendid isolation. And, soon after rehearsals began, the remaining members were convinced that Genesis should continue.

"Once we started rehearsals, we realized that it was worth it," Banks recalled. "The music, even in that primitive form, was really nice." Within days, the group had come up with rough versions of *Dance On A Volcano* and *Squonk*.

The new Genesis had been rehearsing for three weeks when the news broke. In August, 1975, Peter Gabriel typed up the following announcement and personally delivered it to the British music press:

"I had a dream, eye's dream. Then I had another dream with the body and soul of a rock star. When it didn't feel good I packed it in. Looking back for the musical and non-musical reasons, this is what I came up with:

OUT, ANGELS OUT — an investigation.

The vehicle we had built as a co-op to serve our songwriting became our master and had cooped us up inside the success we had wanted. It affected the attitudes and the spirit of the whole band. The music had not dried up and I still respect the other musicians, but our roles had set in hard. To get an idea through "Genesis the Big" meant shifting a lot more concrete than before. For any band, transferring the heart from idealistic enthusiasm to professionalism is a difficult operation.

I believe the use of sound and visual images can be developed to do much more than we have done. But on a large scale it needs one clear and coherent direction, which our pseudo-democratic committee system could not provide.

As an artist, I need to absorb a wide variety of experiences. It is difficult to respond to intuition and impulse within the long-term planning that the band needed. I felt I should look at / learn about / develop myself, my creative bits and pieces and pick up on a lot of work going on outside music. Even the hidden delights of vegetable growing and community living are beginning to reveal their secrets. I could not expect the band to tie in their schedules with my bondage to cabbages. The increase in money and power, if I had stayed, would have anchored me to the spotlights. It was important to me to give space to my family, which I wanted to hold together, and to liberate the daddy in me.

Although I have seen and learned a great deal in the last seven years, I found I had begun to look at things as the famous Gabriel, despite hiding my occupation whenever possible, hitching lifts, etc. I had begun to think in business terms; very useful for an often bitten once shy musician, but treating records and audiences as money was taking me away from them. When performing, there were less shivers up and down the spine.

I believe the world has soon to go through a difficult period of changes. I'm excited by some of the areas coming through to the surface which seem to have been hidden away in people's minds. I want to explore and be prepared to be open and flexible enough to respond, not tied in to the old hierarchy.

Much of my psyche's ambitions as "Gabriel archetypal rock star" have been fulfilled — a lot of the ego-gratification and the need to attract young ladies, perhaps the result of frequent rejection as "Gabriel acne-struck public school boy". However, I can still get off playing the star game once in a while.

My future within music, if it exists, will be in as many situations as possible. It's good to see a growing number of artists breaking down the pigeonholes. This is the difference between the profitable, compartmentalized, battery chicken and the free-range. Why did the chicken cross the road anyway?

There is no animosity between myself and the band or management. The decision had been made some time ago and we have talked about our new direction. The reason why my leaving was not announced earlier was because I had been asked to delay until they had found a replacement to plug up the hole. It is not impossible that some of them might work with me on other projects.

The following guesswork has little in common with truth:

Gabriel left Genesis
1) To work in theatre.
2) To make more money as a solo artist.
3) To do a "Bowie".
4) To do a "Ferry".
5) To do a "Furry Boa round my neck and hang myself with it".
6) To go see an institution.
7) To go senile in the sticks.

I do not express myself adequately in interviews and I felt I owed it to the people who have put a lot of love and energy supporting the band to give an accurate picture of my reasons. So I ask that you print all or none of this."

Although the announcement caused many to question the future of Genesis, the loss of Gabriel ultimately cleared the way for a new approach, and a sound that would lead the group to much greater commercial success. The remaining four were very enthusiastic about the new songs they had been writing and rehearsing, but the announcement must have taken them down a notch or two. They went from making new music in private to having to defend their decision to stay together in the press.

"Peter's leaving isn't the blow that some people seem to think it is," Phil told the *NME*. "The Press have always seized upon Peter and sort of pushed him more than everybody else." Collins was quick to counter the notion that Gabriel had written most or all of the group's lyrics. "Mike and Tony write nearly as much and in very much the same style. It's a band style of writing, not Peter's alone."

The band members expressed their view that, during the latter part of the Gabriel era, the visuals and theatrics had eclipsed the music to some extent.

"The whole situation got out of control," said Banks. In a *Melody Maker* interview, the keyboardist suggested that the group had become a little complacent towards the end of the Gabriel era. "We knew that we could get away with murder. We could, and did, play badly and get off with it. It gets too easy when you get very big. It's good to have some things to keep the edge."

Interestingly, Banks was expressing a viewpoint almost identical to that which Steve Hackett would cite as part of his reason for quitting Genesis two years later.

"Peter left and life goes on," Banks told *Melody Maker*. "We were all sort of sad. We spent some time trying to make him change his mind but, when he didn't, we just carried on. We'll lose people and we'll gain people with the new album. We expect that. The trouble with England is that people decide at an early stage whether they like something or not. What I would like is a reassessment. A lot of people have pre-conceived ideas of what Genesis is about."

Initially, there was some talk of making an album that was mostly, if not entirely instrumental. Tony Banks later commented in *Melody Maker* that A TRICK OF THE TAIL wasn't originally intended to be "such a vocal album. We thought more of doing an instrumental album." After Gabriel's departure, David Hentschel recalls that "the writing was down to mostly Tony and Mike, at least at first."

Although Collins mentioned that Genesis had been auditioning singers, they were obviously moving away from the idea of finding an outside replacement for Peter.

"I do most of the singing, actually," Collins revealed. "There's just the four of us. We start recording soon . . . and we *may* feature one or two singers, as guest vocalists sort of, on a few tracks. And when we next go on the road I should think the concert will be drawn from this new LP's material."

In October, Banks, Hackett, Rutherford and Collins loaded their gear into Trident Studios to start recording. They recruited David Hentschel to co-produce the record with them and a very fruitful partnership was born. (The sessions were engineered by Hentschel and Nick Bradford.)

"After meeting Phil on NURSERY CRYME, he and I became friends and saw a lot of each other socially," says Hentschel. "We even did a bit of artistic collaboration. In addition he often came into the studio where I worked at the time (Trident). When they were looking for a producer for TRICK OF THE TAIL, Phil asked me if I'd be up for it, and then put my name forward to the rest of the band. The rest, as they say, is history."

Hentschel recalls that, by the time Genesis entered the studio to start recording, they had a clearly defined idea of what they were going to record.

"They were very disciplined and organized in their pre-production," he says. "They used to start their writing individually, and then take quite a long time in rehearsal studios to complete the writing with the rest of the band — by committee, if you like. Because their music was so unique, there was never a need for me to get involved in the pre-production. I would go to the later rehearsals just to familiarize myself with the tunes, rather than giving any structural input."

"All my work was really done in the studio," he continues. "I like to think I had a major input in creating their 'sound' of that time, both from a technical (engineering) point of view, and by the choice of sounds they used. Some producers have a musical background, and some do not. Since I do, I am always able to call on that in my productions. I helped with the arrangements, both instrumental and vocal. I also helped Tony quite a bit in the early days, as I had quite a bit of experience in synthesizer programming, although album by album as his experience grew, my role in this diminished. Finally, I guess I was always there as a sounding board. Most musicians need an objective opinion, and confidence and encouragement, from time to time."

Even as the band were recording, they had yet to make a definite decision about finding a new singer. They weeded through forty or fifty tapes and auditioned about ten singers, but no one quite seemed to fit the bill.

"We auditioned vocalists every Monday," said Phil. "We put adverts in the paper. The office would go through all the tapes that were sent, and — who knows? — we might have found Mr. Perfect. We got edited tapes, and every Monday we'd audition the best."

One of the singers, Mick Strickland, had a strong voice but the material wasn't in his key and didn't work out. It has been said that the band recorded all the backing tracks before realizing that Phil could do the job. However, Collins' comments to the NME in September indicate that he was already seeing himself in that role. He was certainly going to be singing some of the quieter numbers, such as Ripples, but he wasn't perceived as a singer of heavier numbers.

"Phil would sing them the melody lines and show them how they went," said Mike Rutherford of the singers who tried out. "Then we started to notice that none of the singers actually sounded any better than Phil."

"We auditioned, unsuccessfully, a few singers in the studio on the new tracks before Phil said, 'I'd like to have a try'," recalls David Hentschel. "He did — it worked." The clincher was the heavy (by Genesis standards) *Squonk*. When Phil sang that number, the others realized that his vocal talent could go beyond quieter numbers, that he could deliver the heavier material, too.

With Phil as the lead singer, the whole group now had more input in the vocal area. They could work closely with Collins, offering suggestions. This contrasted sharply with the approach of Peter Gabriel, who liked to record his vocals in isolation from the others, and let them hear them once they were finished.

Phil's voice was warmer and smoother than Peter's, making the new Genesis instantly more accessible to a wider audience. The energetic Collins gave his all in his new role, although he has said that he doesn't think of himself primarily as a singer.

> "I only sing in Genesis because we don't have another singer," he told *Downbeat* years later. "I don't really think of myself as a singer as such. I think of myself more as a drummer."

Although he had used up a lot of his compositional backlog on his solo album, Steve Hackett still made a strong contribution to A TRICK OF THE TAIL, especially on *Entangled*. "I wrote the lyrics and (the music for) the verse," the guitarist recalls. "The chorus, musically, was Tony's and the outro was based on an arpeggiated figure that Mike came up with, upon which Tony superimposed a choral effect."

> "I thought *Entangled* worked really well," said Banks during the Virgin online chat. "It was a combination of using a bit of (Steve's) and a bit of mine with Steve writing the lyrics. What was fun in Genesis was having the contrasting styles, we had two bits in 3/4 and that's the reason why they ended up together. We ended up doing the bit I originally wrote on piano, the chorus part, on guitar — it sounded very nice like that."

One track from the sessions that didn't find its way onto the album was a lovely acoustic number called *It's Yourself*. Steve recalls that it was,

> "a song that we didn't feel was up to par. We thought it was a bit 'Kensington Market.' That was one of the places that were the focus of the Hippie scene in the Sixties. There were an awful lot of things that sounded a little bit like that tune at the time — slightly ersatz, a bit like the Beatles on Welfare Support."

However, the closing portion of *It's Yourself* evolved into an instrumental number titled *Los Endos*, which closed the record. *Los Endos* is a classic Genesis instrumental. Like much of their best work, it takes the listener on an aural journey, reprising musical themes from other tracks on the album (notably *Squonk* and *Dance On A Volcano*.) This device gives the record a cinematic feel, tying together musical ideas from earlier in the album. Genesis had used a similar device on SELLING ENGLAND BY THE POUND (reprising a riff from the opening *Dancing With The Moonlit Knight* on the closing *Aisle Of Plenty*) and would do so again on WIND AND WUTHERING and on the excellent *Duke's Travels / Duke's End* sequence at the end of the DUKE LP.

The rhythm of *Los Endos* was inspired by one of Phil's favorite Santana albums. "I got that beat from a Santana album that Airto played on called BORBOLETTA . . .," he recalled. "I was really inspired by it." The track also incorporated the drummer's love of jazz fusion, and became a stage favorite for the interplay between Phil and tour drummer Chester Thompson.

All in all, the new Genesis had crafted a very satisfying record, much more accessible than THE LAMB, yet still possessing the epic qualities that had drawn audiences to the earlier incarnation.

"We never doubted ourselves," said Tony Banks of the reinvention of Genesis. "I've always believed that the whole is greater than the individual." The loss of Gabriel brought the other four closer together — at least for the time being.

Even after the album's completion, Genesis contemplated getting a singer for the upcoming tour, since Phil couldn't be expected to sing lead and drum at the same time. They finally decided, to quote Mike Rutherford, "Fuck it, let's get a drummer."

Chapter 11: "A people's band again."

Charisma Records released A TRICK OF THE TAIL in February 1976. Retaining the musical appeal of their best previous work, yet with a more accessible vocal sound, the album was the most successful Genesis release yet. *Melody Maker* sported the headline "Genesis re-born," and praised the album. Barbara Charone of *Sounds* called it a "solid gold success," and the fans concurred. In America it reached No. 31, while in Britain it matched SELLING ENGLAND BY THE POUND'S No. 3 placing.

"With the absence of Gabriel, Genesis now relies on subtlety and melodic continuity more than studio gimmickry," said *Rolling Stone*. "Although the familiar themes are always apparent, A TRICK OF THE TAIL is much more straightforward, possibly because it's more a joint effort than the Gabriel-dominated albums. On their seventh attempt, Genesis has managed to turn the possible catastrophe of Gabriel's departure into their first broad-based American success."

GENESIS

No.1 British Live Band
No.3 British Band

No.1 International Live Band
No.3 International Band

Top British Album
A Trick of the Tail

Top International Album
A Trick of the Tail

No.2 International Arranger
No.3 International Composer

They Don't Come Any Better!

BRITISH AD FOR THE TRICK OF THE TAIL ALBUM.

There was no hit single on either side of the Atlantic, although an edited version of *Ripples* was released in America and *A Trick Of The Tail* itself was offered in Britain. The band even shot promo videos to accompany the singles, furthering their more accessible new image. Charisma promoted the album in Britain by showing "video film" of Genesis at selected record shops.

With a tour planned, the next order of business for Genesis was to find a drummer. When Collins told his old pal Bill Bruford that he was having trouble finding a drummer, Bruford replied, "Why don't you ask me, you fool? I'm not doing anything." So Phil asked him, Bill said yes and soon the ex-Yes stickman was rehearsing with Genesis in the basement of the Una Billings School of Dancing.

Although Phil would man his kit whenever logistically possible, most of the show would see him enjoying his new role as frontman. Bruford rehearsed with the band three times in Britain before they moved over to the U.S. early in March. There they spent two weeks at the Reunion Center in Dallas, Texas, rehearsing the new stage show.

The tour kicked off in late March, in London, Ontario. What was planned as a low-key show in front of a few hundred people ended up with an audience of a few thousand. This show was merely intended to be a warm-up gig, since all the pre-publicity stated that the first show would be at Maple Leaf Gardens in Toronto. Thankfully, the assembled fans were very pleased with the new version of the group. From that very first show, fans were very supportive of the Collins-fronted Genesis. Not only was the group still together, but the new singer was a familiar and likeable presence.

"The audience was very enthusiastic," recalled Phil of his first show as lead singer, "They saw me doing this as helping to keep the group together, and they were very encouraging, and the rest of the group was very encouraging too."

The new show was a mixture of old and new material. The band boldly opened with the new *Dance On A Volcano*, following it with a sequence featuring *The Lamb Lies Down On Broadway, Fly On A Windshield* and *The Carpet Crawlers* (affectionately known as *Lamb Stew*). From there, it was *The Cinema Show*, followed by the new *Robbery, Assault And Battery* and *White Mountain*, which the band hadn't featured in its sets since the TRESPASS era. The Gabriel-less line-up proceeded through *Firth Of Fifth, Entangled, Squonk, I Know What I Like, Los Endos* and *Supper's Ready*. The evening ended with a stunning version of *It*, which segued into a truncated instrumental version of *Watcher Of The Skies*.

A BOOTLEG RECORD FEATURING LIVE GENESIS MATERIAL FROM THEIR U.K. TOUR 1976.

Although Phil was out front singing for most of the show, he joined Bill Bruford on drums for *Los Endos*, and the instrumental sections of *Firth Of Fifth* and *The Cinema Show*. The latter was a highlight of the show for Collins, who described it to *Melody Maker* as . . .

"A showstopper. Everyone is waiting for the drum battle, right? In *Cinema Show*, Bill and I do an unaccompanied eight bars and they think it's going to be a drum solo, but then everybody comes back in again. We just give 'em a taste."

The tour was a typically lengthy affair, as the time was right to consolidate Genesis' foothold in the North American market. The show hit Buffalo, Toronto, Montreal, Ottawa, Quebec City, Philadelphia, Boston, Baltimore, Pittsburgh, Cleveland, Chicago, Detroit, Milwaukee, Grand Rapids, St. Louis, Kansas City, Berkeley, Fresno and Burbank. The April performance at the Beacon Theater in New York was reviewed by *Melody Maker* under the headline "Eat your words, Genesis critics." The paper reported that "the new Genesis . . . is every bit as entertaining as the old one."

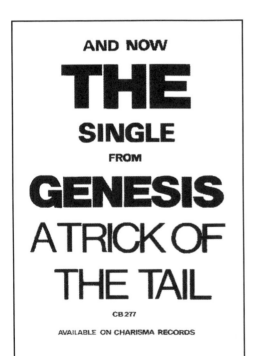

It was no coincidence that the new Genesis had been unveiled before North American audiences. The Gabriel-era group was much less well-established there than in Britain, and audiences were less likely to be disappointed by the new version of Genesis. After a successful series of inaugural gigs, the TRICK OF THE TAIL line-up jetted back to London for a five night stint at the Hammersmith Odeon. From June 9 to 13, the band gave British audiences their first taste of their new incarnation. Tony Banks wanted Britain to reassess Genesis, and Britain proved more than willing to oblige. The reaction was almost entirely positive and it soon became apparent that Genesis was not only alive and well, but was more successful than ever. For every fan mourning the absent flower mask and batwings, there seemed to be several more won over by Phil's easy charm and less idiosyncratic vocal style.

Clive Bennett of the London *Times* found the new show's visual effects especially praiseworthy:

> "Back-projections provided stunningly effective narrative parallels to many of the songs; beautifully composed shots of New York in THE LAMB LIES DOWN ON BROADWAY, a movie version of *Robbery, Assault and Battery* ..." Bennett was also impressed by the "magnificent laser beam display. "And then there was Phil ... Bennett deemed Collins' performance as the new frontman "a near disaster. His witless clowning, severely limited physical capabilities and a shattering inability to sing with any kind of verbal clarity were all profoundly irritating ...'

Luckily for Phil, the critic acknowledged that he was "in a minority" in his negative reaction to the new singer.

The *Daily Telegraph* review echoed the majority:

> "Whether playing tambourine with his head, belaboring his drums opposite the excellent 'deputy' Bill Bruford, kicking imaginary goals, emitting a confident and witty patter, or just singing, the man was magnetic. Gone is the black humor and the distance; Genesis are accessible, a people's band again." Although the arrival of Punk was just around the corner, the *NME* stated that Genesis represented the sound of the 70's: "They are very much what is happening."

Although Gabriel's more theatrical presentation had drawn more attention, it was sometimes at the expense of the music. Collins made more of a personal connection with the audience.

> "I think the distance Peter had was actually good," he told *Circus* in 1978. "I don't think it harmed us. But when you've got nothing in between you and the people, no distraction, then it comes across a lot clearer."

Melody Maker, still firmly behind the band in those pre-Punk days, hailed Genesis at the Hammersmith as "a night to remember" and "sensational." The paper described the show as a mixture of old and new material that left everybody satisfied. It was noted at the time that these shows were being recorded as candidates for a planned live LP.

As the TRICK OF THE TAIL tour moved in Europe, Phil's skills as a frontman became even more apparent. "Phil is very good in foreign countries," Mike Rutherford told *Beat Instrumental*. "He writes things out in huge writing on a bit of paper and does a bit of the foreign language, and his gestures are exaggerated." Phil's exaggerated gestures during this era included a visual representation of Juliet's distinctive anatomical characteristics during the bawdy tale with which he introduced *The Cinema Show*. Like Gabriel, Collins often offset the seriousness of Genesis' music with his lighthearted introductions. It's a shame that none of the group's official live releases (save for the subsequent ARCHIVE box) preserved this element of Genesis' live shows. The inclusion of Collins' and Gabriel's between-song patter would undoubtedly have offset the perceived pomposity of the music.

CHARISMA PLACED THIS AD IN MELODY MAKER TO
CONGRATULATE GENESIS ON THEIR SUCCESS IN
THE PAPER'S READERS' POLL.

With Bill Bruford playing live with the group, there was the question of whether he might appear on any subsequent studio efforts. "There's no plan to use Bill to any extent on the next album," Tony said. "Although it would be nice to have him."

In mid-June, Genesis arrived in Europe. With essentially the same set they had played in North America, they went to Rotterdam, Dusseldorf, Berlin, Brussels, Paris, Lyon, Bern, Munich, Hamburg, Lorelei and Heidelberg.

British fans got short shrift on the TRICK OF THE TAIL tour, with a mere three appearances after the initial Hammersmith dates. The band had to scale back their presentation for their July 8 and 9 dates at the Apollo in Glasgow. Those two shows did not feature the slides and back projections, but still included lasers and smoke. They ended the tour on July 10, at the Bingley Hall in Stafford, which turned out to be Bill Bruford's last show with Genesis.

To capitalize on Genesis' newfound success, Decca Records repackaged the FROM GENESIS TO REVELATION album as part of its ROOTS compilation series. The budget-priced Genesis ROOTS LP appeared in Britain in early 1976, promoted alongside ROOTS collections of vintage tracks by the Zombies, Them and Procol Harum. To make the package more appealing, Decca added the four single sides cut for the label.

In September, Banks, Collins, Hackett and Rutherford traveled to Relight Studios in Hilvarenbeek, Holland, to record WIND & WUTHERING, the follow-up to A TRICK OF THE TAIL. According to Mike Rutherford, Hilvarenbeek was "a little village in the middle of nowhere." It was the first of several excursions abroad to record, in an effort to avoid paying too large a chunk of their earnings to the British taxman. Saddled with debts during the Gabriel years, the group had only broken even financially after A TRICK OF THE TAIL, and recording abroad would allow them to keep an extra twenty-five per cent of their album profits.

They were scheduled to start recording at the beginning of the month, but the sessions were pushed back two weeks due to the birth of Phil's son. Once again, the sessions were produced by David Hentschel, who also engineered, with the assistance of Pierre Geoffroy Chateau and Nick Bradford.

Hentschel feels that the benefits of recording abroad were not merely monetary.

"I think that helped provide a unique focus on that album," he says of the set-up at Relight. "Many people pick WIND & WUTHERING out as the 'purest' Genesis album of all time. I think that was why. It was the first time that they had recorded in a residential studio situation, and I think that the concentration that that situation provides is always a good thing. We did, if I remember correctly, only record in Holland for two weeks. After that we returned to Trident to finish the overdubs and to mix."

The band recorded plenty of material at Relight — more, in fact, than they could fit on the album. The music was a natural progression from the previous album, but the mood was more romantic.

The track that was chosen to open the album was a classic Genesis epic entitled *Eleventh Earl Of Mar.*

"It has a group arrangement on bits that were written by me, and Steve and Mike wrote the lyrics," Tony told the *NME*. "The synthesizer line reoccurs later on in the album. It's a thing that sounds really nice loud as well as soft. Plus the album title is conjured up very well with that line. It's quite an awkward track to open an album. It takes two or three listens before it gets through to you."

Steve added, "One of the reasons we have so many different elements in one song, let alone an album, is that if the listener doesn't respond to one thing, he probably will to another thing. If you're going to lose them there, you'll catch them somewhere else."

"What you do is I sit down in the music room and you play it through two or three times and think what it can be about," Mike Rutherford explained in the same article, in reference to *Eleventh Earl Of Mar.* "I had this idea after reading this history book about a failed Scottish rising. I liked the idea of him — he was a bit gay, a bit camp, and a bit well-dressed."

The bridge of *Eleventh Earl Of Mar* was based on an acoustic piece of Steve's, entitled *The House Of The Four Winds.*

"That middle section was me," he says. "I used a Kalimba — a thumb piano — and a couple of nylon guitars. A pair of nylons, as I'm fond of saying." Steve recalls that the album title "was taken from the idea of that title (*The House Of The Four Winds*). It was taken from a Chinese restaurant, I think, in New York. I thought it sounded quite exotic. I'm now quite glad we didn't use it as a title, but at the time I was disappointed that we didn't use it. But, you see, that's what happens to you when you grow up — you realize that maybe you shouldn't go around naming albums after restaurants!"

The "wuthering" part of the title was a reference to Emily Bronte's novel WUTHERING HEIGHTS. Genesis appropriated part of the last line of that book ("I lingered round them

... and wondered how anyone could ever imagine unquiet slumbers, for the sleepers in that quiet earth.") as the title of an instrumental that appeared on side two of the record. Originally intended to appear as one group written piece, the track was divided up and listed as two separate compositions, in an attempt to give Steve a bigger writing credit. Thus the first section ("Unquiet slumbers for the sleepers . . .") was credited to Hackett / Rutherford, while the second (". . . in that quiet earth.") was billed as a group composition.

Blood On The Rooftops was another number mostly written by Steve. It started out as a love song, but Steve changed the lyrical direction to contrast with the romanticism of the rest of the LP, juxtaposing images from assorted television programs of the day. Hackett's skill as a classical guitarist was showcased on the song's lovely instrumental intro, which later became a feature of his solo performances. The music for the song's chorus was written by Phil Collins. Although Collins' compositional input was less than that of the others in those days, his untrained, three-finger piano technique allowed him to write some strong chord progressions.

A JAPANESE SINGLE OF *YOUR OWN SPECIAL WAY.*

The WIND & WUTHERING sessions also yielded Mike Rutherford's first solo Genesis composition — the lilting *Your Own Special Way*, which would give the group their first American hit. It's a lovely number, although the change between the verses and the chorus is a little awkward, and Rutherford has since expressed dissatisfaction with the track's arrangement.

The majority of the material on WIND & WUTHERING was composed by Tony Banks. The keyboardist contributed two of his strongest compositions, the epic *One For The Vine* and the romantic *Afterglow. One For The Vine* was a song that went through many changes during the sessions. The group tried several different approaches before settling on an arrangement based on acoustic piano.

Technical problems played a part in the recording of *Afterglow*, which became one of the group's best-loved numbers.

"On the last day of recording there was a fault with the machine and it started to chew the tape," recalls Steve. "So Dave Hentschel said, 'Has anyone got any other ideas they want to try out?' And I had this idea of doing vocal loops. So the harmonies that you hear (on the end of *Afterglow*) are done with these vocal loops that were an idea of mine that wasn't a priority until we had the accident, because it meant that I could try this idea out. We had Phil sing on top of himself three times."

By this point, Hackett was becoming dissatisfied with Genesis. One source of his frustration was the material chosen for the album. He couldn't understand why the album should include *Wot Gorilla?*, while stronger tracks like *Pigeons* and *Inside And Out* were left in the can. By this point, Steve's tastes were clearly not always in tune with those of the other three. In fact, Phil Collins cited *Wot Gorilla?* as his favorite WIND & WUTHERING track, proudly deeming it "a real bit of jazz fusion." Part of *Wot Gorilla?* was drawn from a musical theme from *One For The Vine*, developed with a fusion rhythm. Steve still feels that *Wot Gorilla?* was "not really a happening tune. Rhythmically, it was superb. It was a Weather Report rhythm that we'd used. Part of that became part of *Please Don't Touch*, which also used that same rhythm. But I felt we'd left out the best bit."

Hackett's composition *Please Don't Touch* was indeed left out, dropped during rehearsals. Steve, who hadn't originally considered himself a writer, was writing more and more, bolstered by the success of VOYAGE OF THE ACOLYTE. Having had a chance to present his ideas on record without having to get them approved by the Genesis "committee," the guitarist realized that just because Tony, Mike and Phil didn't like an idea, that didn't mean the record-buying public wouldn't like it.

"*Please Don't Touch* was something that was being rehearsed with a view to potential inclusion on the WIND & WUTHERING album," Steve recalls. "It wasn't used. It didn't quite gel with the band." Apparently, although the rest of the group liked the number, Phil's inability to "get behind" it caused it to get dropped from the running. Steve felt it was one of the best instrumentals they'd done for a long time and its rejection pushed him closer to his decision to leave. After he left Genesis, Steve re-recorded *Please Don't Touch* as the title track of his second solo album.

By the time Genesis arrived at Relight Studios, the group had decided which songs were to be recorded. Such decisions tended to be made during rehearsals, before the producer was brought in. Nonetheless, David Hentschel had a sense that there was some conflict regarding Steve's lack of compositional input.

> "I was aware of it, despite the fact that the songs were already decided," he recalls. "There was also a slight sense of unease occasionally in the studio, although I don't think this really affected anyone's work or commitment to the album at the time."

Although his dissatisfaction was growing, Steve doesn't remember much tension being evident during the WIND & WUTHERING sessions.

> "I don't remember any rows," he says. "I think it was quite peaceful. We had less people in the band, less contentious issues to put forth."

Nonetheless, subsequent events suggest that there was considerable tension mounting, although Genesis' very reserved English attitude may have obscured it.

On the surface, things seemed better than ever for Genesis. Although by no means a radical departure from earlier efforts, the WIND & WUTHERING sessions did see the band trying to keep their approach fresh. "This time we consciously avoided things we would do normally," Rutherford told *Melody Maker*. "Where we might use Mellotron, we'd use voices — things like that."

In an interview for the WIND & WUTHERING tour program, Mike attempted to characterize what each of the four members brought to Genesis.

> "I'm good at doing soft things and the very heavy. Steve's romantic ... Tony's style is more classically influenced ... Phil is very jazzy, but he can also sound like John Bonham from Led Zeppelin."

> "Tony, Mike and Steve are the predominant writers," added Phil. "Tony is into the Beach Boys and the classics. He's not interested in pop. He wouldn't rush out and buy an album like I would." Phil also offered some insight into the progression of a Genesis album's creation. "We write the music together and then write the words together. The title of the album is the last thing."

WIND & WUTHERING was released in December 1976, and reached No. 7 in Britain. In America, it peaked at No. 26 — a few places higher than A TRICK OF THE TAIL. Although punk had just exploded in Britain, it had not yet fully taken hold of the British music press. Under the headline "Genesis' musical nirvana," *Melody Maker* opined that "Rock can still have some vestige of pride left in itself when musicians like these are still working, unaffected by the clamorous pursuit of trivia elsewhere."

As Genesis unveiled WIND & WUTHERING, their former frontman was preparing to re-enter the music business. In October 1976, it was announced that Peter Gabriel had started work on a solo with producer Bob Ezrin and members of Alice Cooper's old band. This would be the first of Gabriel's self-titled LP's, and the beginning of a very successful solo career. Gabriel's solo achievements are for a book of their own, but it's worth noting that he has forged a distinct identity on his own. Although it's commonly known that Gabriel once sang with Genesis, his solo success is such that it's almost a footnote in the contemporary view of his career.

A couple of weeks after the announcement of Gabriel's re-emergence, it was revealed that Bill Bruford was to form a "supergroup" with Rick Wakeman and John Wetton. Although the mooted trio didn't materialize, Bruford did not return to Genesis. "Obviously we were thinking it would be nice to have Bill Bruford with us on a loosely permanent basis, and then circumstances changed," Mike Rutherford told *Melody Maker*.

As 1976 drew to a close, the group found themselves in need of a drummer to take Bruford's place for the upcoming tour dates. They found the perfect candidate in ex-Frank Zappa drummer Chester Thompson, who remained with them for the next fifteen years and still plays with Phil. Although Collins was a great admirer of Bill Bruford's playing, there seemed to be a more natural chemistry between him and Chester.

> "Bruford was a little busy," Collins said years later in reference to Bruford's playing style. "And, probably because of my inexperience at playing with two drummers, I was a little busy too in those days. So we never locked together as well as Chester and I do."

> "Everyone tends to regard (Chester) as having a jazzy style," said Rutherford. "But in a way Phil is a jazzy drummer, too, so there is a lot of common ground."

After Christmas 1976, Thompson flew to London to join the band in rehearsal at the newly-refurbished Rainbow Theatre, a favorite Genesis venue from the Gabriel era.

The WIND & WUTHERING tour kicked off with a three night stand at the Rainbow. Those three shows, on January 1, 2 and 3, were Chester Thompson's first appearances with Genesis. The new tour took the emphasis off slide projections and films and showcased the ever more impressive Genesis light show. "We got rid of our screens," said Rutherford, "I think we peaked with THE LAMB and on the last tour they didn't really progress very much."

The group quickly sold out the 8,000 seat Rainbow. In fact, 80,000 fans applied for tickets for the three night stand, leaving about 56,000 disappointed. At the first show, the band opened with *Eleventh Earl Of Mar* but, starting the following night, they opened all the shows with the more straightforward *Squonk*. Band members have observed that audiences generally respond better to familiar material — a lesson they learned on THE LAMB tour. So, since 1977, the group has opened their shows with a song from the previous album. Thus, *Eleventh Earl Of Mar* became the set opener for the ... AND THEN THERE WERE THREE ... tour, *Deep In The Motherlode* kicked off shows on the DUKE tour, *Behind The Lines* opened the ABACAB shows, and so on.

The rest of the show consisted of *The Carpet Crawlers, Firth Of Fifth, Your Own Special Way, Robbery, Assault And Battery, ... In That Quiet Earth, Afterglow, Lilywhite Lilith, Wot Gorilla? I Know What I Like, Supper's Ready, One For The Vine, Squonk* and *All In A Mouse's Night.* Also, *Dance On A Volcano* appeared, linked to *Los Endos* by a Thompson-Collins drum duet. (This medley would remain a staple of the band's concerts for years to come.) While most of the above-mentioned numbers remained in the set, the group soon dropped *Wot Gorilla?* and *Lilywhite Lilith.*

Through the rest of January, Genesis treated British fans to the new set. They played the Odeon Theatre, Birmingham, the Empire Theatre, Liverpool, the Free Trade Hall, Manchester, the Caird Hall, Dundee, the Playhouse, Edinburgh, Newcastle City Hall, the Gaumont Theatre, Southampton, the DeMontfort Hall, Leicester and the Bristol Hippodrome. At the end of the month, they flew to America, where they wowed audiences in Boulder, Tulsa, Kansas City, St. Louis, Minneapolis, Madison, Milwaukee, Chicago, Detroit, Kalamazoo, then traveled up to Canada for dates in Winnipeg and Kitchener, Ontario.

1977 TOUR PROGRAM.

On February 23, the WIND & WUTHERING tour arrived at Madison Square Garden in New York City. The Garden was one of Genesis favorite American venues. Speaking with *Beat Instrumental*, Mike Rutherford called it "an amazing hall. It's a pain in the arse to do, because the unions are a real problem. But the quality of the sound in that hall is very high."

After New York, the tour moved on to Boston, Hartford, Syracuse, Cleveland, Buffalo, Montreal, Quebec, Toronto, Ottawa, Philadelphia, Baltimore, Pittsburgh, Nashville, Atlanta, New Orleans, Houston and Austin. Genesis were making progress in America, but the group members still felt they had a long way to go.

"The trouble with the American scene is that . . . it is very difficult to break in without a singles hit," Tony Banks had lamented the previous year. In March 1977, *Your Own Special Way* peaked No. 62 in the *Billboard* charts — Genesis' first American hit single. Not a huge hit by any means, but a start.

On March 24, the group played to a crowd of 18,000 at the Los Angeles Forum. One overly enthusiastic fan managed to get on stage and, seeing that Phil's drum kit was vacant, decided to play along. The would-be stickman was forcibly removed from his throne by three roadies.

During this Los Angeles visit, Phil spoke with *Melody Maker* about the group's future plans. "We'll be doing the next studio album with Chester," he revealed. "But there will be a double live album first . . ." He didn't make it clear what Chester's exact involvement was to be but, obviously, there was a change of plans over the next few months, since Thompson never appeared on a Genesis studio album.

"We're going to Australia in August," said Collins. "Then we're gonna rehearse the new album, by which time the live album will be out. We'll be doing a lot more writing together this time."

This last comment may have been a reference to Steve's unhappiness with the amount of his input. The other three may have intended moving back towards group writing so that

100

everyone had more equality. Interestingly, Genesis did move in that direction, although not until the DUKE / ABACAB era.

In late March / early April, Genesis wound up the WIND & WUTHERING tour with a few more dates, mostly on the West coast, in San Francisco, San Diego, Phoenix, Portland, Vancouver and Seattle.

1977 saw the long-awaited release of Anthony Phillips' first solo album. Entitled THE GEESE AND THE GHOST, this great LP featured some material that dated back to Ant's Genesis years. Much of THE GEESE AND THE GHOST sounds a lot like a Genesis circa TRICK OF THE TAIL / WIND & WUTHERING. Aside from Ant's gorgeous playing and writing contributions, the album also features Mike Rutherford and Phil Collins. Mike co-produced the LP, co-wrote several songs and plays a variety of instruments, while Phil sang lead on two of the three vocal tracks. Collins' vocals, on *Which Way The Wind Blows* and *God If I Saw Her Now*, are gorgeous. On the former, he harmonizes with himself in a blend that recalls A TRICK OF THE TAIL-era tracks like *Entangled* and *It's Yourself*. Any fans of 1976-77 period Genesis would be well-advised to track down a copy of THE GEESE AND THE GHOST. A great introduction to the talents of Anthony Phillips, it gives plenty of insight into what his contribution to Genesis was.

Chapter 12: Inside and Out

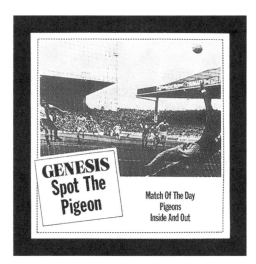

In May 1977, Charisma released the SPOT THE PIGEON EP, which consisted of three leftover tracks from the WIND & WUTHERING sessions. In Britain, it was a 7 inch record, although a Canadian version appeared as a 12 inch. The cover was a spoof of the "Spot the ball" contests that were very popular in Britain. These entailed a photo of a soccer match from which the ball had been airbrushed out. The aim of the contest, which was a regular feature of some newspapers, was to correctly identify the ball's location. The EP's title appears to be a play on "Spot the ball" and "Stop the pigeon!", the latter being the catch phrase of Hanna-Barbera's cartoon villain Dick Dastardly. The latter was also a reference to the song *Pigeons*, which appeared on the EP, along with the soccer-themed *Match Of The Day* and *Inside And Out*.

"In many ways we'd have liked those three songs to have been on the WIND & WUTHERING album," Tony Banks said years later on the American radio show *Rockline*. "I like the WIND & WUTHERING album very much, but it perhaps came across a little heavier than it was originally intended. What we left off were certainly two of the simplest tracks, and one sort of midway-simple track. We put them together on this EP called SPOT THE PIGEON."

1977 EUROPEAN TOUR PROGRAM.

In early June, the band hit the road again, playing dates in Stockholm and Berlin. By this point they had added *Inside And Out* (from the SPOT THE PIGEON EP) to their set, as well as a great medley of *The Lamb Lies Down On Broadway* and the closing section of *The Musical Box*.

In June, David Hentschel traveled to Paris to record the band's five nights at the Palais des Sports, from June 11 to 15. Although concerts from the Bill Bruford tour had been recorded, almost all of the subsequent SECONDS OUT live album would be culled from these Paris shows. (Most of what appeared on the album came from the fourth show.)

On June 17, they played the Open Air Festival in Cologne, followed by a show in Offenbach on the 19th. From June 23 through the 25, Genesis took over London's massive Earl's Court arena, playing three sold-out shows at the 15,000 capacity venue, with Richie Havens as their support act. The stadium was filled with anticipation as M.C. Alan Freeman introduced the band: "Ladies and gentleman, they have their own special way ... And they are ... GENESIS!"

Phil, Mike, Steve, Tony and Chester played *Squonk, One For The Vine, Robbery, Assault And Battery, Inside And Out, Firth Of Fifth, The Carpet Crawlers, In That Quiet Earth, Afterglow, I Know What I Like, Eleventh Earl Of Mar, Supper's Ready, Dance On A Volcano*, Phil and Chester's drum duet, *Los Endos, The Lamb Lies Down On Broadway / The Musical Box* medley, and finished up with *The Knife*, which proved to be just as effective a show-closer as it had done seven years earlier.

Even without Gabriel's theatrics, Genesis presented a visually stunning show, due largely to their increasingly ambitious stage lighting.

"The light show is literally dazzling," wrote Peter Douglas in his review of the Earl's Court show for *Beat Instrumental*. "There are two rows of Boeing 747 aircraft landing lights sending down a blinding waterfall of light which is diffused and refracted by the clouds of smoke hanging over the stage and swirling out into the audience. When they come on at the end of *In That Quiet Earth* the stage explodes into a glorious rainbow umbrella of coloured lights, like a Mormon vision of heaven, and the gasp that goes up is almost loud enough to drown out the music."

In his review for *Melody Maker*, Chris Welch enthused about the Earl's Court shows, noting that Phil Collins "showed more confidence and energy than ever, singing with particularly moving effect on *Supper's Ready*, while Chester Thompson drummed with such blistering attack, one might imagine he had been with Genesis since its inception."

EARL'S COURT BOOTLEG LP

A recording of one of the Earl's Court shows was widely circulated on a bootleg LP (entitled simply EARL'S COURT), popular with fans for its inclusion of *One For The Vine* and *Inside And Out*, neither of which were included on the SECONDS OUT album.

In the years that followed, Genesis became very popular with bootleggers, and the group's unauthorized releases soon greatly outnumbered the legitimate ones. Early Genesis bootlegs — which included AS THOUGH EMERALD CITY and EARL'S COURT — were LP's in a plain sleeve, with a photocopied cover insert. As time went by, the packaging became more ambitious. The professional looking cover of the LAMB tour boot SWELLED AND SPENT made it appear to be an authorized release, an illusion that was quickly dispelled by the murky sound quality of the records inside. The majority of Genesis bootlegs are live recordings, but an increasing number of studio recordings and demos have seeped out over the years. The quality has improved over time, but even some vintage efforts — such as the 1978 live recording on LIVE FROM THE MOUTH OF THE MONSTER — are very listenable. Some vintage albums appeared to have been assembled by someone not terribly familiar with the band, with some rather

LIVE FROM THE MOUTH OF THE MONSTER, 1978

unusual song titles adorning the sleeves. *Behind The Lines* becomes *Written In The Book* on one bootleg, while *Dance On A Volcano* appears as *Best Are Doin' It Right* and *Me And Sarah Jane* is inexplicably re-titled *Me And Ser Yack*.

Genesis themselves seemed to have a healthy attitude towards the bootlegging of their material.

> "To be honest, I've never known anyone buy a bootleg in preference to buying the standard material," said Tony Banks in a radio interview. "It's normally an addition for people, you know, they like to have extra things — there are people who collect this sort of stuff. They're quite fun in some ways, and haven't really proved to be a problem for us."

After a couple of further European dates, the band returned to England in June 1977. There they set about mixing the live album they had been wanting to do since the TRICK OF THE TAIL tour. But not everyone retained their enthusiasm for the project. Sitting in Trident Studios listening endlessly to *Supper's Ready*, *Squonk*, etc., Steve Hackett's dissatisfaction came to a head. Having just come off the road, having played these songs almost every night for the previous seven months, Steve wasn't in the mood to hear them again. Since VOYAGE OF THE ACOLYTE, he had become a prolific writer, and Genesis could no longer accommodate his creative needs. And now, with a backlog of music he couldn't wait to record, Steve was stuck listening to mixes of songs he had played hundreds of times, to the point of boredom. It was all starting to sound weak to him and, one July day, he decided not to come to Trident for the mixing session. Instead, he called the studio and told the others that he was leaving the band. The fact that little effort was made to convince Steve to stay says a lot about how much his contribution to Genesis was valued by the other members.

> "I think once you've had the chance to not put your things in front of a disparaging committee, you realize that things don't have to be that way," Steve says of how VOYAGE OF THE ACOLYTE influenced his decision to leave Genesis. "You can be your own judge, you can be your own editor. You can be just as demanding of yourself, without feeling that good things are being lost or put on a backburner — sometimes infinitely. I think it's a case of feeling more security within yourself, certainly more security within your ideas."

> "I think the band was heading more towards a pared down kind of format, really," he reflects. "There were a number of factors but, basically, I wanted to work with other people. It wasn't that I felt the (Genesis) material wasn't up to par. I wanted to work with other people and have a free hand to do the things I wanted to do."

By 1977, Hackett thought of himself as a writer, whereas he had previously regarded himself primarily as a guitarist. In the early days with Genesis, he was encouraged to write but now, ironically, he was writing much more than the other group members were willing to use. "I ended up scrapping a huge percentage of my material," he recalled. In those days — after Gabriel's departure but before Collins' solo success — Tony Banks definitely dominated the group in terms of songwriting.

As previously stated, the politics of the 1971-75 line-up tended to have Rutherford allied with Banks, Hackett allied with Gabriel, with Collins in the middle. With Gabriel out, the

PLEASE DON'T TOUCH

BAY OF KINGS

balance of power shifted, leaving Steve Hackett in a weak position. The Banks / Rutherford unit was the majority and Steve felt that Phil tended to go along with their decisions. So he left to pursue a varied and successful solo career, leaving Genesis to reinvent itself once more.

"When Steve left it was something which took us by surprise," reflected Tony Banks during the Virgin online chat two decades later. "It was something we didn't want, but you just kind of adapt to it and you accept the cards you've been dealt at that time."

After leaving Genesis, Steve set to work on a second solo album, enlisting the talents of Richie Havens, Chester Thompson, brother John Hackett and members of Genesis-influenced progsters Kansas. The album, PLEASE DON'T TOUCH, included the composition of the same name whose rejection by Genesis was a factor in his departure. Since then he has released a succession of fine albums, and truly made good on his promise to challenge himself musically. While Genesis' post-Hackett releases have tended to stay within certain musical parameters, Steve has made a career out of changing styles and taking chances. Having established a solid progessive group sound on the excellent SPECTRAL MORNINGS AND DEFECTOR, he chucked it in favor of stripped down pop on CURED and made his debut as a lead singer. 1981's superb HIGHLY STRUNG was a more varied collection and even gave Steve a hit single in *Cell 151*. After having a pop solo hit, Hackett turned the tables again and made BAY OF KINGS, a gorgeous album of classical guitar pieces, including a great update of *Horizons*. In 1986, he dallied with arena rock with GTR, a "supergroup" collaboration with Yes-man Steve Howe, had a big hit, then ditched the arenas to make another acoustic album. Since then Steve's loyal followers have learnt to expect the unexpected, as he has gone from rock to classical to blues and all points in between.

Chapter 13: A More Commercial View

The remainder of Genesis didn't waste much time mourning Steve Hackett's departure. By August 1977, Phil, Mike and Tony were writing and rehearsing new material for their next LP. If anything, they were probably a little relieved by Steve's decision.

The fruitless search for a replacement for Peter Gabriel had undoubtedly put the group off the notion of trying to integrate an outsider, so they decided not to recruit a lead guitarist for recording purposes. Instead, Rutherford expanded his role to include lead guitar. His lead playing was a little tentative at first, but progressed a great deal over the next few years. Still, Hackett's contributions as a writer and a player had been an important part of Genesis. Musically, the group lost a key part of their sound when he left, and Steve's haunting electric leads and classical acoustic parts are particularly missed on the post-1977 releases.

In September, Collins, Banks and Rutherford returned to Relight Studios in Hilvarenbeek to record the tracks that would form their next album. In a lighthearted acknowledgement of their reduced membership, they dubbed the record ... AND THEN THERE WERE THREE ... The trio worked through September and October with David Hentschel producing. Engineering duties were handled by Hentschel, assisted by Steve Short and Pierre Geoffroy Chateau.

As always, the loss of a group member spurred the others into new creative areas.

> "The air had been cleared," says Hentschel. "And the personnel change became a new motivation for all of us to make it succeed — not least for Mike who had to pick up his guitars rather more often!"

AND THEN THERE WERE THREE ALBUM 1978.

During the ... AND THEN THERE WERE THREE ... sessions — with the public still unaware of Steve's departure — *Melody Maker* published the results of its latest readers' poll. For

Genesis, it was nothing short of a triumph: they appeared on the cover, with the headline "GENESIS SUPREME!" and were voted Top Band (Britain), Best Live Act and Best Arrangers. Despite the arrival of the Sex Pistols the previous year, Genesis and their ilk were still favorites with many British listeners. "The so-called old was are still a major, fighting force in rock," noted the paper, whose readers' top five British bands were (in descending order) Genesis, Yes, Led Zeppelin, ELP and the Sex Pistols. Although Genesis were busy with sessions for the next album, Phil flew back to London to accept the *Melody Maker* awards.

A couple of weeks after the *Melody Maker* triumph, Steve Hackett went public with his split from Genesis. In an exclusive interview with the paper, he revealed that:

> "Even before VOYAGE OF THE ACOLYTE, I had given up writing specifically for the band's capabilities, and I was getting involved in material that was a challenge for me. By the time we got to WIND & WUTHERING, I felt that the challenge within the band had really diminished ... It seemed to be a foregone conclusion that every time we stepped on stage we would go down beautifully." In the same article, Mike Rutherford said, "We will carry on as we always do ... With a change like this you lose some and you gain some. There was a flare-up at the end of the U.S. tour and problems came to a head. I'm glad he left when he did and made a clean cut, otherwise this album would've suffered."

More than anything, the remaining three seemed relieved by Steve's decision, noting that with less band members it was easier to work in the studio.

In October, as Phil, Mike and Tony were mixing their new studio album at Trident, Charisma released the double live set SECONDS OUT. A fine souvenir of their recent live dates (some of the last with Steve Hackett), it provided a great chance to hear Phil's vocal interpretations of numbers from the Gabriel years. Particularly effective were his renditions of *The Carpet Crawlers* (listed as *The Carpet Crawl* on SECONDS OUT) and *I Know What I Like*. Just in case anyone needed to be reminded of what a huge success the new Genesis was, here was proof, spread across two records. Although they had recorded a number of shows from the previous tour, most of the record came from the WIND & WUTHERING tour, with only *The Cinema Show* remaining as an example of Bill Bruford's stint with the band.

It's worth noting that Steve Hackett's guitar is kept suspiciously low in the mix throughout SECONDS OUT. (Perhaps he should have waited until the mixing was complete to leave the band!) Whether a deliberate case of revenge-by-mixing or not, the depth of Steve's guitar in the SECONDS OUT mix does rob the album of the kind of power his playing unleashed on GENESIS LIVE. While technically superior and smoother than its predecessor, SECONDS OUT tends to lack the raw energy of the band's first live album. Tellingly, the remaining members of Genesis had the more powerful GENESIS LIVE withdrawn from the British market in the late 70's / early 80's, citing its technical inadequacies as the reason.

Although Phil had predicted a return to group writing, it didn't really happen on ... AND THEN THERE WERE THREE ... Although there were group-written tracks, the majority were solo compositions. In these cases, the individual composers would exert a lot of influence over how their tracks would sound. Not quite solo efforts, but far from the group spirit that Genesis would soon rediscover. Solo compositions by Mike and Tony dominate the album. In particular, Rutherford's *Snowbound* and Banks' *Undertow* stand out as two of their best-ever compositions. *Scenes From A Night's Dream* marked the first time Collins had written a complete set of lyrics on his own, although its fantasy lyric (inspired by the vintage comic strip *Little Nemo In Slumberland*) gave no hint of the very personal creative outpouring that was to come from the drummer before the next Genesis album.

Because Mike Rutherford was just starting out as a lead player, the guitar presence on this album was fairly subdued. . . . AND THEN THERE WERE THREE . . . remains one of the band's most keyboard-dominated efforts.

> "Tony is using a new poly-moog and a lot more grand piano and we're not using a Mellotron except for a little bit," Phil revealed. "There's not so much acoustic material; also, it's more sparsely arranged as opposed to having layers and layers."

Although there wasn't much group-written material on the album, the Banks-Collins-Rutherford collaboration *Follow You, Follow Me* was a definite indicator of things to come. A simple, laid back number, it grew from extended jamming on a guitar riff of Mike. Colored by some warm synth chords from Tony, lyrics by Mike and a sincere vocal by Phil, it was a compelling work that introduced Genesis to a new audience.

> "I'd just written a simple love lyric for *Many Too Many*, and I think Mike was keen to try the same thing," said Tony. "Maybe *Follow You Follow Me* was almost too banal, but I got used to it. I think we find it much easier to write long stories than simple love songs."

Although it has been suggested that David Hentschel was not particularly fond of *Follow You, Follow Me*, the producer denies this. In any case, the single was unlike anything they had done before, and became Genesis' biggest hit to date, reaching No. 7 in Britain and No. 23 in America.

The American single of *Follow You, Follow Me* featured a remixed version of the track.

> "It had a Brazilian or Calypso feel to it originally," Phil told *Trouser Press*, "but Ahmet Ertegun remixed the American single and gave it more of a Bee Gees beat because he thought it had a funkier quality than we got out of it."

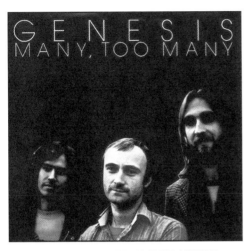

PICTURE SLEEVE FOR *MANY, TOO MANY* EP.

In addition to the tracks that appeared on the album, Genesis recorded at least two other tracks during the . . . AND THEN THERE WERE THREE . . . sessions: Tony's *The Day The Light Went Out* and Phil and Mike's *Vancouver*, both of which appeared on the flip side of the *Many Too Many* 45. Although there's no obvious reference in the lyrics, the title for *Vancouver* was presumably in reference to Phil's domestic situation, in which he was pondering a move to that city in an effort to save his marriage. It's possible that the lyrics — which tell the story of a girl who runs away from home in the middle of the night, then changes her mind and sneaks back in before dawn — could be a metaphor of sorts for Phil's domestic crisis.

Although it contains some excellent tracks, . . . AND THEN THERE WERE THREE . . . has not aged as well as the other albums from the 1975-80 era.

"It's a bit like NURSERY CRYME this album, it's not one of my favourites," commented Tony Banks in the late 80's. "I can't work out why. I listened to it the other day because we had it on compact disc. The best tracks were *Undertow, Follow Me* and *Say It's Alright, Joe.*"

Aided by the success of *Follow You, Follow Me*, . . . AND THEN THERE WERE THREE . . . became Genesis' biggest-selling album to date. Although it's British peak of No. 3 only matched the success of SELLING ENGLAND BY THE POUND and A TRICK OF THE TAIL, in America it reached No. 14 — Genesis' first showing in the American Top 20. It was certainly the group's biggest success yet, at least in commercial terms. Like each of the albums that followed it, it won Genesis new fans, while alienating those weened on the band's earlier efforts. And then there were the critics:

"AND THEN THERE WERE THREE lumbers about in a pea-soup fog of electronics, twists through a maze of odd tempos and dropped beats and ultimately spends itself in gratuitous effects," said the review in *Rolling Stone*. "The melodies have never been less substantial, while the songs revel in pettiness and two-bit theatricality. In short, this contemptible opus is but the palest shadow of the group's earlier accomplishments. Not only is the damage irreversible, it's been highly endorsed: AND THEN THERE WERE THREE is Genesis' first U.S. gold record."

The *Melody Maker* review, by Chris Welch, was much more favorable, calling the new record "an album as good as any they have made in recent, post-Gabriel years."

In December, with the new studio record finished and scheduled for a January release, Collins, Banks and Rutherford were making plans for their first post-Hackett tour. Although they had decided to remain a three-piece for their studio recordings, Phil, Mike and Tony needed a guitarist to take Steve's place in their live shows. It didn't take them long to find a suitable replacement: an American named Daryl Stuermer, formerly of Jean-Luc Ponty's band.

> "I know they auditioned about thirty guitarists from England," Stuermer recalls. "It didn't work out, and they had a list of about five guitar players — as far as I knew — from the United States. And I was on that list of five. I was recommended by a bass player named Alphonso Johnson. He was from a band called Weather Report and he knew Chester Thompson." Johnson was on Genesis' short list of potential guitarists, but didn't quite fit the bill. "They also needed a guitarist who could also play bass," Daryl explains. "But Alphonso was more of a bass player that could play some guitar. They needed a stronger guitar player who could double on bass, and that's something I could do. Most of my role at that time was going to be pretty much picking up where Steve Hackett left off, but Mike Rutherford was going to be starting to play more guitar from . . . AND THEN THERE WERE THREE . . . on."

> "I was with Jean-Luc Ponty for many years and they got my number through him," Daryl recalls. "They flew me to New York. I was the first out of the five guitar players auditioning that day, at S.I.R. Studios. They had sent me a tape previously of about four Genesis songs — *Squonk, Dance On A Volcano, Down And Out* and one of the other new ones (from . . . *And Then There Were Three* . . .). So I came there prepared for all those songs. And after I auditioned, Mike Rutherford said, 'I think you're the one.' And I said, 'Are you auditioning other people?' And he said, 'Yeah, I have four more guitar players, but I'll call you at five o'clock at your hotel, and I'll get together with you and give you a list of the songs we're going to be doing on the tour.' So I thought, 'Well, maybe he'll call, maybe he won't.' But he was sincere. You know, he and I got along very well. I think part of it was that I came in knowing the music, I was adaptable and also personally, we got along. And I think that's what made it easy for us."

The first few weeks of 1978 were spent rehearsing for the . . . AND THEN THERE WERE THREE . . . tour.

> "They had given me a list of twenty-five songs to learn in a short period of time," Stuermer remembers. "Which was hard to do. I was kind of nervous about learning so many songs. And I wasn't exactly sure how some of this worked. When you listen to the record, sometimes you don't know if what you're hearing is a guitar or a keyboard. So what I did was tried to learn both, not sure which one I was going to do. I came into the first rehearsal thinking, 'These guys are going to come right in and start rehearsing and go through all the songs.' Well, the first day, we didn't play a *note*. We were basically getting equipment together. And then the second day that we got together, we rehearsed maybe

two songs. And those guys were a little rusty themselves, with those songs, because they hadn't played them for quite a while."

Based on his experiences in other groups, Daryl had assumed that he was required to have mastered all the songs by the first day of rehearsal. He soon found that this wasn't the case with Genesis.

"In this band, you just kind of came in and slowly you started learning the songs and getting it together. Everybody wasn't clear on the chords and things. Which surprised me, because I was — I felt I had to be. In the first week of rehearsal, Tony Banks actually walked up to me and said 'Do you know what the chords are in that part?' So I told him what they were. It was kind of funny to me."

"A lot of things that you try at rehearsal, that are on the record, don't necessarily translate to a live performance," Stuermer explains. "We did that with a lot of songs. We'd try everything, but certain songs just didn't feel right to play live. Because you have more of a controlled situation in a studio and maybe you have an overdub of a second guitar. And you can do that in the studio, but live you'd actually have to have another guitar player. So, sometimes things didn't work out."

One new song that didn't last long in the set was *Down And Out*, the opening track from . . . AND THEN THERE WERE THREE . . . Genesis had finally written a song so complex that band members had trouble coming in on the right beat!

"The working title for that song was '5/8'," Daryl remembers. "Because a lot of the song is in 5/8. But the funny part of that song was everybody's position on where the beginning of the 5/8 bar is was different. Mike, Tony and Phil had different places where 'one' was. Tony's was definitely in a different place from Phil's and Mike decided he wasn't even going to think about it!"

Coinciding with the April release of . . . AND THEN THERE WERE THREE . . ., Phil, Mike, Tony, Chester and Daryl unveiled their live show with a lengthy bout of American shows. The goal for 1978 was to 'break' America. They were getting there already, but felt that a relentless onslaught across the nation would finally win over this lucrative market.

They kicked off the shows with a familiar number, *Eleventh Earl Of Mar*, followed by THE LAMB favorite *In The Cage*, which would prove to be one of the most durable numbers from the Gabriel era. *Burning Rope*, *Ripples*, and *Deep In The Motherlode* were followed by a resurrection of *The Fountain Of Salmacis*. Then it was *One For The Vine*, *Squonk*, *Say It's Alright Joe*, *The Cinema Show* and *Afterglow*. They saved their new hit single, *Follow You, Follow Me*, for near the end, then wound it all up with *Dance On A Volcano* and *Los Endos*, linked by Chester and Phil's drum duet. Some dates featured *The Lady Lies* while the first few shows included the tricky *Down And Out*.

Los Angeles Times writer Richard Cromelin, who had championed the group's Gabriel-era performances, offered an astute appraisal of the latest version of Genesis:

"Moments of tough rock excitement occasionally emerge from the generally restrained surroundings, but in its newer music Genesis seems more interested in maintaining the status quo than broadening its ambitions. Originally, the facet that separated Genesis from the mellotron brigade was the offbeat nature of the departed Peter Gabriel's lyrics and stagemanship. Today, Genesis' verbal content is virtually nil, and vocalist / drummer Phil Collins serves as emcee. His hammy monologues range from the 'jes folks style of "people's bands" to introductory tales inherited from Gabriel but transformed from whimsical / surreal to grossest common denominator."

Although they focused their efforts on "breaking" America, Genesis remained quintessentially English.

"I'd like a nice cup of tea," Mike complained to *Melody Maker* during the U.S. tour. "I've even brought my own kettle for this trip, but there is something wrong with the milk and water here. I just can't seem to make a proper cup of tea." Even after a decade away from Charterhouse, Genesis still weren't exactly the epitome of rock and roll. Tony Banks seemed equally unaffected by rock stardom: "I'm a composer really," he explained. "I just play because no one else would want to play my stuff."

After Stateside shows in Buffalo, Rochester, Philadelphia, Bloomington, Kalamazoo, Normal, Chicago, Cleveland, Dayton, St. Louis, Oakland and Los Angeles, the band left America for a European tour. During May and June, Genesis took their show across the Continent, playing Cologne, Frankfurt, Munich, Brussels, Paris, St. Etienne, Oslo, Hamburg, Dortmund and Helsinki.

REVELATORY GENESIS 80:78 BOOTLEG ALBUM,
FEATURES THREE LIVE KNEBWORTH FESTIVAL
RECORDINGS.

On June 24, Genesis made their only British appearance of 1978, at the huge Knebworth Festival (which was billed as "A Midsummer Night's Dream"). The band's decision to focus their energies on America was a disappointment to the faithful British fans, but at least they chose a big venue: 100,000 fans got to see Genesis at Knebworth. Sharing the bill with them at the one-day festival were Devo, Brand X, Jefferson Starship, Tom Petty and the Heartbreakers and the Atlanta Rhythm Section.

July was spent back in North America building on the newfound success of . . . AND THEN THERE WERE THREE . . . and

PROGRAM FOR THE 1978 JAPANESE TOUR.

Follow You, Follow Me, with dates in Toronto, Montreal, Clarkston, Milwaukee, Cincinnati, Pittsburgh, Syracuse, Columbia, Hampton, Providence and Saratoga Springs. At a New York City performance, Peter Gabriel himself showed up to sing along on the encore.

In late August and early September they were back in Europe, before crossing the Atlantic again for a third bout of North American dates. One of these, an October 13 show at Chicago's Uptown Theater, was recorded for a radio broadcast. This high-quality recording became the source for a number of bootlegs, including LIVE FROM THE MOUTH OF THE MONSTER.

Genesis ended 1978 with a brace of dates in Japan — at the Kosei Nenkin Hall in Osaka and the Sun Plaza in Tokyo. Exhausted after a year of touring, and with Phil's marriage on its last legs, the group members decided to give Genesis a rest for the next ten months.

Chapter 14: Duke's Travels

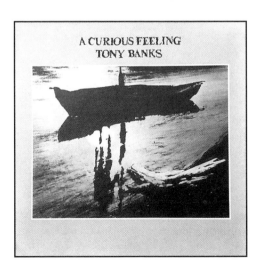

Although there was no new Genesis product released in 1979, the group members were not idle. While Phil relocated to Vancouver, in a last-ditch attempt to save his marriage, Tony and Mike recorded their first ever solo albums. Both Banks' A CURIOUS FEELING and Rutherford's SMALLCREEP'S DAY featured guest vocalists, with neither the keyboardist or guitarist ready to make their lead vocal debut (yet).

Tony's album, A CURIOUS FEELING, appeared in late 1979.

"There were things I wanted to do but couldn't within Genesis," Banks told *Sounds* that October, during rehearsals for the next Genesis record. "Like not using drums on all the tracks and orchestrating things my way. Obviously I can't help sounding a bit like Genesis on everything I do but I wanted to take certain things further; such as using chord sequences that wouldn't go down too well with Genesis."

Banks had also recently completed work on his first film score, for the Alan Bates picture THE SHOUT. Although Banks would provide music for several subsequent movies — including THE WICKED LADY and QUICKSILVER — he has never quite made a name for himself in that area. A shame, since his music has always had a cinematic quality that seemed ideally suited to the big screen.

Mike Rutherford enlisted Anthony Phillips to play keyboards on his solo album, entitled SMALLCREEP'S DAY. The album featured one side based on the short story "Smallcreep's Day" and another side of individual shorter songs. Like Banks' solo debut, it was not outstanding, but was a nice chance to hear Mike's talents given full creative reign, especially since he had only penned a handful of solo compositions for Genesis.

Despite his new status as Genesis' frontman, Phil Collins was, in some ways, an unlikely candidate for a solo career. Although he had co-written and contributed to many Genesis songs over the years, he had never written a whole song on his own. All that changed in 1979, when the untrained keyboard player began writing and demoing an amazing batch of songs. The hiatus after Genesis' 1978 world tour was supposed to give him a chance to sort out his personal life, but Phil soon realized there was no saving his marriage. He returned to England and began pouring his emotional turmoil into songwriting. The songs he wrote were very personal and direct, much more so than one would have expected from a member of Genesis, but Collins gave the band first refusal of several of his songs. The timing was certainly right for an increase in his songwriting contribution, with Tony and Mike having used up most of their recent material on their solo efforts.

In October, the trio reconvened at Phil's house to work on new Genesis material, which would appear on their next album, DUKE. Although punk rock had drastically altered the musical climate, particularly in Britain, Genesis were more popular than ever.

"Funnily enough, punk rock helped us a lot," said Tony Banks. "Because a lot of bands didn't survive and it meant we had less competition in our area and I always thought we were better. This kind of confirmed it in a way. I always thought it was wrong for us to be lumped with other bands. We had technique and complexity but the basis of our songs has always been in melody and sound."

The band commandeered Phil's bedroom and transformed it into their rehearsal room. Inspired by the success of the group-written *Follow You, Follow Me,* Phil, Mike and Tony, decided to write more songs together for the new record. As the threesome spent more and more time jamming, their new music evolved rapidly. They developed a fresh, vital sound, yet the energy was reminiscent of such early Collins-Banks-Rutherford collaborations as the closing section of *The Cinema Show.* As well as group jamming, another factor in Genesis' changing style was the influence of the outside musicians brought in to tour with the band.

"The (original band) was a very good band," observes Daryl Stuermer. "But they were all kind of brought up together, so they didn't have a lot of outside influences. I think as they got, say, Bill Bruford in the band, and then Chester, then myself, there was a little bit of outside influence. And Phil got influenced by having his own band (Brand X) and having other musicians influencing him as well, and then he brought that back to Genesis. He was a big fan of a lot of American music, so he was bringing that in with the British music."

As well as writing together, each member of Genesis brought individually penned songs for the new album. Phil offered up *In The Air Tonight, If Leaving Me Is Easy, I Missed Again, Misunderstanding* and *Please Don't Ask.* Amazingly, Banks and Rutherford passed on the first three (two of which later became solo hits for Phil), and chose the last two numbers as candidates for Genesis. Banks brought in a typically romantic, melancholy quartet of tunes — *Guide Vocal, Evidence Of Autumn, Heathaze* and *Cul-de-sac* — while Rutherford contributed *Man Of Our Times, Open Door* and *Alone Tonight.*

The rest of the songs grew out of group jam sessions. *Behind The Lines, Duchess, Turn It On Again* and *Duke's Travels / Duke's End* were the most powerful songs Genesis had written since Steve Hackett's departure, and represented a newfound creativity that would reinvigorate the band for the next few years.

Mike has said that *Behind The Lines* started out as more of a "traditional" Genesis song, but took on more of a "Supremes feel" as it evolved. Phil took a stab at writing the words, penning a cynical lyric inspired by the music press' criticism of the band, but that idea was ultimately abandoned.

Another group-written highlight was *Duchess*, which Tony Banks cites as one of his all-time favorite Genesis songs. *Duchess* tells the story of the rise and fall of a singer and, although it concerns a female vocalist, it's easy to draw a parallel with Genesis' own career: the early days when "times were good" and they didn't worry about the future, the gruelling years of touring and eventually rise to the top, when all they had to do was step on stage to make the crowd roar. In its last verse, *Duchess* dealt with the artist's decline. Genesis wouldn't get to that point for quite some time, but when they did, *Duchess* seemed to mirror the group's career arc.

Having written such strong material as a group, Phil, Mike and Tony originally envisioned the new album as featuring one side on which all the group-written material would appear together as a "suite." The plan was to record one twenty-five minute group-written piece and devote the other side of the LP to six individual songs, two written by each group member.

The twenty-five minute piece would probably have consisted of *Behind The Lines, Duchess, Guide Vocal, Turn It On Again, Duke's Travels* and *Duke's End.* which were subsequently played together in that sequence in concert. (This is commonly referred to by fans as the "Duke

Suite.") Interestingly, *Turn It On Again* began life as a "throwaway" instrumental passage linking two other pieces (probably *Guide Vocal* and *Duke's Travels*), but the group grew so fond of it that they developed in into a song — and a hit single to boot.

Although the "Duke Suite" would have made for a very powerful album side, the group abandoned the plan, feeling that the other side would've sounded weak by comparison. They were probably right, in that the solo compositions on DUKE were nowhere near as strong as the group-written numbers.

"There were problems with DUKE, specifically with the long and short tracks," David Hentschel recalls. "Phil was really beginning to do more writing on his own and, as his own solo career went on to prove, had always had a love of shorter (in particular Tamla Motown) tunes, and he naturally wrote these himself. There were also other influences — notably Earth, Wind and Fire — that he and I were very keen on at the time — hence his later collaboration with Philip Bailey. So, really, I guess there was a conflict in styles emerging. Various options were discussed and tried, but I don't remember exactly what was said, or how we arrived at the decisions we did."

As well as the tracks used on the album, the group also recorded Tony's *Evidence Of Autumn* and Mike's *Open Door*. Those tracks appeared first as B-sides and then on the North American version of THREE SIDES LIVE. Tony has said that he felt that *Evidence Of Autumn* should have been included on DUKE, perhaps at the expense of Mike's *Alone Tonight*, which he felt was a slightly weaker number. Interestingly, *Evidence of Autumn* was issued as a single in Poland a couple of years later (to promote the THREE SIDES LIVE album), and made the Top 10 there.

"All the tracks which ultimately became B-sides were always written and recorded with a view to being included on the corresponding album," Hentschel points out. "They were only left off in order to make a stronger, more focused and more concise album. This didn't in anyone's view at the time mean they were inferior tracks — just that they didn't necessarily fit in so well with the rest of the album."

To get the better of the British taxman, Genesis once again traveled abroad to record. During November 1979, they spent two weeks at Polar Studios in Sweden (a facility owned by the group ABBA), where they recorded all the instrumental tracks for the new album. The vocals were reportedly added later on at Maison Rouge in London, although the album credits state only that the record was recorded at Polar, presumably for tax purposes.

The sleeve of DUKE credits Phil with supplying drums, vocals, drum machine and ... duck. In a radio interview with *Rockline*, Collins explained the latter credit.

"The 'duck' was in fact the duck call. Its one of those little things that like, you know, if you shoot rifles and stuff and you're trying to capture, you know, trying to kill ducks or whatever, you have duck calls and crow calls and things like that.

Before I got to know Earth, Wind & Fire, and we wanted to get the horn sound on *Behind The Lines* and *Turn It On Again*, the only way to do it was for me to trigger a vocoder and a synthesizer, and I was fooling around with a duck call, which I played into a microphone, that went through a synthesizer, from the synthesizer to a vocoder. It ended up sounding like a horn section, but we thought if we put 'horn section' on it, people would think that it was a horn section when it wasn't. So we called it the duck. So really, it was the beginning of my association with Earth, Wind & Fire because, you know, you can't go through life with just a duck call, you have to get the real thing eventually."

In February 1980, shortly before the release of the new Genesis material, Mike Rutherford released his SMALLCREEP'S DAY LP and the single *Working In Line*. The album sold respectably on both sides of the Atlantic, but the single slipped by without much notice.

Towards the end of February, after putting the finishing touches on DUKE at Maison Rouge, Genesis began rehearsing for their next tour. Before rehearsals for a tour began, Phil, Mike and Tony would send an advance tape of the new album to Chester Thompson and Daryl Stuermer.

"They would usually send me a note, or call me, and say 'These are the ones we're thinking of doing,'" Stuermer recalls. "They knew I could pick it up off the tape, but sometimes Mike would say he was playing guitar on this one and I'd be playing bass, or on another one he's playing bass."

Much of the ... AND THEN THERE WERE THREE ... tour had been devoted to American dates and British fans had been neglected, save for the Knebworth performance. For DUKE, the band decided to treat their U.K. fans to a full tour, playing smaller venues. It was generous gesture but, because of the band's rapidly growing fanbase, there were logistical problems. When the tickets went on sale for the nationally announced dates, many fans were disappointed to find out that the shows had already sold out. Those who applied in advance for tickets through the mail had been the lucky ones, it turned out. In an effort to meet the demand, Genesis added a few extra London shows to the schedule, but were limited by commitments to American dates.

On March 3, just before the tour began, Genesis released a new single, *Turn It On Again*. It was followed later in the month by the DUKE LP, which quickly reached the top of the British charts.

"It was well worth the wait," proclaimed the ads that heralded DUKE's release. Not everyone agreed. Chris Bohn's review of the album in *Melody Maker* played upon the recent publicity about the demand for tickets, and sported the headline, "Yes, half a million can be wrong." Bohn called Genesis "an essentially mediocre group way past its peak" and opined that "post-Gabriel, Genesis have never been about raw excitement." By this point, punk and new wave had taken hold of the trendy British music press, and Genesis were seen as representing exactly what the new groups were supposed to wipe out.

JAPANESE *TURN IT ON AGAIN* 45.

Many readers took exception to the *Melody Maker* review. In fact, an entire issue's letters column was devoted to fan reactions to Bohn's assessment, under the headline "Duke Box Jury." "In several paragraphs he reduced almost a decade of instrumental and compositional wonder to a few unjustified statements," wrote one fan, echoing the reaction of the majority. There were those who agreed with Bohn's assessment, however. "Full marks to him for slagging off Mike Rutherford's and Tony Banks' nauseatingly narcissistic rubbish," wrote one disappointed fan. "Congratulations to Phil Collins on almost saving the album."

And the negative press wasn't limited to the U.K. In America, *Rolling Stone* concluded that:

> "in the six years since their psycho-opera, THE LAMB LIES DOWN ON BROADWAY, Genesis have lapsed into a stylistic predictability that sorely misses Gabriel's perverse wit and the sensual near-Indian strains of Hackett's guitar. Yet the familiar, almost anesthetic sound of DUKE is comforting; a reassurance that Genesis aren't ready for an exodus yet."

Twenty years later, DUKE holds up very well, a fine balance of Genesis' epic work and their shorter catchier songs. Tony Banks said as much in a recent interview, calling DUKE his favorite Genesis album and citing *Duchess* as his favorite song.

After the difficult-to-fathom cover design of . . . AND THEN THERE WERE THREE . . . , Genesis stopped working with Hipgnosis and sought out a fresher, simpler look for the DUKE sleeve. By 1980, Hipgnosis had a certain stigma attached to their work, which was associated with bands like Yes, Pink Floyd and . . . Genesis. The artwork on the *Duke* sleeve was by French artist Lionel Koechlin.

> "We were looking for some ideas to try and get away from the usual kind of Genesis cover that we had been associated with," said Phil on the *Rockline* radio show. "And we saw his crayon drawings, which were . . . very childlike. We just thought that it would be very nice. Originally, it was part of an A-B-C book for children, and it was Q for question, and it had a picture of Albert looking out the window like on the cover, but with a Q above it and a question mark. We just got rid of the Q. We just tried to get away from the usual Genesis type cover and that was what we went for."

The early dates in the DUKE tour were warm-up gigs that weren't announced nationally, including shows at Paignton's Festival Hall, Exeter University and the Civic Hall, Guildford. Perhaps the most significant of the warm-up shows was the March 22 date which saw the band return to Friar's, Aylesbury. Even though the gig was only advertised locally, there was a huge demand for tickets, with fans lined up overnight for tickets. David Stopps and his staff stayed with the fans overnight and brought them a wheelbarrow full of porridge for breakfast in the morning.

The fans' perseverance was worth it. On March 22, they were treated to a powerful mixture of old and new Genesis: *Deep In The Motherlode, Dancing With The Moonlit Knight, The Carpet Crawlers, Squonk, One For The Vine, Behind The Lines, Duchess, Guide Vocal, Turn It On Again, Duke's Travels, Duke's End, Ripples, The Lady Lies, In The Cage, Afterglow, Follow You, Follow Me, Dance On A Volcano, Los Endos, I Know What I Like* and a revival of the Gabriel-era set-closer *The Knife*.

Aside from the ticket fiasco, the DUKE tour suffered another setback. A March 26 appearance at Winter Gardens, Bournemouth — originally announced as the first "official" date of the tour — had to be cancelled when Phil came down with laryngitis.

Once, Phil's throat had recovered, the "official" tour began. Genesis played at Hammersmith Odeon on March 27, 28 and 29 and Oxford's New Theatre on the 31st. On April 1, they played the Gaumont, Ipswich, followed by the ABC in Great Yarmouth and the ABC in. Peterborough ABC. Next was the following dates:

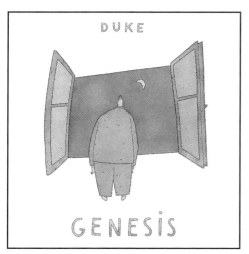

- o Odeon in Birmingham,
- o The Blackpool ABC,
- o Trentham Gardens in Stoke,
- o Sophia Gardens in Cardiff,
- o The Gaumont in Southampton,
- o Brighton Centre,
- o Brighton, Coventry Theatre,
- o Leicester DeMontfort Hall,
- o The Assembly Rooms in Derby,
- o Sheffield City Hall,
- o The Manchester Apollo,
- o St. George's Hall in Bradford,
- o The Edinburgh Odeon,
- o Caird Hall in Dundee,
- o The Capitol in Aberdeen,
- o The Glasgow Apollo,
- o Newcastle City Hall,
- o Market Hall in Carlisle
- o Two nights at the Empire Theatre in Liverpool.

CANADIAN SINGLE FOR *MISUNDERSTANDING*.

A May 5 appearance at the Theatre Royal, Drury Lane had been added to the agenda to help accommodate the thousands of fans disappointed by the tour's quick sell-out. The Drury Lane show sold out immediately and the band added two more London shows, on May 6 and 7 at the Lyceum Ballroom. From there, it was off to North America, where *Misunderstanding* was heading for the Top 20.

"Some of the old fans don't even like it when you have a hit single," Collins told *Rock Scene.* "Like *Misunderstanding* was. *Follow You, Follow Me* was a hit here, too, and in England, and we'd get letters saying 'Well, that's it, Genesis — you sold out!' But if they could see behind the scenes, they'd know that those tunes — both hits — were written the same way as some of the more esoteric stuff."

With each album since GENESIS LIVE, the group had achieved a higher placing on the American charts, and DUKE continued this trend. The album reached No. 11, three places higher than ... AND THEN THERE WERE THREE ...'s peak position.

"We've a lot of much younger fans now," Collins explained. "You see, the fans we had when we started have grown up, got mortgages and kids and don't go to concerts anymore. They still buy albums, of course — maybe one a week, but if they can't buy yours, well, they might go get somebody else's. But these kids now — a lot of them teenagers — surprisingly don't even remember when Peter was in the group. Or even Steve. They might even have just picked up on our last couple of albums. And perhaps a lot of them have become fans because of 'Misunderstanding.' The kids on the fringe heard that record. They heard the band that did it was coming to town. And they came out to see us."

The North American DUKE tour kicked of on the 17th and 18th of May with dates in Edmonton and Calgary. On May 25, the band treated Los Angeles fans to a surprise show at the Roxy, before their announced appearance at the outdoor Greek Theater. With the catchy *Misunderstanding* perched at No. 16 on the *Billboard* chart, Genesis could afford to do a less extensive tour than they had in 78, but their six-week North American jaunt offered plenty of great shows to their burgeoning Stateside following.
In the *Los Angeles Times*, Robert Hilburn acknowledged the quality of the DUKE material, but was largely unimpressed.

"Mostly ... the band's lyrics and themes continue to lag behind the instrumental sheen. We know the writer (or singer) is lonely here or insecure there, but we aren't given insights or depth. We are left, with Genesis operating from an extremely conservative format, one that neither reaches for the bravado of the progressive rock era nor the relevancy and bite of the new-wave contingent."

After the U.S. dates, Genesis returned to England for a well-deserved break. But the energetic Mr. Collins had his own backlog of songs to deal with and was soon hard at work on his first solo album. Playing keyboards as well as drums, he laid down backing tracks in his eight-track home studio, inspired by the freedom to work on his music whenever he felt like it. With Genesis' previous records, the group had to adhere to the hours and days during which they had booked studio time, but now Phil could work on his music anytime he wanted to.

Collins' attitude to recording had been profoundly affected by his work with Brian Eno on ANOTHER GREEN WORLD.

> "It showed me that anything could work," he told *Melody Maker*. "We did three days of just blowing. I learnt that you could do something at home, and it didn't have to sound good — that it was the idea that counted. The logical extension of that was for me to do something at home that did sound good and feel good."

With a looser recording set-up, Collins crafted a powerful, personal collection, including moody pieces like *In The Air Tonight* and *The Roof Is Leaking*, as well as uptempo R&B-flavored pop tunes such as *I Missed Again*. As if to make a point, Phil threw in a barely-recognizable funk interpretation of Genesis' *Behind The Lines*. Everything about the album begged for a complete re-appraisal of Phil Collins. Not too long after its release, Phil ceased to be perceived as "the singer / drummer from Genesis." To many listeners, Genesis would soon be regarded as "that group that Phil Collins plays with."

Essential to the re-evaluation of Phil Collins was the fact that FACE VALUE came out on Virgin Records. At the time, Virgin was a much hipper label than Charisma, and the latter was very much associated with Genesis. (Ironically, Virgin took over Charisma a few years later and is now home to Genesis and their back catalog.)

> "FACE VALUE delights in confounding the familiar parameters of that band's style," said the *Melody Maker* review. "Listening to this album is like meeting someone you thought you knew and disliked and discovering that they've got far more going for themselves than you ever imagined ... While Genesis may have their heads in the clouds, Phil Collins has got his feet on the ground."

Chapter 15: Who Dunnit?

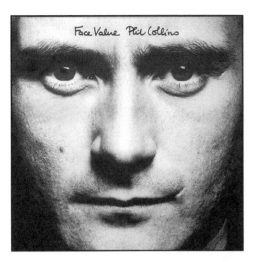

PHIL COLLINS' IN THE AIR SINGLE.

Phil Collins' experience with working at home on FACE VALUE had unleashed in him a newfound creativity. The relaxed approach to recording was something he'd never experienced with Genesis, but that was about to change. Towards the end of 1980, the group purchased a farm in Surrey, some thirty miles Southwest of London, and set about converting it into a recording facility where they could work at their own pace, unhampered by the restrictions of working at someone else's studio.

The renovation was barely finished when the band started recording there in March of 1981. As they settled into the studio, which they had simply dubbed "The Farm," they were eager to forge a new Genesis sound, influenced to some extent by Phil's solo work, especially in terms of the approach to recording. Significantly, David Hentschel — whose production style had become synonymous with the post-Gabriel group — was gone.

"I think deep down we all knew that DUKE would be our last collaboration, though nothing was said at the time," says Hentschel. "There was from time to time a sense that we were re-treading familiar ground, rather than boldly going where we had not been before! When that happens in any creative relationship, it's usually time for one or all of the people involved to move on. Phil's solo success and the sound he was getting with Hugh (Padgham) were surely a big influence as well, not only on my position, but very obviously on the future of Genesis as well . . ."

In Hentschel's place was Hugh Padgham, who had worked with Collins on FACE VALUE, and had previously worked with the Police and XTC. Phil had first encountered Padgham while drumming on Peter Gabriel's third self-titled album. During those sessions, Collins had developed a powerful new drum sound that would become his trademark and would be widely imitated for years to come. The heavily compressed sound was achieved with assistance from Padgham, but also owed a lot to an unorthodox suggestion Gabriel made

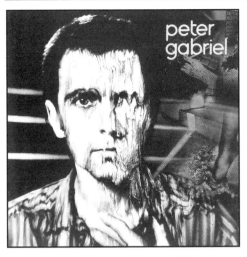

GABRIEL'S THIRD SOLO ALBUM.

when Phil arrived at the studio: "No cymbals." Collins tried to get Gabriel to let him at least use his hi-hat, but his ex-bandmate would have none of it. It was an audacious move, but the results speak for themselves, particularly on the stark, eerie opener *Intruder*. This kind of radical approach to recording was just what Genesis needed to invigorate their sound. They weren't about to match the Clash or the Sex Pistols in the "credibility" sweepstakes, but they were about to shed some of their "dinosaur" image.

Phil, Mike and Tony took their time writing and recording their new material. They worked hard, but strived to capture on tape a looser feel — closer to what they sounded like in their rehearsal room. On this new album, the *studio* was also the rehearsal room. If they got the right feel in rehearsal, the tape machine would be rolling and they wouldn't have to worry about recreating the magic later on. Six years on from THE LAMB LIES DOWN ON BROADWAY, Genesis finally achieved the kind of spontaneity they'd hoped to capture at Headley Grange.

"I had worked with Hugh Padgham on my album and was confident he would make us sound different," said Phil. "On ABACAB we sound much more the way we do at rehearsal. We always had a rough edge, but it was cleaned up by David (Hentschel), or ourselves."

Although, Chester Thompson and Daryl Stuermer were an integral part of their live shows, Phil, Mike and Tony preferred to work as a trio in the studio.

"I have a lot of admiration and respect for them but it's easier for the three of us to work in the studio," said Banks. "I used Chester and Daryl on my solo album. They are people I really like to play with, but on the albums, it's better to keep it to the three. Why fly them over from America when we can put a bit of guitar and drums on in the studio right away?"

Also, when Genesis had gone down to a three-piece, they had ceased to have the type of conflicts over songwriting contributions that had contributed to the departures of Hackett and Gabriel. If Daryl and Chester had worked on the studio sessions, the others would probably have felt obliged to let them contribute as writers, which could have resulted in a more strained working environment.

Years later, during a Virgin online chat, Tony Banks pointed to ABACAB as the album on which Genesis most consciously tried to change their sound and their approach to creating it: "We made a definite change to prevent boredom setting in."

The trio wrote a lot of material, but didn't use anything that sounded too much like "Genesis." When Phil, Mike and Tony found themselves instinctively veering towards the "traditional" Genesis sound, they scrapped what they were working on. "We had one track which had the working title *Fast Bass*, which we went ahead and recorded," Phil told *Melody Maker*. "We started thundering along on this *Fast Bass* tune, and suddenly we all stopped. We said, 'This is what people expect to hear from Genesis.' " The track was quickly abandoned, and the group continued searching for fresher sounds.

> "I urge people to forget what they think of as Genesis," Phil said. "There is definitely much more immediacy on this record, which I think is us getting better at writing and not clouding it up with shit. We shied away from stock Genesis devices such as sustained keyboards, and just honed everything down to its barest essentials. A lot of the songs are very, very unlike Genesis."

In an interview with *Sounds*, Collins put it bluntly: "I can't really expect anyone who liked us in 1972 to like us now."

After a few weeks of writing and rehearsing, Banks, Collins and Rutherford began recording, utilizing The Farm's 24-track facilities. They recorded at least fifteen new songs and for a time considered putting out a double album. Ultimately, they settled for a single LP. At the time, a double album would have further cemented Genesis image as a 70's "dinosaur" act. A single LP, packaged in a cover with minimalist artwork (no Squonks, lawnmowers or angels on this sleeve), would help Phil, Mike and Tony reinvent the group's image.

ABACAB ALBUM 1981.

There were four different versions of the ABACAB cover. Each featured the same design, but with a different color scheme. The album's packaging was also notable for not including the lyrics to the songs. Previously, including the lyrics was a standard procedure for Genesis and the decision not to include them with ABACAB was another part of their attempt to alter people's perceptions of the group.

"I do think that ABACAB is a definite step forward in terms of Genesis," Phil told *Melody Maker*. "By saying that, I guess I'm denouncing what we've done already, though without meaning to sound as though I'm saying that. I'm just proud, though, that we're thinking more ... modern."

In a *New York Post* interview, Collins explained that, "I did feel that people tended to categorize Genesis as something pompous, and I wanted to shake them by the neck and say, 'Listen, we're not what we were in the 70's.' "

Phil was eager to explain why Genesis were nothing like Yes and Pink Floyd.

"We're totally unlike all those bands that have synthesizers and lights," he told *Melody Maker*. "Recently I did a Radio One Pop Quiz with Dave Gilmour, and he was exactly what I hoped he wouldn't be. Also, though I really like Jon Anderson as a person, I completely hate that Yes kind of music. So its a double insult to be compared with stuff that I really can't stand."

Interesting comments, in that Collins had been an avid Yes fan when he joined Genesis back in 1970. But Phil's change in attitude was no doubt due in part to the direction Yes had taken through the 70's, straying ever further into the land of concept albums, mystical lyrics and extended soloing — just as Genesis were heading in the other direction. Also, Genesis were desperately striving for some credibilty in the post-punk climate and it was important for them to disassociate themselves from the 70's prog-rock image. The truth is, they *had* always had a quite different attitude from Yes, Pink Floyd and ELP, but ABACAB proved the point.

U.K. *ABACAB* SINGLE

The album opened with ABACAB itself, a track that really couldn't have worked with the old Genesis sound. The stripped-down, driving number opened the album, unveiling the new Genesis in an unapologetic manner. The song's title was derived from the group's working method, whereby they labeled the three different sections "A," "B" and "C" during the songwriting process. At one point, the structure spelled out "ABACAB" and it was adopted as the title. The finished track had a different sequence, but the group liked the title and kept it anyway.

Even more un-Genesis-like was the soulful blast of horns that kicked off the next track, *No Reply At All*. Although it featured a LAMB LIES DOWN ON BROADWAY-esque grand piano part from Tony, there was no mistaking this for vintage Genesis. *No Reply At All* featured stunning contributions from the Earth, Wind and Fire brass section, an addition that would have seemed unthinkable on any previous Genesis record. Phil flew over to America to overdub their parts on this track (as well as another number, *Paperlate*), completely uncertain of what Mike and Tony's reaction would be. When he returned to England with the tapes, they agreed that his instinct was correct, and Genesis took another bold step forward.

Me And Sarah Jane was a solo composition by Tony, incorporating several different song snippets all set to the same drum machine rhythm. At first he thought of working one or two sections into a more traditional song. However, he decided that since other songs on the album tended to keep to one mood throughout the song, it would be good to do a track covering many different moods. It's a brilliant piece of work, retaining the romanticism of earlier Banks efforts, but in a vital new sonic setting.

Keep It Dark, which closed the album's first side, started with a garage rock riff, that caught the listener off guard, even after the revelations of the first two tracks. The song, whose working title was *Odd*, featured the group playing against a looped drum track. In an admirable display of restraint, Tony didn't play a single chord on his keyboard until the chorus, but when he did, the effect was all the more powerful. Genesis had always used musical dynamics to great effect, but this minimalist approach was truly refreshing. Banks has said that *Keep It Dark* is his favorite track on ABACAB.

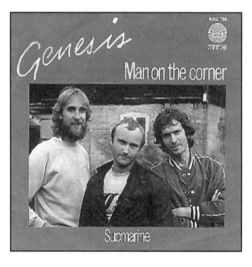

The repetitive, new wave-flavored *Who Dunnit?* was the album's most radical departure, but has not aged as well as the rest of the album. The *Dodo / Lurker* medley recalled the classic Genesis style of songwriting, but was performed and produced in the stripped-down manner of all the other ABACAB tracks. Rutherford's *Like It Or Not* and Collins' *Man On The Corner* were less striking, merely re-treading familiar ground, albeit with more up-to-date production.

Overall, the album is a little inconsistent, but even some of the weaker numbers served an important purpose. For better and for worse, ABACAB was the reinvention of Genesis.

(ABOVE) CANADIAN *MAN ON THE CORNER* SINGLE. (BELOW) GERMAN *MAN ON THE CORNER* SINGLE.

In addition to the tracks that appeared on the album, the group finished several others which were used as B-sides and on the 3X3 EP: the upbeat *Paperlate*, the atmospheric instrumental *Submarine, You Might Recall* (working title: *Jangly*), *Me And Virgil*, and *Naminanu*. All these tracks would presumably have been included if ABACAB had been a double LP. Another track that would undoubtedly have found space on a double album was a fifteen-minute version of ABACAB itself. "We were quite keen to put out the whole 15-minute version," Tony once remarked, "because it all sounded good."

Banks has said that he really wanted *You Might Recall* on the album, but when it came down to a choice between that and *Who Dunnit?*, the group opted for the latter. With hindsight, *You Might Recall* was the better number, but *Who Dunnit?* was a strong indication of the group's desire to redefine themselves, and it served a purpose.

In August 1981, British fans got their first taste of the new Genesis with the release of the single *Abacab*. If there were older fans who were alienated by the very current sound of the record, there were plenty more willing to embrace this song. *Abacab* quickly climbed the chart. It was a fine single but, to those weaned on 70's Genesis, it was an indicator that the good old days were well and truly over. It was clear at that point that there would be no return to the *Firth Of Fifth* or the *Fountain Of Salmacis*. Just as Peter Gabriel had pushed the group out of the 60's with THE LAMB LIES DOWN ON BROADWAY, Phil Collins yanked them out of the 70's with ABACAB.

After all the uproar over the *Melody Maker* review of DUKE, the paper was somewhat more charitable in its treatment of ABACAB. The review praised *Keep It Dark* and *Who Dunnit?* in particular, calling them "the most exciting and innovative music Genesis have made for years." While criticizing the album's inconsistency, the review conceded that it was "far more promising" than . . . AND THEN THERE WERE THREE . . . or DUKE.

ABACAB was released in September 1981, just as the group were gearing up to take their new music on the road. Old school fans could take heart in the fact that Genesis still featured plenty of pre-ABACAB material in their live sets. But the balance was shifting, and Gabriel-era standards such as *The Carpet Crawlers* and *Firth Of Fifth* made up an increasingly small percentage of the set. However, it's unlikely that those fans won over by *Misunderstanding* and the new American hit *No Reply At All* were too broken up over the absence of *The Knife*. Six years on from Gabriel's defection, "oldies" now meant *Afterglow* and *Dance On A Volcano*.

In a somewhat uncharacteristic move, the band performed the ABACAB outtake *Me & Virgil* at a few shows early in the tour. Not since the early 70's had Genesis featured an unreleased song in their increasingly conservative set lists. But they quickly dropped the tune, which at that time sported the working title *Chunky*, when they decided to record the tour for another live album. The group also tried Mike Rutherford's ABACAB ballad *Like It Or Not* on a few American dates, but it didn't quite gel. At New York and Los Angeles shows, the band was joined by the Earth, Wind and Fire horn section for *No Reply At All* and *Paperlate*.

The standard set for the ABACAB tour was: *Behind The Lines, Duchess, The Lamb Lies Down On Broadway, Dodo / Lurker, Abacab, The Carpet Crawlers, Me And Sarah Jane, Misunderstanding, No Reply At All, Firth Of Fifth, Man On The Corner, Who Dunnit?*, a medley of *In The Cage, The Cinema Show, The Colony of Slippermen* and *Afterglow*, followed by *Turn It On Again, Dance On A Volcano / Los Endos* (linked by the now-customary drum duet) and *I Know What I Like*.

It was quite usual for Mike and Daryl to switch back and forth between bass and guitar during Genesis' live shows. Since Rutherford had taken over the lead guitar position from Steve Hackett in the studio, he tended to play lead on the newer songs, while Daryl handled the earlier stuff. But Mike did play bass on some newer songs, such as *No Reply*

At All. However, when the group played *Who Dunnit?* live, Mike took a seat behind Phil's drumkit and played alongside Chester, while Daryl played bass. The sight of Mike Rutherford pounding the drums was yet another sign that Genesis were loosening up.

The ABACAB tour kicked off at the end of September, starting with shows in Germany, France and Switzerland. In early November, Genesis flew to America, where *No Reply At All* had just peaked at No. 29. This time out, they played Madison, Chicago, Milwaukee, South Bend, Detroit, Pittsburgh, Cincinnati, Cleveland, Philadelphia, Uniondale, Largo, Hartford, Montreal, Ottawa, Toronto, East Rutherford and New York City. In mid-December, the tour arrived in Britain, where Genesis played at Wembley Arena on the 17th, 18th and 19th. After that, the tour wound up with four nights at the National Exhibition Centre in Birmingham, on December 20, 21, 22 and 23.

For North America, the band chose *Abacab* as the second single from the album (the first having been *No Reply At All*), and it peaked at No. 26 at the end of December. For the British market, *Keep It Dark* was picked for the next single. Intent on shaking up people's perceptions of them, they came very close to releasing *Who Dunnit?* as a single, but dropped the idea at the eleventh hour. As it was, *Keep It Dark* was by no means a "safe" choice for a Genesis single. Unfortunately, this was reflected in its chart performance. Even the inclusion of the non-album *Naminanu* on the flip couldn't push it higher than No. 33.

Chapter 16: Three By Three & Six Of The Best

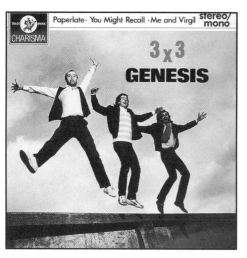

In May 1982, Charisma released a new Genesis EP, entitled 3X3, in Britain. This 7" record was to ABACAB as SPOT THE PIGEON was to WIND AND WUTHERING — three tracks left over from the album sessions. And — as with SPOT THE PIGEON — this EP showed that the band had not necessarily chosen their best material for the album. It seems unlikely that many fans would disagree with Tony Banks suspicion that ABACAB might have worked better had it included *You Might Recall* in place of *Who Dunnit?* The latter track served a purpose in terms of the group's image, but hasn't aged as well as the chiming, romantic *You Might Recall*.

3X3 was packaged in the style of an old Beatles EP circa 1963 — complete with a *Twist And Shout* cover pose and liner notes by onetime Fabs press officer Tony Barrow. "To call these three 'out-takes' might foster a wrong impression," said the group in the sleeve notes. "They are all group-written stuff which we felt very into." Although the EP didn't get a North American release, *Paperlate* came out as a single there. Backed by *You Might Recall*, it reached No. 32 in May.

Paperlate! was what British newspaper vendors used to shout on street corners in days gone by, and had been incorporated into the lyrics for *Dancing With The Moonlight* on the SELLING ENGLAND BY THE POUND LP. Genesis revived the number for their 1980 tour and, at a soundcheck before one of the shows, the sound engineer asked Phil to sing "paperlate" over and over while he set the echo level. The repetition took on a life of its own, and the rest of the group started playing along with Phil's "paperlate's". The following year, during the ABACAB sessions, the band developed the jam into the finished song.

TONY BANKS' SOLO ALBUM THE FUGITIVE, 1982.

During the early months of 1982, Tony Banks recorded his second solo album. Taking a cue from Collins' FACE VALUE recording method, the keyboardist worked on new material in his home studio, then added overdubs at The Farm. He decided not to use another lead singer on this effort, instead filling the lead vocalist position himself. The result, released in May, was a superb album called THE FUGITIVE. Although Tony didn't go so far as to put his photo on the cover, the sleeve's minmalist artwork (a la ABACAB / THREE SIDES LIVE) did feature a drawing of him. (The sleeve for the accompanying single, *This Is Love*, did sport a photo of the reticent musician.)

Following in the footsteps of FACE VALUE and ABACAB, THE FUGITIVE's sound was stripped down and modern. Like Phil's album, it had the potential to win Tony a new audience. You didn't have to be a Genesis fan to appreciate the album, and Banks' vocals were surprisingly confident and enjoyable.

In early 1982, Mike Rutherford also recorded a second album and, like Banks, decided to try his hand at singing lead. Although not as strong as THE FUGITIVE, Rutherford's ACTING VERY STRANGE album certainly had its moments, including the excellent single *Halfway There*. Although not technically great, Mike's voice was well suited to the harder-edged material on ACTING VERY STRANGE and it was a treat to finally hear his voice up front. Unfortunately, neither THE FUGITIVE nor ACTING VERY STRANGE achieved much commercial success and both Banks and Rutherford would return to using other singers for their subsequent extracurricular projects. It's a shame that Banks' album didn't fare better, since he seemed to be heading in a very interesting direction, one hinted at on *Me And Sarah Jane*. However, the infectious *This Is Love* did sneak into the Top 20 in Poland.

Meanwhile, Phil Collins was heading out on his first solo tour, in support of his second album, HELLO, I MUST BE GOING. As well as his many new fans, a contingent of Genesis

BRITISH PICTURE SLEEVE FOR MIKE RUTHERFORD'S
HALFWAY THERE SINGLE, 1982.

die-hards inevitably turned up and there were a few cries for *Supper's Ready*. Phil obligingly regaled them with an abridged, ten-second rendition: "A flower? . . . Six six six . . . Jerusalem . . ." Apart from that, Phil didn't include any Genesis material in his set, although he did perform his solo arrangement of *Behind The Lines*.

There were inevitably many questions about Phil's future with Genesis. In an interview with the *New York Post*, he reassured fans that he would stay with the group until they got it right. "I'm not sure we'll ever get it completely right, because the band is a compromise of three different musical tastes." However, he did stress to the *Hamilton Journal News* that:

"The main thing, the most important thing to me, is my solo career. That doesn't undermine my feelings for Genesis, but it does put them into perspective . . . I make more money on my own than I do with Genesis, so the bottom line, mercenary level, is that there's no reason for me to be in Genesis except that I enjoy it."

In August, there was a new group album, the double THREE SIDES LIVE, featuring recordings from the ABACAB tour. In most of the world, the album contained three sides of new live material, with the fourth side comprising five non-album tracks from the 1980-82 era: *Paperlate, You Might Recall* and *Me And Virgil* had all appeared in Britain on the 3X3 EP, while *Open Door* and *Evidence Of Autumn* had been B-sides to singles from DUKE. For the British market, it was decided that fans wouldn't appreciate the duplication of tracks they already owned on singles, so the fourth side was filled with live recordings from earlier tours. British fans were treated to a recording of *The Fountain Of Salmacis* from the 1978 Knebworth show, *One For The Vine* from the 1980 tour and the *Watcher Of The Skies / It* medley from the 1976 tour, with Hackett and Bruford.

Both versions were eventually issued on CD in their respective markets. However, when the Definitive Edition remasters came out in 1994, the British version of *Three Sides Live* became the only version available anywhere in the world. Therefore, CD copies of the version with the studio tracks have become sought after by fans and collectors.

In August the band hit the road again, in support of the live album. The set for these dates consisted of *Dance On A Volcano, Behind The Lines, Follow You Follow Me, Dodo / Lurker, Abacab,* the last full performances of *Supper's Ready, Misunderstanding, Who Dunnit?, The Carpet Crawlers, Me And Sarah Jane,* a medley of *In the cage, Cinema Show, The Colony Of Slippermen* and *Afterglow, Turn it on again,* Phil and Chester's drum duet, *Los Endos,* a medley of *The Lamb Lies Down On Broadway* and *Watcher Of The Skies,* and a closing *I Know What I Like.* Considering the group's (in particular Collins') apparent desire to disassociate themselves with their past, there was a generous amount of vintage material in these shows, with the inclusion of the epic *Supper's Ready* a definite concession to the old school fans.

They spent August in North America, playing Peoria, Chicago, Berkeley, Los Angeles, Phoenix, Dallas, Houston, Oklahoma City, St. Louis, Detroit, Columbia, Philadelphia, Forest Hills, New Haven, Saratoga Springs, Rochester, Toronto and Montreal. The first of the two Los Angeles dates (at the Inglewood Forum) featured a surprise guest appearance by none other than Bill Bruford, who showed up to add his percussive skills at the end of the show.

Although the shows seemed to offer something for all the fans, the *Los Angeles Times'* Steve Pond felt the mix of old and new was ill conceived, describing it as:

> "a schizophrenic, confusing evening . . . The overall feeling was that this band is stuck at a crossroads. It can commit itself to the newer material or stick with an evening of one from Column A, one from Column B. If it persists in the second option, it had better resign itself to the fact that few people will head home completely satisfied."

In early September, the band returned to Europe, playing dates in Geneva, Frejus, Pisa, Rome, Hamburg, Stockholm, Copenhagen, Gothenburg and Brussels. These gigs were followed by a British tour. It was not quite as extensive as the DUKE trek, but certainly more so than the British leg of the ABACAB tour. They started on September 18 at the Coliseum in St. Austell, then played the next day in Shepton Mallet. The next two nights were spent in Birmingham which, along with London, almost invariably got penciled in whenever Genesis toured Britain. A few not-so-predictable stops followed: Deeside on the 22nd, Leeds on the 23, Ingliston on the 24th and 25th, then down to London for the last few days of the month.

The group closed the tour with a surprise appearance at the Marquee. The £4 tickets were soon selling on the street for £50. Those who did snag a ticket certainly got a treat. *Melody Maker* reported that the audience "seemed awed by being allowed to approach so close to normally such distant figures." Onstage, Phil noted that it had been "ten years since we were here last — it took a whole decade to get a repeat booking!" According to *Melody Maker,* Genesis "played incredibly well, treating us to the full Genesis set and more and coping admirably with the cramped conditions."

The conditions for Genesis' next live appearance were anything but cramped. The "Six Of The Best" show was staged at the massive Milton Keynes Concert Bowl. The concert was an unexpected reunion with Peter Gabriel, designed to recoup the losses incurred by Gabriel's ambitious WOMAD Festival. On October 2, a crowd of 60,000 — some of whom traveled from North America and Japan — were treated to a set of vintage Genesis, complete with Gabriel's costumes and stories.

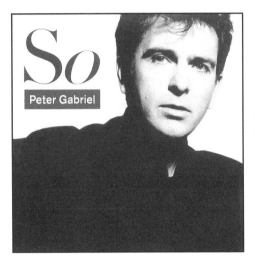

The decision to get back with Genesis cannot have been an easy one for Peter Gabriel to make. Since leaving the band in 1975, Gabriel had worked very hard to forge a strong identity as a solo performer. By 1982, he had released four albums, each breaking new musical ground, each simply titled *Peter Gabriel* (in a gesture of compromise, he had allowed his American label to give the fourth album a "proper title" — SECURITY). Gabriel had enjoyed some chart success with numbers like *Solsbury Hill, Games Without Frontiers* and *Shock The Monkey*, but he was not yet at the peak of his career, commercially speaking. He would hit the top of the American charts in May 1986 with the R&B—inflected *Sledgehammer*, from the very successful SO album. (Coincidentally, Genesis also had their first American No. 1 in May 1986.) However, in late 1982, Gabriel was not in a secure enough financial position to cover WOMAD's losses and he was worried. He had reportedly been receiving threats about his unpaid debts, and desperate measures were called for.

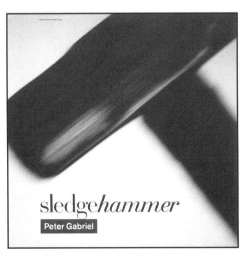

"I'm sure that, as with anyone reliving their youth, I'm going to feel a lot of nostalgia about the gig," said Gabriel. "Although, in terms of career moves, it's probably not a very good idea for them or for me. But financially it's going to be very useful for the WOMAD Festival and I'm certainly going to enjoy it."

"It will be nice for people to hear some of the old songs with Pete again," wrote Tony Banks in the program. "We'll do the songs we still play in our set together with some of the early classics and one or two other bits we feel like playing. I don't know if we can really live up to what people are expecting. What's strange is that the last tour we did with Pete playing THE LAMB LIES DOWN ON BROADWAY we were playing town halls and not even filling most of them but now there's an awful lot of people who want to hear it. I just hope they haven't built it up into something it can never be. It will be a bit like a first night for us in some ways but it will certainly be interesting. I just hope we can get through it without too many mistakes."

"I don't think any of us realized how much work this was going to be," Rutherford revealed. "It can take a surprising amount of time to learn a song you haven't played for ten years — when I played a tape of *Musical Box* the other day there were about four minutes in the middle that I'd completely forgotten! We've been learning the old songs on the bus between gigs on our British tour because we haven't got much time to rehearse them."

"The real fans put on a Genesis album and listen to it," Phil explained to the band's fan club magazine *Genesis Information*. "But we haven't listened to *The Musical Box* since Pete left. We played the last part of it in a medley which we did in the SECONDS OUT period, but as a whole you know you really have to go back and listen to the whole thing and dissect what everybody did; like sort of relearn it. There's a lot of mental hard work ... stuff like *Supper's Ready* which I haven't played the drums on since 1973, and *Musical Box* I hadn't played, and *The Knife* I haven't played since then, and stuff like that. I'm finding it very difficult for my hands to translate into, like now; there's different speeds and everything and my hands will insist that it's still 1973. They don't wanna know anything about it."

The most telling comment came from Daryl Stuermer, who said of Gabriel and Genesis, "Personally, I find it hard to see how they were ever in the same band because the way Genesis is now, it's very hard to see a connection."

The "Six Of The Best" program started at two in the afternoon, with an unexpectedly early appearance by John Martyn. As a result, many audience members didn't arrive early enough to see the set by Martyn, whose most recent album had been produced by Phil Collins. Next up was the Blues Band, followed by a young Talk Talk.

The only downside to the event was the weather. *Melody Maker* stated that "Of course it pissed down and continued to drizzle for most of the day, quickly reducing the Bowl into a slippery lake of stinky mud. The conditions were *revolting*."

Approximately two hours after Talk Talk finished their set, none other than Jonathan King appeared onstage to introduce the headliners. A blue light bathed the stage and a most unusual sight greeted the audience. Pallbearers carried a coffin onstage, out of which leapt ... Rael. Gabriel was back, in the makeup and leather jacket of the 1974-75 tour.

"In return for your cash, we will try and give you what you think you would like of this combination," he promised the crowd, before leading the band through an enticing selection of oldies: *Back In New York City*, *Dancing With The Moonlit Knight*, *The Carpet Crawlers*, *Firth Of Fifth*, *The Musical Box*, Gabriel's solo hit *Solsbury Hill*, *Turn It On Again* (on

Milton Keynes Concert Bowl

SATURDAY 2nd OCTOBER 1982

PROGRAM FOR THE SIX OF THE BEST CONCERT.

which Gabriel manned the drum kit), *The Lamb Lies Down On Broadway*, *Fly On A Windshield*, *Broadway Melody Of 1974*, *In The Cage* and a very emotional *Supper's Ready*. "It's been a long, long time, hasn't it?" sang Gabriel. As if that wasn't enough to delight the old fans, Steve Hackett walked onstage for the encore of *I Know What I Like* and *The Knife*.

"Playing with the guys again felt wonderful, just for one night," says Hackett. "It was very nice, particularly the circumstances under which we came together, which was to help the WOMAD Festival pay off its debt. I think it was a great buzz for everybody."

"That was my first time playing with Peter Gabriel," recalls Daryl Stuermer. "But we had done a couple of rehearsals prior to that. It was a lot of fun for me, because I had to learn old Genesis songs that I had never played before. It was really a great show for us. Also, Steve Hackett came out for the encore, and that was the first time I had met him."

Although some of the playing was a little shaky — the group was playing a great deal of material that they hadn't played for years — a good time was had by all. It was, according to *Melody Maker*, "The rock event of the year."

As a footnote to the reunion show, Gabriel and Rutherford made a guest appearance at a Steve Hackett concert at Guildford Civic Hall in January 1983, performing Gabriel's solo numbers *Here Comes The Flood* and *Solsbury Hill*, followed by *Reach Out (I'll Be There)* and *I Know What I Like*.

Chapter 17: Just A Job To Do

The "Six Of The Best" reunion show satisfied the pangs of nostalgia for many old school Genesis fans. Those who couldn't be at Milton Keynes could take heart in bootleg records of the show, bearing titles like GABACABRIEL and THE LAMB WOKE UP AGAIN.

In March 1983, Phil, Mike and Tony returned to the present tense and set to work on some new Genesis material, which appeared on an album that was simply called GENESIS. If anyone expected the reunion show to clear the path for a return to the vintage Genesis

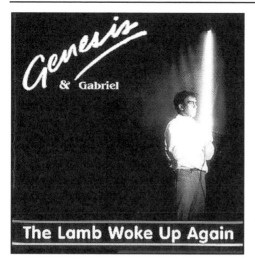

The Lamb Woke Up Again

THE LAMB WOKE UP AGAIN, ONE OF SEVERAL BOOTLEG RELEASES OF THE SIX OF THE BEST REUNION CONCERT.

sound, they were mistaken. Settling back into The Farm, the trio spent the next few months crafting songs that were a natural evolution from the ABACAB sound. Once again, Hugh Padgham joined the band as co-producer.

Daryl Stuermer feels that the album — simply titled GENESIS — was something of a turning point for the band.

"The reason why they called it GENESIS was that they decided to write everything together, the three of them," he says. "Because everybody had started doing solo albums, they decided that when it came to Genesis they would all come in with maybe just a half of a song and then have somebody else finish it. Their outlet (for individually written songs) was their solo albums."

PICTURE SLEEVE FOR *HOME BY THE SEA* SINGLE.

A typical example of the group writing approach was a track called *Home By The Sea*.

"Phil started playing this drum riff that Mike and I found attractive," Tony recalled in an interview with *Keyboard* magazine. "We jammed on it for about two hours one day and an hour or two the next. And then we learned exactly what we played, down to the last detail . . . We worked on a few bits, extended some, changed others, just trying to get it into some cohesive form."

The new music was a continuation of the direction taken on ABACAB, increasingly simplified and straightforward.

"You can't mystify people if you want to sell records," Collins told *Rolling Stone*. "Genesis only began to break when the lyrics became less story-oriented. The basic difference between me and Pete and Tony and Mike is that lyrically they're a bit emotionally screwed up. They went to boarding school all their lives, only saw their families on holidays, while I went to regular school, went home every day."

135

"I think a lot of people think of us as still the art-rock group that we might've been eight or nine years ago," Collins told *Creem*. "We don't do that kind of stuff anymore. We pull on it — we use it as a tool. If one of us writes a piece of music that sounds like it should be really pompous, then we use that tool that we've managed to perfect over the years of sounding very large and grandiose. But, at the same time, we write a lot of stuff that's very simple. And I think ABACAB is obviously the best example of that because it's the last example of that. The next album (GENESIS) will be a better example of that."

MAMA BRITISH 12" SINGLE.

The album was preceded by a superb single, *Mama*, released in Britain in August 1983. *Mama* was a truly stunning piece of work, a moody, passionate song, built around a drum machine pattern devised by Rutherford. When the drums kicked in at the song's climax, the influence of Phil's solo work was very evident. "The drum entry was a bit like *In The Air Tonight*," admitted Banks. "But it seemed so right for the song, we wouldn't fight it." The flipside, *It's Gonna Get Better*, started off in classic Genesis fashion, with an atmospheric Mellotron-ish intro, played by Tony on his Emulator. Shades of *Watcher Of The Skies* at first, then the soulful bass line kicked in — a masterful mix of old and new Genesis.

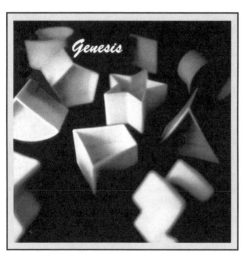

GENESIS ALBUM, 1983

The album itself appeared in October. Overall, it was something of a disappointment, and it seemed that the best songs were the two that already appeared on the single. There were many strong moments, but there was a very noticeable dip in the overall quality level. This may have stemmed from the band's determination to use only group-written tracks. While some of the group-penned numbers were excellent, there weren't enough of them to sustain the album. Even one track each from the individual writers — as on ABACAB — might have brought GENESIS up to the previous album's level. For their part, Phil, Mike and Tony have said that they feel the first side of GENESIS is very strong, but the second is much weaker.

Phil's solo career was undoubtedly now more important to him than Genesis, so it followed that he would want to save his songs for his own albums. And Tony and Mike — still no doubt hoping for some solo success of their own — were certainly happy to put aside their own finished songs for solo efforts. But the new approach didn't always work. When it did — as on *Mama* — it was incredibly powerful. When it didn't, it tended to sound like a watered down version of the group's previous efforts. *Just A Job To Do* was a lackluster attempt to capture a Michael Jackson vibe, while *That's All* was a pleasant but uninspired pop song, with a vague country flavor. *Home By The Sea* was musically very strong, but was dragged down by lyrics that sounded like a limp attempt to recapture the mystical Genesis style of years gone by. On the whole, the lyrics seemed particularly weak compared to previous efforts.

For many of the old school fans, each new Genesis album seemed to have less to offer. It wasn't a question of fans being stuck in the 70's — nobody expected them to do a new *Watcher Of The Skies* or *Supper's Ready* — but even the DUKE material seemed much stronger than the GENESIS album. The group may have felt that the old fans just didn't like them doing shorter simpler songs, but that wasn't really the case. *Turn It On Again* was a perfect example of a fairly straightforward pop song that worked, but much of the GENESIS material was nowhere near as good. Even the album's sleeve design seemed half-hearted, a blurred photo of tumbling shapes, with a dull new Genesis logo.

One song that drew its share of negative attention was the second side's opener (and the album's third extracted single), *Illegal Alien*. This wacky number featured Phil singing in a quasi-Mexican accent, lamenting that "it's no fun being an illegal alien." A catchy tune, to be sure, but a questionable approach to the subject matter and one that has not worn well over the years.

PHIL RESPONDS TO THE CRITICS ON THE COVER OF THE *ILLEGAL ALIEN* BOOTLEG.

Melody Maker's review of the album was devoted mostly to *Illegal Alien*, which the paper cited as an example of what was wrong with the 1983 version of Genesis.

"Cheap laughs or cheap credibility?" asked the reviewer. "What motive, other than the decadent pursual of novelty for novelty's sake, could possibly account for a piece as blatantly insensitive as *Illegal Alien?*"

Although Genesis genuinely seemed to feel they were breaking new ground artistically, *Rolling Stone* hit the nail on the head with the observation that GENESIS was their safest album to date:

"Instead of resolutely pushing forward, as ABACAB did, or merely refining the achievements of its predecessors, as was the case with SELLING ENGLAND BY THE POUND, GENESIS seems little more than an attempt to be all things to all fans."

137

If the GENESIS album was a bit of a let down, the accompanying tour was not. The new shows offered plenty to please both old and new fans. The group used their time-honored practice of opening the show with a number from their second-newest album. The *Dodo / Lurker* medley from ABACAB was a great opener, and much of the new material proved more effective in concert. Second up was *Abacab* itself, then two new numbers, *That's All* and *Mama*. After that, longtime fans were treated to a medley of three older pieces — the intro from *Eleventh Earl Of Mar*, segueing into *Squonk* and *Firth Of Fifth*. Next came a sequence of songs from the two newest LP's: *Illegal Alien, Man On The Corner, Who Dunnit?, Home By The Sea, Second Home By The Sea, Keep It Dark* and *It's Gonna Get Better*. Then the band took a little trip back to play *Follow You, Follow Me* and more oldies, medley-style: *In The Cage, The Cinema Show, In That Quiet Earth, The Colony Of Slippermen* and *Afterglow*, followed by the drum duet and the show-closing *Los Endos*.

As is usually the case with arena rock shows, the two encores were clearly predetermined. The first was *Misunderstanding*. The second encore, *Turn It On Again*, was spun out into a medley which incorporated various rock and roll oldies plus the occasional contemporary cover. Songs featured in the medley included *Everybody Needs Somebody To Love, Satisfaction, Twist And Shout, Pinball Wizard, All Day And All Of The Night* and *Karma Chameleon*. In that seven-minute stretch, Genesis laid to rest their policy of not playing covers and furthered their efforts to "lighten up" their image. A recording of the medley was released in early 1984, on the flipside of the *Illegal Alien* single.

The light show was one aspect of Genesis that kept on improving, and it dazzled those who witnessed the 1983-84 tour. And Phil was more confident than ever onstage, not only as the singer, but as the show's Master of Ceremonies. His charming Steve Martin-esque stage patter and clowning were perfect antidotes to the generally serious tone of the music.

The tour started in November in Normal, Illinois, proceeding to, Ames, St. Paul, Milwaukee, Detroit, Landover, New York City, Montreal, Toronto, Philadelphia, Worchester, Hartford, Syracuse, Buffalo, Pittsburgh, Cincinnati, Greensboro, Nashville, Atlanta, Jacksonville, Tampa and Miami. The group flew home for Christmas, but was back in North America on January 6th for another tour. This time they played San Francisco, Vancouver, Los Angeles, Phoenix, Denver, Tulsa, Dallas, Houston, Austin, New Orleans, Memphis, St. Louis, Kansas City, Lexington, Indianapolis, Ottawa, Peoria, Madison, St. Paul, Winnipeg, Calgary, Edmonton, Boise, Reno, Las Vegas and Oakland.

In February, the MAMA tour arrived in Britain. Unfortunately for the band's U.K. following, the band's British "tour" consisted of a few nights at Birmingham's National Exhibition Centre. Although the band were undoubtedly tired after three months of gigs in North America, it seemed that such an approach gave short shrift to the British fans. Those dates at the NEC would be the last Genesis activity for the next year and a half, as Phil, Mike and Tony took time off and pursued their respective solo projects.

Chapter 18: Invisible Touch

1985 proved to be Phil Collins' most successful year ever. He racked up a total of three American No. 1 hits: *One More Night, Sussudio* and *Separate Lives* (the latter was a duet with Marilyn Martin, from the movie WHITE NIGHTS). Phil's big flop of the year was *Don't Lose My Number*, which only made it to No. 4! This was surely the year in which Phil well and truly surpassed Genesis in terms of household-name status. His appearances at Live Aid were legendary, since he was the only performer who managed to appear at the British and American concerts. It now seemed that Genesis needed Phil more than he needed them. But, whether out of loyalty or love of the music (probably a bit of both), Collins would stick it out with Genesis for a few more years.

In a mid-80's interview, Phil stressed that he had no plans to quit Genesis.

> "The next one to leave the band will finish it," he said. "I feel happier with what we're doing now, because I feel it's closer to me. I won't be the one."

ONE OF TWO VIDEO CASSETTES COLLECTING GENESIS PROMO VIDEOS.

In late 1985, Mike Rutherford unveiled his new extracurricular project, a group called Mike and The Mechanics. For this project, Rutherford had opted out of the vocal role, no doubt because of ACTING VERY STRANGE's failure to take the world by storm. There was a very commercial, radio friendly feel to the band, which featured Paul Young and Paul Carrack on lead vocals. If Mike was looking to shift a few more units, this new venture certainly worked. The group's debut self-titled album spawned two top ten American hits, *Silent Running (On Dangerous Ground)* and *All I Need Is A Miracle*. It was catchy pop, but certainly didn't have much in common with Rutherford's Genesis work.

"I think he's diluted himself quite a lot," commented Tony Banks. "It's very polished but it doesn't really sound like Mike to me. It's good, you know — and certainly at times it's very good, but it sounds like a lot of people." In comparing his own lack of solo success to Mike's hits with the Mechanics, Tony told *Keyboard Review*, "Maybe his material is more radio-friendly — it's certainly more commercial. I always put in one chord too many, one note or one abrasive lyric that I can't resist. I've never been able to compromise . . ."

Banks' comments, and a comparison of the three members' solo releases, suggest that whatever was left of Genesis' "progressive" inclinations was mostly down to him. Still, by the mid-80's, the group was pretty much locked into a radio-friendly formula, and even Tony Banks would eventually try his hand at a Mike & the Mechanics-style project. Even the risk-taking Steve Hackett succumbed briefly, joining Yes-man Steve Howe in supergroup GTR, who stormed the American charts with their self-titled album and the arena-rock single *When The Heart Rules The Mind*. In contrast to the approach of his ex-bandmates, however, Hackett used his GTR earnings to fund the recording of MOMENTUM, a decidedly uncommercial album of solo acoustic guitar pieces.

In October 1985, Genesis reconvened at the Farm to start work on some new material. As with the previous album, the sessions were devoted entirely to new, group-written material. Working through until the following March, the trio recorded the songs that would comprise their next album, INVISIBLE TOUCH. As on the ABACAB sessions the band actually recorded more songs than they could fit on the album, leaving *I'd Rather Be You, Feeding The Fire* and *Do The Neurotic* to be used as non-album B-sides.

Overall, as with the GENESIS album, one gets the sense that INVISIBLE TOUCH could have been stronger if Genesis hadn't stuck so rigidly to the group-writing-only format. There was another drop in the level of quality, and the group began to sound like they were repeating themselves. *Tonight, Tonight, Tonight* was a perfect example: an inventively atmospheric musical setting was hobbled by lyrics that sounded too familiar. The monkey-on-your-back image had already been used in *Man On The Corner*, while the chorus felt too much like a retread of the "tonight, tonight" hook from DUKE's *Man Of Our Times*.

Although the music was a product of group jamming, the three members still tended to write the words on their own. Phil penned the lyrics for *In Too Deep, Tonight, Tonight,*

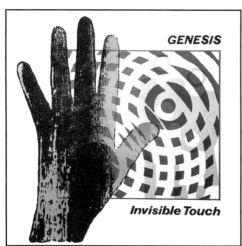

GENESIS

Invisible Touch

Tonight, Invisible Touch and *I'd Rather Be You*, which was left off the album but showed up as a B-side. Tony supplied the words for *Anything She Does, In The Glow Of The Night, The Last Domino* and the B-side *Feeding The Fire*. Mike only wrote two sets of lyrics for the album, *Land Of Confusion* and *Throwing It All Away*.

INVISIBLE TOUCH came out in June 1986, preceded by a single release of the catchy title track, a perfectly executed pop record. In Britain, the album shot to No. 1, although the single inexplicably stalled at No. 15. In America, *Invisible Touch* gave Genesis their first No. 1 single, while the album peaked at No. 3.

Inevitably, the band planned an extensive North American tour to promote the album. Since their increasingly complex touring machine cost a lot to run, Genesis agreed to accept corporate sponsorship for the INVISIBLE TOUCH tour. This in itself would have been seen as "selling out," but what upset many observers was the fact that Genesis' tour sponsor was a beer company, Michelob. To make matters worse, the group allowed their song "Tonight Tonight Tonight" — a song which dealt with the problems of addiction — to be used in Michelob commercials. Although the fans still turned out in droves, the Michelob deal was a clear sign that Genesis was now a very big business, for better and for worse.

PICTURE SLEEVE FOR THE CANADIAN *THROWING IT ALL AWAY* SINGLE, 1986.

The tour kicked off September 18 at the Joe Louis Arena in Detroit. The set list for the new shows included *Mama, Abacab, Land Of Confusion, That's All, Domino, In Too Deep, The Brazilian, Follow You, Follow Me, Home By The Sea, Throwing It All Away*, an oldies medley of *In The Cage, In That Quiet Earth, Apocalypse In 9/8* and *As Sure As Eggs Is Eggs, Invisible Touch*, the drum duet and *Los Endos*. The evening wound up with the *Turn It On Again* medley that had been such a crowd-pleaser on the previous tour.

From Detroit it was up to Toronto, then back to the U.S. for a few nights at Madison Square Garden. Next up, the Rosemont Horizon, Chicago, the Los Angeles Forum and the Oakland Coliseum Arena. Then Phil, Mike, Tony, Daryl and Chester journeyed Down Under for the first time, for dates in Auckland, Sydney, Adelaide, Perth and Melbourne.

After a couple of weeks off for Christmas, the quintet jetted back to the States for the next leg of the INVISIBLE TOUCH tour. This time, their agenda included stops in Houston, Dallas, Kansas City, Chapel Hill, Indianapolis, Cleveland, Atlanta, Orlando, Worcester, Hampton, Greensboro, Atlanta and Miami. This was followed by a brief trip to Japan, and a European tour. In mid-June, the epic tour finally brought the band back to Britain for a handful of stadium dates — four nights at Wembley Stadium and one each in Glasgow and Leeds.

Chapter 19: Fading Lights

After the INVISIBLE TOUCH tour, Phil, Mike and Tony spent the next few years pursuing their respective solo careers. They reconvened briefly in May 1988 to perform at the Atlantic Records 40th Anniversary concert at Madison Square Garden, where they played a twenty minute medley of *Turn It On Again, Land Of Confusion, Misunderstanding, Throwing*

It All Away, You Can't Hurry Love (Phil's solo hit), *Shortcut To Somewhere* (a Tony Banks solo number, from the QUICKSILVER soundtrack), *All I Need Is A Miracle* (the Mike & The Mechanics hit), *That's All, Tonight Tonight Tonight, Invisible Touch* and a reprise of *Turn It On Again*.

Tony's solo follow-up to THE FUGITIVE was the SOUNDTRACKS album, which collected together the material he had written for the movies QUICKSILVER and LORCA AND THE OUTLAWS. Interestingly, one track — *Shortcut To Somewhere* — featured a vocal by Fish, the lead singer of Marillion. A young progressive rock outfit, Marillion had drawn many comparisons to Gabriel-era Genesis when they surfaced in 1982. They had gone on to massive success in Britain with the concept album MISPLACED CHILDHOOD and its single *Kayleigh*. SHORTCUT TO SOMEWHERE was an enjoyable record, but didn't do much to boost Banks' solo career. Clearly, though, Tony's talents were well suited to film scoring and he was disappointed when plans for him to score 2010 (the much-anticipated sequel to 2001: A SPACE ODYSSEY) fell through.

SELF-TITLED RELEASE BY TONY BANKS' GROUP BANKSTATEMENT.

Banks continued his solo career through the mid-90's, in various permutations, releasing the albums STILL, BANKSTATEMENT and STRICTLY INC, the latter two being self-titled efforts by one-off bands assembled by Tony. Despite the fact that he was a major contributor to Genesis, Tony's solo career has attracted little attention, apart from devoted Genesis fans.

"People don't realize I do anything between Genesis albums," he told *Keyboard Review*. "I've talked to people who've asked, 'What have you been doing while Phil and Mike have been top of the charts?' I get so frustrated. I do as much as I can . . . I try to make myself available, but I'm naturally introverted, so maybe I'm not as good at promoting myself as the others are."

In early 1991, Phil, Mike and Tony reconvened at the Farm to start work on a new Genesis album. Working from March until September, the group once again crafted songs from scratch, as they had done on the two previous albums. One notable difference was the absence of Hugh Padgham, who had played a major part in the development of their post-DUKE sound. Ten years on from ABACAB, it was time for another change. This time out, the sessions were co-produced by Nick Davis, who had co-produced Tony Banks' STILL album and engineered Mike and the Mechanics' LIVING YEARS. "I think they were looking for new input," says Davis. "Though not necessarily in the sound of the album." Davis also engineered the sessions, with assistance from Mark Robinson.

TONY BANKS' STRICTLY INC ALBUM.

One of the album's highlights was *Fading Lights*, a number whose writing process typified the group's approach. It grew from a three or four-hour session, in which the trio jammed on the main riff, with the tape machine running. After reviewing the tape of their efforts, they condensed the number down, singling out the best elements and distilling them into a cohesive song structure.

"We meet on day one with no complete song," Phil told *Music Express Sound*. "Sometimes we play one piece a whole day and finally erase it, simply because we can't play it how we'd like it to sound. We record our rehearsals on DAT tapes and in the end we take the pick of the bunch. During the recordings for WE CAN'T DANCE, we filled twenty DAT tapes. Half of them sound awful, lots of wrong notes and hot chords, but on the rest there are some of the best things we've probably ever done."

"Perhaps that's also the reason why Genesis still exists," Mike added. "We have the freedom to realize our solo projects — but when we do something together, we are a band - three guys bombarding each other with ideas."

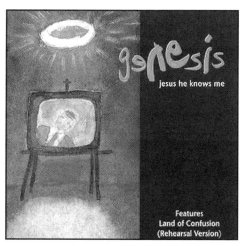

CD SINGLE FOR *JESUS HE KNOWS ME*.

According to Nick Davis, the music "grew out of studio jams. When I came along there were no lyrics. Nearly all the arrangements were sorted but there were still bits missing. For instance, the middle eight of *Jesus He Knows Me* was an unknown quantity."

The almost-title track, *I Can't Dance* was, according to Tony,

"probably the most minimalistic piece we've ever done." "The track more or less sounds like we originally recorded it," Phil told *Music Express Sound*. "Tony and I were playing around a bit, because Mike had salmonella poisoning and couldn't come into the studio for a few days. Tony was playing drums, and it took me about one hour to write the lyrics. If we had given the song the typical Genesis treatment, we would have destroyed it."

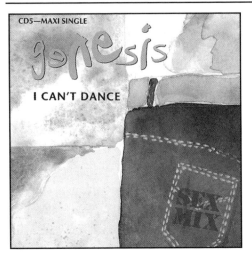

CD5—MAXI SINGLE

I CAN'T DANCE

I CAN'T DANCE CD SINGLE, 1992.

The idea for the lyric came when Rutherford started playing a guitar riff that Phil thought sounded like something out of a jeans commercial. The song became a spoof of British jeans ads and the "hunks" who star in them.

"*I Can't Dance* is my comment on these beaus in those jeans spots," Collins explained. "That all look so cool and sexy — unless they open their mouths. I know plenty of them. They're permanently posing in front of the mirror, but in their heads there's nothing going on."

Despite comparisons between Genesis and Phil's solo work, Collins' contributions in the group context were often quite distinct from his solo output. The epic *Driving The Last Spike* was a good example. Phil's lyric about 19th century railway workers was not something he would have come up with for one of his own albums, but the Genesis framework inspired him to do it. Working with Banks and Rutherford tended to push him into areas that he might not have discovered on his own.

Often, Phil's vocal improvisations in the studio would be developed into full song lyrics. *Dreaming While You Sleep* was such a number, growing from two improvised lines — "dreaming while you sleep" and the Collins standby "all my life." Using those phrases as a starting point, Mike Rutherford developed a storyline and finished the lyrics.

"Those two phrases suggested a story to me — not true, by the way — about a driver who hits a girl and doesn't stop, only to come back to the hospital and find she's in a coma for the rest of her life," Rutherford told the *Chicago Tribune*. "From the moment on he's entwined, obsessed, with her, for the rest of his life."

Although the new material bore little resemblance to the epics of the 70's, there was one trip down memory lane. During the sessions, Mike Rutherford brought his old double-neck Rickenbacker guitar out of retirement, using its 12-string neck on two tracks, *Tell Me Why* and *On The Shoreline*. The latter number was one of two tracks that didn't make the album but turned up as B-sides, the other being *Hearts On Fire*.

In an interview with *Music Monitor*, Mike reflected on how the group's sound had changed since the early days:

"I think when we started off we were keen to prove how brilliant we were in those days. You've got a lot to prove. Later on, you learn more about your craft. You realize that if a particular song requires someone to play one note the whole way through, that's what's good and that's what you'll play. You learn to arrange and write for the bit, not for anything else."

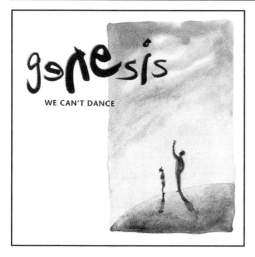

WE CAN'T DANCE

A particularly appealing aspect of WE CAN'T DANCE was the lovely cover artwork by Felicity Roma Bowers, a great improvement on the uninspired covers of the two previous albums. Even Collins acknowledged that the cover was "a lot stronger" than the previous two. As for the music, it was solid and commercial but, like the previous two albums, WE CAN'T DANCE didn't really feel like a step forward for Genesis — at least not from the perspective of older fans. From the band's point of view, it didn't matter. As far as they were concerned, their music was progressing and they were winning new fans with each new album.

In April 1992, the mighty Genesis touring machine kicked in for another international onslaught. The band rehearsed for the WE CAN'T DANCE tour in the Goodyear blimp hangar in Houston. This was one of the few spaces large enough to accommodate the group's new live setup, which now included a $5 million Sony Jumbotron video projection setup.

"We were down there for a few weeks," recalls Daryl Stuermer. "We had rehearsed originally in England as a band. We would always do that first — we'd get together as a band in a smaller place. And then you'd have to bring it to a production stage. And that's when things slow up. You've got the music rehearsed and then you want to run through this stuff. But what happens is you have to start dealing with staging, lighting, things like that. That was probably the most difficult tour, from a technical point, because we were doing such huge venues. And then to have these brand new Jumbotrons — there were always problems with those. There were always parts of the screen that weren't coming on — there was always a glitch somewhere."

One notable change on this tour was that the set included less of the 'oldies.'

"But, I mean, In the Cage — we've played it every tour since 1978 or something," Tony Banks protested in an interview with Musician. "There's a time when you stop playing something. You've got to feel comfortable with what you're doing. What's the point if you're just going through the motions?" The We Can't Dance tour was also characterized by its emphasis on huge stadium shows. "We're doing this tour of stadiums because we don't want to be on the road forever, like a lot of other bands are," Phil told Musician. "I don't think we can sit here and justify it and say, 'Well, we love stadiums,' because I don't think any of us do. But we just take on that challenge and see if we can try and make it work better than other people, really."

With the larger venues came huge noisier crowds and poorer acoustics. For these reasons, the group didn't bother rehearsing any quieter acoustic numbers for this tour. It was a compromise, to be sure, but the British DUKE tour had proved that booking smaller venues would result in many fans being unable to get tickets.

The tour turned out to be the last Genesis tour not only for Phil Collins, but also for Chester Thompson and Daryl Stuermer. Reflecting on how the Genesis sound changed during his fourteen-year tenure, Stuermer says,

> "I saw the music getting tighter and more sophisticated. Maybe it was more 'pop', but the band got better musically, the musicianship got better. The standard got a little higher as they went along. And I'm hoping that Chester and I had something to do with it, because we came from bands where the standard was real high, anyway. It seems like Genesis started growing also, and so did I. We started learning how to play together better live than we did originally."

The set for the new tour kicked off with a brace of newer numbers — *Land Of Confusion, No Son Of Mine* and *Driving The Last Spike*. This was followed by the *Old Medley* which encompassed parts of *Dance On A Volcano, The Lamb Lies Down On Broadway, The Musical Box, Firth Of Fifth, I Know What I Like, That's All, Follow You Follow Me, Stagnation* and a reprise of *I Know What I Like*. Then it was back to the newer stuff for the rest of the show: *Throwing It All Away, Fading Lights, Jesus He Knows Me, Home By The Sea, Second Home By The Sea, Hold On My Heart, Domino*, the obligatory drum duet, *I Can't Dance, Tonight Tonight Tonight, Invisible Touch* and *Turn It On Again*.

The tour began on May 8 at Texas Stadium in Irving, followed by dates at the Houston Astrodome and Joe Robbie Stadium in Miami. The May 17 show at Tampa Stadium in Tampa, Florida was canceled after just two songs.

> "Phil came up on stage and he couldn't sing," recalls Daryl Stuermer of this aborted show. "We came out and did *Land Of Confusion*, I think, and then *Mama* — something that's really, incredibly hard to sing. And he just had nothing there. And we had to actually walk off stage at that point. Sometimes Phil would have a bad throat before we'd go on stage, but somehow, as he'd start singing, it would get better. So he chose not to cancel before we went on, thinking that maybe if he started singing, it would all come back. But he actually opened his mouth and nothing came out."

The WE CAN'T DANCE tour was back on track on May 19, in time to play RFK Stadium in Washington, DC. After that it was on to Indianapolis, Columbus, Pontiac, Cleveland, Pittsburgh, Foxboro, Montreal, Philadelphia, East Rutherford, Syracuse, Toronto, Madison, Minneapolis, and Edmonton.

Vancouver's B.C. Place, where the band played on June 14, was typical of the sort of oversize stadiums Genesis played on the tour. Now that the group was such a big moneymaker, with so many fans to accommodate, there was clearly a great deal of compromise involved. As they had learnt on the British DUKE tour, choosing smaller venues meant that many fans couldn't get tickets. Having said that, it seems that Genesis themselves were aware that the venues they had lined up were not ideal from their fans' point of view.

> "I know (B.C. Place is) a bit of a barn, apparently," Phil admitted in a radio interview prior to the tour. "My kids live in Vancouver and they keep telling me it's a rotten place for gigs, but I think we're going to try to make the best of it, and try to make it sound good and look good."

After Vancouver, the quintet headed south for dates in Tacoma, Los Angeles, Sacramento, Oakland, Ames, Iowa, The North American leg of the tour ended with a June 24th show in Chicago. The WE CAN'T DANCE tour resumed just four days later at the Festival Grounds in Werchter, followed by dates in France, Germany and Spain, through the end of July.

On July 31, Genesis was back in England for a show at Roundhay Park in Leeds. This was followed by two Knebworth shows, on the 1st and 2nd of August. The band played a few smaller venues — such as the Manchester Apollo and Edinburgh Playhouse — as well as six nights at Earl's Court. The WE CAN'T DANCE tour was Genesis' most extensive British jaunt since the DUKE tour and the THREE SIDES LIVE tour a decade earlier. It was also the last time most British fans would see Phil Collins perform with Genesis.

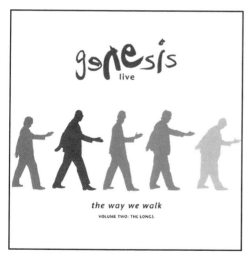

THE WAY WE WALK - VOLUME 2: THE LONGS CD.

Having released three studio albums since THREE SIDES LIVE, Genesis decided they were due for another live collection. In 1993, they decided to release not one but two live albums, aimed at different sections of the group's following. For those fond of the newer stuff, there was THE WAY WE WALK — VOLUME ONE: THE SHORTS. A few months later, Virgin released THE WAY WE WALK — VOLUME TWO: THE LONGS.

"Basically, the two albums are the live show," Mike Rutherford told *Music Monitor*. "We tried to make it one, but we couldn't seem to make it work. It meant losing quite a lot of material, especially some of the old stuff, like an old twenty-minute medley which wouldn't fit onto one CD. Also, probably more important than that, what works on stage over two-and-a-half hours, which is alternating with short and long songs and building the set up and down, didn't work on record. It felt kind of weird, you know, two or three short songs and the two or three fifteen or ten-minute songs. And then we had the idea to split it up and sort of keep a different mood for different albums and it seemed to work straight away when we did that. As quite a lot of people seem to prefer one type of song over the other, they can now make their own choice."

A concert in September 1993, prompted Phil Collins to make a choice of his own.

> "In the middle of my writing and making BOTH SIDES, Genesis did a concert with Queen," he told *Hello* magazine several years later. "But I didn't enjoy it . . . As I was singing these songs, it didn't feel natural. Obviously, it was bad timing, going just like that from doing my most personal thing to a Genesis thing and back. But it definitely felt like, 'What am I doing here?', like shoes that don't fit anymore."

Phil couldn't shake this feeling and gave the matter a lot of thought. Aside from his recent onstage revelation, Genesis also added a lot of commitments to his already-busy schedule. The once-tireless musician now found that the pressures and demands of Genesis and his solo work were making his life "very complicated." A couple of weeks later, he had reached a decision: he would leave Genesis. Although his departure would not be announced for a year and a half, Phil now considered himself to be an ex-Genesis member.

> "I don't think that we would continue, if any of us were to leave," Tony Banks had told *Replay* earlier that year. "Genesis has become very much what the three of us do together now. I can't say definitely that we would split up, as it would depend very much on how it happened, but I think it's unlikely we would continue."

> "We get asked this question from time to time, and I wouldn't have thought we'd continue, but you never quite know, do you?" added Mike Rutherford. "But we've got to stop somewhere along the line though!"

In 1994 — with the rest of the world unaware of Phil's decision — Virgin began to reissue the Genesis back catalog (from TRESPASS to THREE SIDES LIVE) in improved, remastered versions. These releases — touted by Virgin as the "Definitive Editions" — came out in two stages: the albums from TRESPASS through THE LAMB LIES DOWN ON BROADWAY appeared in the summer, while the remaining titles appeared in Autumn. (TRESPASS was not reissued in North America, where Virgin didn't have the rights to it.) Although the sound was a vast improvement over the previous versions, fans were displeased at some of the errors in the packaging. The band members were also displeased by the errors, Mike Rutherford in particular, over his omission from the writing credits for *Ripples*, on the new TRICK OF THE TAIL CD. But, overall, the reissues were a great improvement and offered new sonic perspectives on the Genesis catalog. After the reissues, nothing much was heard of Genesis until early in 1996. And when it was, the news wasn't good . . .

Chapter 20: . . . And Then There Were Two . . .

On March 28, 1996, Phil Collins officially announced his departure from Genesis. He told a press conference, "I felt it was time to change direction . . . I wish the guys the very best. We remain best friends."

Out of all those who quit Genesis, it was Phil whose departure proved to be the biggest blow to the group. Collins was not just a great singer, points out Daryl Stuermer, but also . . .

> "A great entertainer. He really was the entertaining side — outside of the light show and all that. He was the personality of the band when he was out there. And, of course, he's also a great drummer."

Having had some time to consider their options, Mike and Tony announced that they planned to continue as Genesis. Although they had yet to find a new vocalist, Banks and Rutherford began working on a new Genesis album. In June 1996, they began recording tracks that would eventually appear on CALLING ALL STATIONS.

> "When a change like this comes about, it brings something different, and that's what we've found with the direction out music is now taking," said Rutherford, in reference to Phil's departure. "The new Genesis album that Tony and I are working on will be much darker and heavier." Banks characterized Collins' departure as "an opportunity, rather than a problem . . . This gives us a chance to take Genesis to the next stage."

Between late 1996 and early 1997, as the group began assembling the first of several Genesis box sets, Banks, Collins, Rutherford, Hackett and Gabriel participated in a new recording of *The Carpet Crawl*, co-produced by Trevor Horn. The track was initially slated for the first ARCHIVE box set, but wasn't finished in time.

In a recent interview with the Intermusic.com web site, Mike Rutherford explained how *The Carpet Crawlers* was chosen for the remake treatment:

> "Other songs on THE LAMB had a lot of character, arrangement wise, so it would have been quite hard to redo them. So *Carpet Crawlers* was quite a simple song and didn't have too tricky an arrangement. It was also Trevor's choice — that helped, as he was very much involved in how it came out."

In the meantime, there was new music to make. During the initial post-Collins Genesis sessions there was still doubt about whether the group would continue.

> "We were not sure whether we would continue the album," recalls Nick Davis. "Even when we had a short-list of singers, we just didn't know whether it would work out." The writing and recording process was different this time out because, as Davis points out, "we were missing our drummer and vocalist for the writing stage. Before, we would put down a guide (drum machine part), keyboard, guitar and guide vocals for a song and then go into the studio straight away and do the drums. But on this album we worked with drum machines for quite a while because we also had to find a drummer. We were also working without a melody on some of the songs for a longer time than usual."

The uncertainty didn't last long. In June 1997, more than a year after Phil Collins' departure from Genesis, Mike and Tony announced that they had found a new lead singer,

Ray Wilson. Born in 1968 in Dumfries, Scotland, the singer's previous bands had included The End and Guaranteed Pure. But it was Wilson's work as the lead vocalist of Stiltskin that brought him commercial success. A Stiltskin track called *Inside* had been featured in a Levi's TV commercial in Britain and the exposure had pushed the song to the top of the singles charts there in 1994.

During the initial post-Collins sessions at The Farm, Tony Banks had heard Stiltskin's album and was suitably impressed by the vocals. In particular, he felt that Ray's voice would suit a song called *Congo* that he and Rutherford had been working on. Apparently, Mike and Tony had considered recruiting ex-Marillion singer Fish to handle the vocals and had discussed this with him. Ultimately, though, Fish was as much a writer as a singer, and would have needed an equal contribution to the writing process, which was not really what Tony and Mike wanted from a new singer. There was also the stigma of the Gabriel / early Genesis comparisons that Marillion had drawn in their early days. To have Fish become the lead singer of Genesis might have been too bizarre a notion to realize.

The sessions for the first Genesis album since TRESPASS not to feature Phil Collins progressed at a leisurely pace. The tracks that would make up the CALLING ALL STATIONS were recorded between June 1996 and July 1997 at The Farm. Production duties were shared by Nick Davis, Tony Banks and Mike Rutherford, and Davis engineered the sessions, with assistance from Ian Huffam. In addition to the tracks that appeared on the album, the new Genesis lineup recorded several other numbers, most of which were used as "B-sides" for CD singles: *Anything Now, Sign Your Life Away, Nowhere Else To Turn, Run Out Of Time, Papa He Said, Banjo Man, 7/8* and *Phret.*

Although Ray Wilson had joined towards the end of the recording process, he did receive a co-writing credit on three of the album's tracks — *Not About Us, Small Talk* and *There Must Be Some Other Way.* Drumming duties on the album were divided between Nick D'Virgilio (of Spock's Beard) and Nir Z.

On July 31, Virgin held a launch party for the album, in the revolving restaurant atop the B.T. Tower. There, assembled media types got their first chance to hear the new version of Genesis. Among those present was Virgin President Paul Conroy, who truly went back a long way with Genesis. Conroy had been Charisma's Press officer in the early 70's, and it was he who had suggested Gabriel don the fox head and dress to promote FOXTROT.

Ray Wilson's first live appearance with Genesis came on August 26 at the Alexanderplatz in East Berlin. It was the first of two "launch concerts" for the CALLING ALL STATIONS album. The new lineup did a four-song acoustic set for the assembled members of the media, comprising the *Lover's Leap* section of *Supper's Ready, No Son Of Mine, Not About Us* and *Turn It On Again.* The choice of material seemed designed to show that Wilson could handle material from the various eras of Genesis' career, theoretically providing a worthy replacement not only for Collins, but also for Gabriel. Indeed, the press release announcing Wilson's recruitment joked that after twenty-one years of Collins filling in, Genesis had finally found a replacement for Peter Gabriel!

Two days after the Berlin appearance, the new Genesis arrived at the Kennedy Space

Center in Florida — a particularly appropriate venue for the second CALLING ALL STATIONS "launch concert." This appearance featured the same acoustic set as the previous show, showcasing the new line-up for the American media.

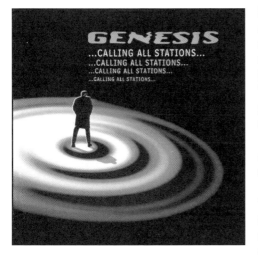

In September, Virgin released CALLING ALL STATIONS, and the public at large got their first chance to hear the post-Collins Genesis line-up. It went to No. 2 in Britain, despite the absence of Collins. The album fared less well in America, peaking at No. 54, the lowest placing for a Genesis album there since 1973.

Although the album sold well in Britain, the critics were less receptive.

"It was a long, hard search," sniped the *NME*. "Through a process of elimination, the Other Two Blokes In Genesis found him: the only vocalist in the universe smug and emotionless enough to replace Phil Collins ... Still, the guy should be thankful. A few years back, joining the least credible band ever would have incited mass ridicule. These days, the world probably doesn't care enough about Genesis to make the effort." The paper also pointed out that "Like the rest of the population, they've forgotten why they were once any good."

David Wild's review in *Rolling Stone* correctly pointed out that Ray Wilson wasn't to blame for the somewhat lackluster album: "The ultimate problem here is the usual one: the dearth of decent material beyond a few pleasant if generic FM-rock tunes like *Shipwrecked* and *Not About Us*." Indeed, Wilson's renditions of earlier Genesis numbers revealed that the new material didn't give him enough of a chance to showcase his considerable abilities.

"Eleven new songs and barely a cheery moment among the lot of them," read the review in *Q*. "Just darkness, confusion, individual isolation and relationships falling apart at the seams, all pinned to a series of dense, heavily mannered, airless rock settings whose foundations have barely shifted in the past 20 years. One-paced and one-dimensional, their time might just be up ..."

Clearly, Mike and Tony were trying to revert to a more "progressive" sound, but their musical approach had changed a lot over the years and they couldn't quite get back to the kind of atmospheric style that had worked so well in the 70's.

The first single taken from the album was *Congo*. Released as a CD single — accompanied by the non-album cuts *Papa He Said* and *Banjo Man* — *Congo* was a modest hit in Britain, reaching No. 29. The other two British singles from CALLING ALL STATIONS each appeared in two formats, one with non-album studio cuts and the other with live tracks from the album launch concerts. *Shipwrecked* came backed with either *Phret* and *7/8*, or live versions of *No Son Of Mine, Lover's Leap* and *Turn It On Again*. The third single, *Not About Us*, added either *Anything Now, Sign Your Life Away*, and *Run Out Of Time*, or live renditions of the opening section of *Dancing With The Moonlight Night, Follow You, Follow Me* and *Not About Us*.

With the album in stores, it was logical for Genesis to hit the road in support of CALLING ALL STATIONS. As with the first tour after Peter Gabriel left, Genesis decided to first introduce their new line-up to their fans in North America. A typically extensive tour was announced, comprising shows in large venues. It was a pretty typical Genesis itinerary, but the tour didn't happen, even after it was rescheduled into smaller venues. Initially, "technical problems" were cited as the reason, but it came to light that disappointing ticket sales were what prompted the cancellation.

> "Our support there isn't as strong now as it was," Mike Rutherford said, adding inexplicably, "I think there's something of an anti-English movement."

> "We were geared up for the wrong type of tour," Rutherford conceded. "We were aiming to play the big venues when we should have been more humble."

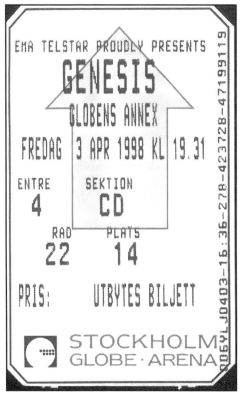

A TICKET STUB FROM ONE OF GENESIS' EUROPEAN SHOWS.

The European leg of the tour still went ahead, but the cancellation of the American dates was a huge blow to Genesis' ego, especially coupled with the album's poor chart showing. Although they surely didn't need the money, Genesis had clearly become used to being big in America. So much so that, two years later, when Banks finally broached the idea of ending Genesis, he would cite the (lack of) American reaction to CALLING ALL STATIONS as a key factor.

Not only was Phil Collins absent for the CALLING ALL STATIONS tour, but so were Chester Thompson and Daryl Stuermer.

"What happened there is, they were planning on doing a tour without Phil," says Daryl. "And there was no way I could do the tour, because I had already planned on doing a tour with Phil and it was going to run into their tour. But I have a feeling that they also wanted to make a total change. I don't know if that's true or not — it's just a feeling I got."

Instead of Thompson and Stuermer, the new shows featured Nir Z on drums and Anthony Drennan on guitar. But the absence of Daryl and Chester onstage just made the whole thing seem even less like Genesis.

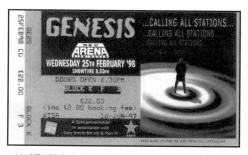

ANOTHER TICKET FROM A GENESIS CONCERT IN THE U.K.

On January 29, 1998, the new Genesis began a European tour at the Sports Hall in Budapest, Hungary. Their set consisted of: *No Son Of Mine, Land Of Confusion, The Lamb Lies Down On Broadway, Calling All Stations, Hold On My Heart, Alien Afternoon, There Must Be Some Other Way, Domino, The Carpet Crawlers*, a portion of *Firth Of Fifth, Congo, Home By The Sea* and *Second Home By The Sea*. Next came the acoustic portion of the set, in which Tony Banks played acoustic guitar alongside Rutherford and Drennan. The acoustic portion included the introduction from *Dancing With The Moonlit Knight*, followed by *Follow You Follow Me* and the *Lover's Leap* section of *Supper's Ready*. After that they turned electric again with *Mama, The Dividing Line, Invisible Touch, Turn It On Again, Throwing It All Away* and *I Can't Dance*. For old school fans, the acoustic set was a treat, with Wilson doing a great job of the vocals on *Moonlit Knight* and *Lover's Leap*. If nothing else, those performances showed that if CALLING ALL STATIONS was something of a disappointment, Ray was not to blame.

From Budapest, the band traveled to Warsaw, Poland, then the Czech Republic, then on to Germany for shows in Mannheim, Leipzig and Berlin. On February 8, they crossed the border into France to play at Le Galaxie in Amneville. Then Dortmund, Stuttgart, Zurich, Vienna, Bologna, Milan, Geneva, Lyon and Bercy.

The European tour was generally a positive experience for the new Genesis, especially the dates in Eastern Europe.

> "We really enjoyed it actually, I think Poland particularly, and Prague — they were all good," said Tony in the Virgin online chat. "Katowice took us kind of by surprise because people didn't only know us from our early days but also seemed to like our more recent stuff as well. We needed that. It was the first few gigs we did with Ray as singer, we went there because people had no comparisons and we thought that was a good place to start and get confidence. It was quite gratifying really because it gave us a bit of self confidence, particularly with Ray just to see what it was like being out there and to get used to the idea of it all."

On February 25 and 26, Ray, Tony, Mike, Nir and Anthony did their first British dates, at the NEC in Birmingham. On the 27th, they returned to Earl's Court, the site of those triumphant 1977 shows. This was followed by arena dates in Glasgow, Newcastle, Cardiff, Manchester and Dublin.

On March 10, it was back to the continent for shows in Brussels, Rotterdam, Lille, Angers,

Bordeaux, Pau, Madrid, Barcelona, Marseille, Clermont, Caen, Strasbourg, Munich, Efrurt and Hamburg. A planned March 31 gig in Bielfeld, Germany was canceled due to Ray having lost his voice, and a show in Copenhagen the following day suffered the same fate. By the 2nd of April, Ray was well enough to belt out the Genesis set at the Spektrum in Oslo, concluding this leg of the tour with shows in Stockholm and Helsinki. The group played a couple of dates at the end of May. The Rock Am Ring Festival in Koln, Germany in the 30th and the Frankenstadion in Nurnberg the following day. And that was it for the new Genesis.

Chapter 21: Afterglow

In the summer of 1998, Virgin finally released the much-delayed GENESIS ARCHIVE box set. The plan to do a series of Genesis box sets had originally been revealed in 1994. It was first announced that there would be three four-CD box sets - one spanning the Gabriel years, the next covering the period from mid-'70s to the early '80s, and the last covering the mid-'80s through early '90s. Originally, the sets were each to have contained two discs of the best previously released material from each period, with the other half collecting unreleased gems and rarities.

Over the next four years, there were numerous delays and changes. On a positive note for fans, it was decided that the sets would comprise nothing but rarities and unreleased tracks. However, it was also decided that there would only be two sets released: the first, as originally planned, would cover 1967-1975, but the second set would attempt to cram the other two decades of Genesis into one package. (Certainly there was less need to include live material from this period, since most of the band's repertoire had appeared on the three Collins-fronted live albums.) The band had also overseen the creation of a CD-ROM containing rare archival material which was, at one point, mooted as the fourth disc in the proposed third box set.

The first box set, provisionally titled The Gabriel Years, was originally scheduled for release in November 1995. It didn't appear, for a variety of reasons, including Phil Collins' departure and the difficulties of tracking down and licensing suitable material. (Jonathan King still owned the rights to some of the band's early recordings.) In the next year or so there was quite a bit of speculation as to what would be on the set. Among the rumored tracks that didn't make the final cut were demos of White Mountain, Fourteen Years Too Long, Barnaby's Adventure, Through The Looking Glass, and live versions of The Light and The Battle Of Epping Forest. Also rumored to be on the set were recordings of Supper's Ready and Watcher Of The Skies from an October 30, 1973 performance at Shepperton Studios.

The track line-up was finalized in 1996, although the box set wouldn't find its way into stores for another two years. When it finally did, fans seemed to agree it had been worth the wait. By the time it appeared in 1998, the title had been changed to GENESIS ARCHIVE. (Apparently, it was Tony Banks who vetoed the original title, probably uncomfortable with the emphasis on Gabriel.) The discs were laid out in an unorthodox manner, almost in

reverse chronological order. The first two CDs featured a full live performance of THE LAMB LIES DOWN ON BROADWAY, recorded at the Shrine Auditorium, Los Angeles in 1975. The performance wasn't quite as "live" as it seemed, however, since the original tapes were touched up quite a bit for release. The biggest flaw through most of THE LAMB tapes was the poor quality of the vocals. Due to the ambitious nature of the staging, Gabriel was often out of breath from running around the stage, or had to sing from inside a mask. For the box set release, Gabriel re-recorded all the vocals for THE LAMB, at his Real World Studio, in 1995. These new vocals were substituted where necessary for original performances. To some fans, this had a jarring effect, with the new vocal parts easily distinguishable as the late '90s Peter Gabriel, rather than his mid-'70s counterpart. Steve Hackett also felt that, due in part to his hand injury, some of his LAMB solos warranted re-doing, including *The Lamia* and *Riding The Scree*. The last LAMB track, *It*, had to be redone from scratch, since the tape machine at the Shrine performance apparently ran out partway through the song. A new version was assembled, incorporating a remix of the studio version and a new Gabriel vocal.

The third disc offered several live tracks recorded in October 1973 at London's Rainbow Theater: *Dancing with the Moonlit Knight, Firth of Fifth, More Fool Me, Supper's Ready* and *I Know What I Like*. (There was some "tarting up" done on these live recordings, too: Steve touched up some of his lead work on *Firth Of Fifth* and part of *Dancing With The Moonlit Knight*, while Peter re-did some of *Supper's Ready*.) Then there was a 1972 BBC recording of *Stagnation*, plus the non-album *Happy The Man*, a remix of the B-side *Twilight Alehouse*, and a remix of the single version of *Watcher Of The Skies*.

The fourth disc contained a great assortment of demos and out-takes from the '67-'70 era: a rough mix of *In the Wilderness*, 1970 BBC recordings of *Shepherd, Pacidy, Let Us Now Make Love* and *Dusk*, the 1969 demo of *Going Out to Get You*, rough mixes of *Build Me a Mountain, The Image Blown Out* and *One Day*, demo versions of *When the Sour Turns to Sweet, In the Beginning, The Magic of Time, Hey!, Hidden in the World of Dawn, Sea Bee, The Mystery of the Flannan Isle Lighthouse, Hair on the Arms and Legs, She is Beautiful, Try a Little Sadness*. The box set ended with a track from the very first demo session, the instrumental *Patricia*.

"The fun part was mixing the old live material," says Nick Davis of his work on the first Archive set. "And it was great having repairs done by Peter and Steve. Mixing *It* again from the original multitrack was great." However, Davis doesn't share the fans' enthusiasm for all the unreleased material. "The not-so-fun bit was cleaning up the demos," he says. "I personally don't see the great appeal in listening to things that never were good enough to become released, though I suppose other people may find them of interest."

On May 11, 1998, there was a brief reunion of past and present group members at Heathrow Airport. To promote the release of the ARCHIVE set, Tony Banks, Peter Gabriel, Anthony Phillips, John Silver, Phil Collins, Steve Hackett and Mike Rutherford all gathered together for the first time, were filmed and posed for photographs.

At around the same time as the ARCHIVE box set, there appeared another disc of great interest to fans of early Genesis. Anthony Phillips' ARCHIVE COLLECTION CD included several demos recorded with Mike Rutherford in 1969, including a very early version of *The Musical Box* (under its original title of *F Sharp*).

"It was planned to come out quite independently of the box set," Phillips explains. "But, because they suddenly brought the box set forward, it came out at a not-too-dissimilar time and people probably thought, 'Ah, he's trying to do it at the same time to get interest.' And in fact we conspicuously didn't use any kind of advertising that would seem to be going off the back of the Genesis thing. I think we possibly went too far the other way."

"We managed to find recordings that Mike and I had done as a duo during the period just before we went on the road," Phillips says. Aside from *F Sharp*, the other early tracks also provided much insight into Phillips' importance to the Genesis sound.

Not all the newly unearthed Phillips-Rutherford duets were deemed worthy of inclusion on the ARCHIVE COLLECTION.

"There was a very early version of 'The Silver Song,'" Phillips reveals. "It's dreadful. It was so awful we couldn't use it. We couldn't use virtually anything that was vocal, because our vocals were so bad. Not the kind of shy shrinking-violet stuff, but the kind of really robust, rugged, almost sort of pub-type singing, very loud and unpleasant!"

In October 1999, Genesis released their first official compilation CD, TURN IT ON AGAIN - THE HITS, which closed with the long-awaited remake of *The Carpet Crawlers*. The recording of this new version was finally completed in May 1999, with the addition of backing vocals by Phil Collins (who also sings lead on a verse) and Peter Gabriel. The sound of Phil and Peter harmonizing, with Steve's ghostly guitar in the background was a moving experience for old school fans. The NME naturally panned the *Carpet Crawlers* remake, while conceding that the original LAMB album was "quite splendid in parts actually." For those fans who didn't want to buy a CD full of tracks they already had,

Carpet Crawlers 1999 was made available as a free download on Genesis' official Web site, as well as Steve Hackett's site.

Genesis Archive #2
1976-1992

In July 2000, Virgin announced that the second ARCHIVE box set would be released in November. Disappointingly (at least for die-hard fans), it was revealed that the second and last installment would only consist of three discs. Covering the 1975-1992 era, the set included non-album tracks (including 12" mixes), live versions of songs that haven't previously appeared on a live album and a working version of *Mama* featuring the band jamming in the studio. The press release also mentioned that the set would even include "a note from the band as to why certain tracks often requested by fans, didn't make it on to the box set!" A wise move, since the set had some glaring omissions: Although the set included almost all the group's non-album tracks from '75-'92, it curiously omitted the excellent *Match Of The Day* (from SPOT THE PIGEON) and *Me And Virgil* (from 3X3).

Twenty-three years after *The Silent Sun*, interest in Genesis seems to be as strong as ever. However, much of it seems to be nostalgic, for the Gabriel era, or the late '70s/early '80s era. Over the last few years a number of Genesis tribute bands have formed, including The Musical Box, In The Cage and ReGenesis. With Genesis themselves reluctant to delve too far into their past, such groups may be the closest many fans will come to experiencing the classic line-up. Steve Hackett has been to see ReGenesis at least once and was impressed by their show. Mike Rutherford reportedly saw a video of a tribute band and mistook it for the real thing! There was even a one-off performance by a Tony Banks tribute act called Strictly Banks. There are numerous Internet sites devoted to Genesis, where fans can delve into the minutia of the band's career.

While fans speculate about the group's future, the past and present members of Genesis are busy with their own projects. Steve Hackett continues to make new albums at an incredible pace, so much so that he's had to form his own label! Camino Records is Steve's label, but also includes a mail order division that sells all Steve's back catalog, as well as the entire Genesis catalog and solo releases by other members. In 1999, Steve unleashed Darktown, a superb release that sounds more "progressive" than anything Genesis has done in the last decade or two. True to form, he followed it with another classical project - Sketches of Satie, comprising duets between his classical guitar and his brother John's flute. Camino Records is also now home to Chester Thompson, who re-released his first solo album, A JOYFUL NOISE, on the label in May 1999. Daryl Stuermer also recently released a new solo album, ANOTHER SIDE OF GENESIS including his own interpretations of Genesis songs.

Peter Gabriel is, typically, taking his time. A new Gabriel album, reportedly to be titled UP, has been expected for some time now, the latest reports predicting its appearance in late 2000. He did, however, show up on the 1999 Academy Awards program, singing the Oscar-nominated *That'll Do*, with the song's composer Randy Newman providing piano accompaniment. In 2000, he released OVO, featuring music composed for Britain's Millenium Dome.

Mike Rutherford's latest project is a self-titled MIKE AND THE MECHANICS album. Released in May 1999 in Europe, Mike & The Mechanics drew a lukewarm response from some fans, furthering the feeling that Mike and Tony are stuck in a bit of a rut. (However, the album did chart in Britain, reaching #14.) Phil Collins was heard by a new generation in the summer of 1999, providing the songs for Disney's animated version of Tarzan, and winning an Academy Award for his efforts. For the older fans, Phil also released a live album with his Big Band, entitled A HOT NIGHT IN PARIS, and is currently working on another Disney score. And Phil's replacement, Ray Wilson, released an album with his band Cut and is currently working on a new project.

Tony Banks is said to be writing new material, though it is uncertain what form his new music will appear in. Banks has had limited success as a solo artist. Even at the height of his songwriting powers, his records made only a modest chart showing, so it seems doubtful that he will ever find much success on his own. Indeed, this may well have been the reason for his desire to continue on with Genesis after Collins' departure.

Although there has been no announcement of a break-up, the future of Genesis is very much in doubt. In early 1999, it was reported that the Tony, Mike and Ray line-up had booked time at The Farm in November of that year to record a follow-up to CALLING ALL STATIONS. This plan became increasingly vague, with reports that the recording sessions would have to be pushed back to accommodate Mike's promotional activities for the new Mechanics album. When November arrived, things looked even more doubtful. In interviews, Tony Banks began to broach the possibility that Genesis might call it quits.

"We need to decide if we want to do another record," he told ABCNews.com. "I think the lack of response in America for CALLING ALL STATIONS was a bit depressing for us, really, though it did well in Europe. It wasn't so much that it was badly received as it wasn't received at all ...There's no way we can reinvent ourselves to say we're new, young, and fresh. It's a question of whether we want to keep on with that kind of thinking or if we want to stop. I still want to make music, but there's no point in making music through Genesis if Genesis itself isn't going to be the answer."

In June 2000, Ray Wilson revealed that Banks and Rutherford had decided in 1999 not to continue with the CALLING ALL STATIONS line-up. "I will not be doing another Genesis album but the band will probably tour with Phil again," Wilson told journalist Oystein Hage. He revealed that Mike and Tony's decision not to make another album with him was based on "the lack of success in America and the fear that no one would buy a new Genesis album." Wilson said that his deal was for two Genesis albums and he had been willing to continue. "I have mixed feelings when I look back," he reflected. "I did enjoy the experience but feel they should have had the balls to do another album."

Despite the dissolution of the CALLING ALL STATIONS line-up, Genesis doesn't seem to be over yet. There was a planned appearance of the Collins, Banks, Rutherford, Stuermer and Thompson line-up at a farewell show for Wembley Stadium. Genesis was confirmed for a short set at the gig, which was scheduled for August 26, 2000, but the show was canceled when the promoter couldn't secure enough other big name acts for the line-up.

A reunion of sorts did take place on September 21, 2000, although it was a private performance at the London Hilton, in honor of their longtime manager Tony Smith. The event was the British Music Roll of Honour gala, and Smith was awarded the Peter Grant Award (named after Led Zeppelin's legendary manager) for his achievements. After performances by Artful Dodger and Lionel Ritchie, Genesis performed a four song set: *Invisible Touch, Follow You Follow Me, Tonight Tonight Tonight* and *I Can't Dance*. The line-up for this performance was: Phil on vocals, bongos and maracas, Mike and Daryl on acoustic guitars and Tony on keyboards. Peter Gabriel attended the event and joined the group on stage to preform the number *Turn It On Again*.

In a TV interview at the time, Tony Banks was non-committal about the possibility of further reunions, saying,

> "If we got together, even for those who liked us, it would be a major disappointment. Most revivals are. And that's one good reason for avoiding them. But, if you just do something retrospective and you play old songs or as Phil says you get together and do something that is not trying to be the group, then that is very different I think."

So it would seem that Phil, Mike and Tony may still work together again, but perhaps not under the Genesis name. However they don't seem to be in a hurry to announce that Genesis is over. A new official web site is about to be launched, which suggests we haven't heard the last of Genesis. Whatever they choose to do, there are plenty of devoted fans waiting to hear some new Genesis music, and interest in the group is still surprisingly strong. Thirty years after the Charterhouse boys delivered their humble demo tape to Jonathan King, Genesis has carved out a secure place in rock history.

Put Another Record On:
The Genesis Discography:

U.K. Albums:

Since Genesis' album releases have been the same all over the world, I have just included the British releases in this discography, along with the original international version of *Three Sides Live*.

1969:
FROM GENESIS TO REVELATION
  (stereo LP: Decca SKL 4990; mono LP: LK 4990)
    Where the Sour Turns to Sweet
    In the Beginning
    Fireside Song
    The Serpent
    Am I Very Wrong
    In The Wilderness
    The Conquerer
    In Hiding
    One Day
    Window
    In Limbo
    The Silent Sun
  (Note: As Genesis' popularity began to grow in the early 70's, reissues of *From Genesis To Revelation* began to surface. Since then Decca and/or Jonathan King have served up a multitude of reissues, many of which have added the first two Decca singles to the line-up.)

1970:
TRESPASS
  (LP: Charisma CAS 1020; CD: CASCD 1020; remastered CD: CASCDX 1020)
    Looking For Someone
    White Mountain
    Visions Of Angels
    Stagnation
    Dusk
    The Knife

1971:
NURSERY CRYME
  (LP: Charisma CAS 1052; CD: CASCD 1052; remastered CD: CASCDX 1052)
    The Musical Box
    For Absent Friends
    The Return Of The Giant Hogweed
    Seven Stones
    Harold The Barrel

Harlequin
The Fountain Of Salmacis

1972:
FOXTROT
   (LP: Charisma CAS 1058; CD: CASCD 1058; remastered CD: CASCDX 1058)
   Watcher Of The Skies
   Time Table
   Get 'Em Out By Friday
   Can-Utility And The Coastliners
   Horizons
   Supper's Ready

1973:
GENESIS LIVE
   (LP: Charisma CLASS 1; CD: CLACD 1; remastered CD: CLACDX 1)
   Watcher Of The Skies
   Get 'em Out By Friday
   The Knife
   The Return Of The Giant Hogweed
   The Musical Box

SELLING ENGLAND BY THE POUND
   (LP: Charisma CAS 1074; CD: CASCD 1074; remastered CD: CASCDX 1074)
   Dancing With The Moonlit Knight
   I Know What I Like (In Your Wardrobe)
   Firth Of Fifth
   More Fool Me
   The Battle Of Epping Forest
   After The Ordeal
   The Cinema Show
   Aisle Of Plenty

1974:
THE LAMB LIES DOWN ON BROADWAY
   (LP: Charisma CGS 101; CD: CGSCD 101; remastered CD: CGSCDX 101)
   The Lamb Lies Down On Broadway
   Fly On A Windshield
   Broadway Melody Of 1974
   Cuckoo Cocoon
   In The Cage
   The Grand Parade Of Lifeless Packaging
   Back In N.Y.C.
   Hairless Heart
   Counting Out Time
   The Carpet Crawlers
   The Chamber Of 32 Doors
   Lilywhite Lilith

The Waiting Room
Anyway
The Supernatural Anesthetist
The Lamia
Silent Sorrow In Empty Boats
The Colony Of Slippermen
Ravine
The Light Dies Down On Broadway
Riding The Scree
In The Rapids
It

1976:
A TRICK OF THE TAIL
(LP: Charisma CDS 4001; CD: CDSCD 4001; remastered CD: CDSCDX 4001)
Dance On A Volcano
Entangled
Squonk
Mad Man Moon
Robbery, Assault & Battery
Ripples
A Trick Of The Tail
Los Endos

WIND & WUTHERING
(LP: Charisma CDS 4005; CD: CDSCD 4005; remastered CD: CDSCDX 4005)
Eleventh Earl Of Mar
One For The Vine
Your Own Special Way
Wot Gorilla?
All In A Mouse's Night
Blood On The Rooftops
Unquiet Slumbers For The Sleepers ...
... In That Quiet Earth
Afterglow

1977:
SECONDS OUT
(LP: Charisma GE 2001; CD: GECD 2001; remastered CD: GECDX 2001)
Squonk
The Carpet Crawl
Robbery, Assault and Battery
Afterglow
Firth of Fifth
I Know What I Like
The Lamb Lies Down On Broadway
The Musical Box (closing section)
Supper's Ready

The Cinema Show
Dance On A Volcano
Los Endos

1978:

...AND THEN THERE WERE THREE ...

(LP: Charisma CDS 4010; CD: CDSCD 4010; remastered CD: CDSCDX 4010)
Down And Out
Undertow
Ballad Of Big
Snowbound
Burning Rope
Deep In The Motherlode
Many Too Many
Scenes From A Night's Dream
Say It's Alright Joe
The Lady Lies
Follow You Follow Me

1980:

DUKE

(LP: Charisma CBR 101; CD: CBRCD 101; remastered CD: CBRCDX 101)
Behind the Lines
Duchess
Guide Vocal
Man of Our Times
Misunderstanding
Heathaze
Turn It On Again
Alone Tonight
Cul-de-sac
Please Don't Ask
Duke's Travels
Duke's End

1981:

ABACAB

(LP: Charisma CBR 102; CD: CBRCD 102; remastered CD: CBRCDX 102)
Abacab
No Reply At All
Me and Sarah Jane
Keep It Dark
Dodo / Lurker
Who Dunnit?
Man On The Corner
Like It Or Not
Another Record

1982:
THREE SIDES LIVE
  (LP: GE 2002; CD: GECD 2002; remastered CD: GECDX 2002)
    Turn It On Again
    Dodo
    Abacab
    Behind The Lines
    Duchess
    Me And Sarah Jane
    Follow You Follow Me
    Misunderstanding
    In The Cage
    Medley: Cinema Show / Slippermen
    Afterglow
    One For The Vine
    Fountain Of Salmacis
    It / Watcher Of The Skies
  (The British release of *Three Sides Live* was the only version which was comprised entirely of live recordings. In the rest of the world, the fourth side included the following non-LP tracks from the DUKE / ABACAB era:)
    Paperlate
    You Might Recall
    Me and Virgil
    Evidence of Autumn
    Open Door

1983:
GENESIS
  (LP: Charisma / Virgin GENLP 1; CD: GENCD 1)
    Mama
    That's All
    Home By The Sea
    Second Home By The Sea
    Illegal Alien
    Taking It All Too Hard
    Just a Job To Do
    Silver Rainbow
    It's Gonna Get Better

1986:
INVISIBLE TOUCH
  (LP: Virgin GENLP 2; CD: GENCD 2)
    Invisible Touch
    Tonight, Tonight, Tonight
    Land of Confusion
    In Too deep
    Anything She Does
    Domino Part One — In the Glow of the Night

Domino Part Two — The Last Domino
Throwing It All Away
The Brazilian

1991:
WE CAN'T DANCE
  (Virgin GENLP 3; CD: GENCD 3)
    No Son Of Mine
    Jesus He Knows Me
    Driving The Last Spike
    I Can't Dance
    Never A Time
    Dreaming While You Sleep
    Tell Me Why
    Living Forever
    Hold On My Heart
    Way Of The World
    Since I Lost You
    Fading Lights

1992:
THE WAY WE WALK VOLUME 1: THE SHORTS
  (LP: Virgin GENLP 4; CD: GENCD 4)
    Land Of Confusion
    No Son Of Mine
    Jesus He Knows Me
    Throwing It All Away
    I Can't Dance
    Mama
    Hold On My Heart
    That's All
    In Too Deep
    Tonight, Tonight, Tonight
    Invisible Touch

1993:
THE WAY WE WALK VOLUME 2: THE LONGS
  (LP: Virgin GENLP 5; CD: GENCD 5)
    Old Medley (Dance On A Volcano / The Lamb Lies Down On Broadway /
    The Musical Box closing section / Firth Of Fifth / I Know What I Like)
    Driving The Last Spike
    Domino Part 1: In The Glow Of The Night
    Domino Part 2: The Last Domino
    Fading Lights
    Home By The Sea
    Second Home By The Sea / Drum Duet

1997:
CALLING ALL STATIONS
  (LP: Virgin GENLP 6; CD: GENCD6)
    Calling All Stations
    Congo
    Shipwrecked
    Alien Afternoon
    Not About Us
    If That's What You Need
    The Dividing Line
    Uncertain Weather
    Small Talk
    There Must Be Some Other Way
    One Man's Fool

1998:
ARCHIVE 1967-75 (4 CD box set)
  (Virgin GENBOX 6)
    The Lamb Lies Down On Broadway
    Fly On A Windshield
    Broadway Melody Of 1974
    Cuckoo Cocoon
    In The Cage
    The Grand Parade Of Lifeless Packaging
    Back In N.Y.C.
    Hairless Heart
    Counting Out Time
    The Carpet Crawlers
    The Chamber Of 32 Doors
    Lilywhite Lilith
    The Waiting Room
    Anyway
    The Supernatural Anesthetist
    The Lamia
    Silent Sorrow In Empty Boats
    The Colony Of Slippermen (a. The Arrival — b. A Visit To The Doktor —
    c. The Raven)
    Ravine
    The Light Dies Down On Broadway
    Riding The Scree
    In The Rapids
    (All of the above were recorded live in 1975)
    It (Remix of studio version)
    Dancing With The Moonlit Knight
    Firth Of Fifth
    More Fool Me
    Supper's Ready
    I Know What I Like

(Above five recorded live in 1973)
Stagnation (BBC session)
Twilight Alehouse (remix of B-side)
Happy The Man
Watcher Of The Skies (single version)
In The Wilderness (1968 rough mix, without strings)
Shepherd (1970 BBC "Nightride" session)
Pacidy (1970 BBC "Nightride" session)
Let Us Now Make Love (1970 BBC "Nightride" session)
Going Out To Get You (1969 demo)
Dusk (1969 demo)
Build Me A Mountain (1968 rough mix)
The Image Blown Out (1968 Rough mix)
One Day (1968 Rough remix)
Where The Sour Turns To Sweet (1968 demo)
In The Beginning (1968 demo)
The Magic Of Time (1968 demo)
Hey! (1968 demo)
Hidden In The World Of Dawn (1968 demo)
Sea Bee (1968 demo)
The Mystery Of The Flannan Isle Lighthouse (1968 demo)
Hair On The Arms And Legs (1968 demo)
She Is Beautiful — (1967 demo, later "The Serpent")
Try A Little Sadness (1967 demo)
Patricia (1967 demo, later "In Hiding")

1999:
TURN IT ON AGAIN — THE HITS
  (Virgin)
    Turn It On Again
    Invisible Touch
    Mama
    Land Of Confusion
    I Can't Dance
    Follow You Follow Me
    Hold on My Heart
    Abacab
    I Know What I Like (In Your Wardrobe)
    No Son Of Mine
    Tonight Tonight Tonight
    In Too Deep
    Congo
    Jesus He Knows Me
    That's All
    Misunderstanding
    Throwing It All Away
    Carpet Crawlers 1999

2000:
GENESIS ARCHIVE 2 1976 - 1992 (3 CD BOX SET)
 (Virgin)
 Disc One :
   On the Shoreline
   Hearts on Fire
   You Might Recall
   Paperlate
   Evidence of Autumn
   Do the Neurotic
   I'd Rather Be You
   Naminanu
   Inside and Out
   Feeding the Fire
   I Can't Dance 12"
   Submarine

Disc Two
  Illegal Alien (Live - LA Forum 84)
  Dreaming While You Sleep (Live - Earls Court 92)
  It's Gonna Get Better (Live - LA Forum 84)
  Deep in the Motherlode (Live - Drury Lane 80)
  Ripples (Live - Lyceum 80)
  The Brazilian (Live - Wembley 87)
  Your Own Special Way (Live - Sydney 86)
  Burning Rope (Live - Houston 78)
  Entangled (Live - Bingley Hall, Staffordshire 76)
  Duke's Travels (Live - Lyceum 80)

Disc Three
  Invisible Touch 12"
  Land of Confusion 12"
  Tonight, Tonight, Tonight 12"
  No Reply at All (Live - Savoy NYC 81)
  Man on the Corner (Live - Savoy NYC 81)
  The Lady Lies (Live - Lyceum 80)
  Open Door
  The Day the Light Went Out
  Vancouver
  Pigeons
  It's Yourself
  Mama (work in progress)

International album releases

Although TURN IT ON AGAIN — THE HITS was the first compilation sanctioned by the band, a number of Genesis compilations had previously appeared in different countries. The following is a sampling of some of the more interesting ones:

PRESENTING GENESIS
  (Canada, Charisma CAS 101, 1973)
    The Musical Box (live)
    The Fountain of Salmacis
    Time Table
    The Return Of The Giant Hogweed (live)
    The Knife (live)
    Seven Stones
    (Live recordings on this album are from *Genesis Live*.)

70S POP SOUND
  (Spain, Charisma 6369 936, 1974)
    Watcher of the Skies
    Seven Stones
    Looking For Someone
    Harold the Barrel
    The Knife
    Get 'em Out By Friday
    White Mountain

ROCK THEATRE
  (Germany, Fontana 9299 515, 1975; CD reissue: Virgin 610-468-225, 1986)
    I Know What I Like (In Your Wardrobe)
    Harold The Barrel
    Harlequin
    Watcher Of The Skies (single version)
    The Fountain Of Salmacis
    Supper's Ready

THE STORY OF GENESIS
  (Japan, SFX-10061-2, 1978, double LP with booklet)
    The Knife
    The Musical Box
    Watcher Of The Skies
    Supper's Ready
    I Know What I Like
    The Lamb
    Dance On A Volcano
    Squonk
    Ripples
    11th Earl Of Mar
    Your Own Special Way

Burning Rope
Follow You Follow Me

TURN IT ON AGAIN: BEST OF '81-'83
(Vertigo 848 854-2, 1991)
Mama
Home By The Sea
That's All
Illegal Alien
Paperlate
No Reply At All
Taking It All Too Hard
Man On The Corner
Misunderstanding (live)
Follow You, Follow Me (live)
Abacab (live)
Turn It On Again (live) (medley including Everybody Needs Somebody, Satisfaction / The Last Time, All Day An All Of The Night, and In The Midnight Hour.)
Firth Of Fifth (live)

FROM GENESIS TO REVELATION (2 CD set)
(Original Masters 142952, 2000)
(This is just one of numerous CD reissues of the first Genesis album. I've included it here because it includes not only the first four Decca single sides, but also four demos from the same era and an interview with Jonathan King.)
When The Sour Turns To Sweet
In The Beginning
Fireside Song
Serpent
Am I Very Wrong
In The Wilderness
Conqueror
In Hiding
One Day
Window
In Limbo
The Silent Sun
A Place To Call My Own
Patricia (demo)
She Is Beautiful (demo)
The Image Blown Out (demo)
Try A Little Sadness (demo)
A Winters Tale
One Eyed Hound
That's Me
The Silent Sun

UK Singles:
(All are 7" singles unless otherwise specified)

1968:
- The Silent Sun / That's Me (Decca F12735)
- A Winter's Tale / One-Eyed Hound (Decca, F12775)

1969:
- Where the Sour Turns to Sweet / In Hiding (Decca F12949)

1970:
- Looking for Someone / Visions of Angels (Charisma GS1. 1970) (DJ promo single)

1971:
- The Knife (part 1) / The Knife (part 2) (Charisma CB 152)

1972:
- Happy the Man / Seven Stones (Charisma CB 181)

1974:
- I Know What I Like (in Your Wardrobe) / Twilight Alehouse (Charisma CB 224)
- Counting out Time / Riding the Scree (Charisma CB 238)

1975:
- Carpet Crawlers / Evil Jam (The Waiting Room live) (Charisma CB 251)

1976:
- A Trick of the Tail / Ripples (Charisma CB 277)

1977:
- Your Own Special Way / It's Yourself (Charisma CB 300)
- *Spot The Pigeon* EP: Match of the Day / Pigeons / Inside and Out (Charisma GEN 001; CD-Maxi 1988: CDF 40/CDT 40)

1978:
- Follow You Follow Me / Ballad of Big (Charisma CB 309)
- Many Too Many / The Day the Light Went Out / Vancouver (Charisma CB 315)

1980:
- Turn It on Again / Behind the Lines part 2 (Charisma CB 356)
- Duchess / Open Door (Charisma CB 363)
- Misunderstanding / Evidence of Autumn (Charisma CB 369)

1981:
- Abacab / Another Record (Charisma CB 388)
- Keep It Dark / Naminanu (Charisma CB 391)

○ Keep It Dark / Naminanu / Abacab (long version) (Charisma CB 391-12)
(12" single)

1982:
○ Man on the Corner / Submarine (Charisma CB 393)
○ 3X3 EP: Paperlate / You Might Recall / Me and Virgil (Charisma GEN 1)

1983:
○ Mama / It's Gonna Get Better (Virgin MAMA 1)
○ Mama (long version) / It's Gonna Get Better (long version)
(12":Virgin MAMA 112; CD single, June 1988:Virgin CTD 5)
○ That's All / Taking It All Too Hard (Virgin TATA 1)
○ That's All / Taking It All Too Hard / Firth of Fifth (live) (Virgin TATA 1-12)
(12" single)

1984:
○ Illegal Alien / Turn It On Again (live) (Virgin AL 1)
○ Illegal Alien / Turn It On Again (live) (Virgin AL 1-12) (12" single)

1986:
○ Invisible Touch / The Last Domino (Virgin GENS 1)
○ Invisible Touch (extended) / Invisible Touch / The Last Domino (Virgin GENS 1-12)
(12" single)
○ In Too Deep / Do the Neurotic (Virgin GENS 2)
○ In Too Deep / Do the Neurotic (Virgin GENS 2-12) (12" single)
○ Land of Confusion / Feeding the Fire (Virgin GENS 3)
○ Land of Confusion (Extended Version) / Land of Confusion / Feeding the Fire
(GENS 3-12) (12" single)
○ Land of Confusion / Land of Confusion (Extended Version) / Feeding the Fire /
Do the Neurotic (SNEG 3-12) (CD single)

1987:
○ Tonight, Tonight, Tonight / In the Glow of the Night (GENS 4)
○ Tonight, Tonight, Tonight / In the Glow of the Night / Paperlate /
Tonight, Tonight, Tonight (12" remix) (GENS 4-12) (12" single)
○ Tonight, Tonight, Tonight (single edit) / In the Glow of the Night / Paperlate /
Tonight, Tonight, Tonight (12" remix) (DRAW 412) (CD single)
○ Throwing It All Away / I'd Rather Be With You (GENS 5)
○ Throwing It All Away / I'd Rather Be With You / Invisible Touch (live) (GENS 512)
(12" single)
○ Throwing It All Away / I'd Rather Be With You / Invisible Touch (live) (GENSC 512)
(cassette single)

1991:
○ No Son of Mine / Living Forever (Virgin GEN6)
○ No Son Of Mine / Living Forever / Invisible Touch (live) (Virgin GENS6-12)
(12" single)

○ No Son Of Mine / Living Forever / Invisible Touch (live) (Virgin GENDG6)
(CD single)

1992:

○ I Can't Dance / On The Shoreline (Virgin GENS7)
○ I Can't Dance / On The Shoreline / I Can't Dance (Sex Mix) (Virgin GENSD7)
(CD single)
○ Hold On My Heart / Way of the World (Virgin GENS8)
○ Hold On My Heart / Way of the World / Home By The Sea (live) (Virgin GENSD8)
(CD single)
○ Hold On My Heart / Way of the World / Your Own Special Way (live)
(Virgin GENDG8) (CD single)
○ Jesus He Knows Me / Hearts On Fire (Virgin GENS9)
○ Jesus He Knows Me / Hearts On Fire / I Can't Dance (The Other Mix)
(Virgin GENDG9) (CD single)
○ Jesus He Knows Me / Hearts on Fire / Land of Confusion (rehearsal version)
(Virgin GENDX 9) (CD single)
○ Never A Time / Dreaming While You Sleep (live) / Turn It On Again (live) /
Tonight Tonight Tonight (live 1986) (Virgin GENE 11) (CD single)
○ Invisible Touch (live) / Abacab (live) (Virgin GENS 10)
○ Invisible Touch (live) / Abacab (live) / The Brazilian (live) (Virgin GENDX10)
(CD single in box, with booklet, limited edition)

1993:

○ Tell Me Why / Dreaming While You Sleep (live) (Virgin GENS 11)
○ Tell Me Why / Dreaming While You Sleep (live) (Virgin GENSC 11) (cassette single)
○ Tell Me Why / Dreaming While You Sleep (live) / Turn It On Again (live)
(Virgin GENDG 11) (CD single)
○ Tell Me Why / Dreaming While You Sleep (live) / Tonight Tonight Tonight (live)
(Virgin GENDX 11) (CD single)

1997:

○ Congo / Papa He Said / Banjo Man (Virgin GENSD12) (CD single)
○ Congo / Second Home By The Sea (Virgin GENSDX12)
(Enhanced CD single, featuring the video for "Congo.")

1998:

○ Not About Us (radio edit) / Dancing With The Moonlit Knight (part)* /
Follow You Follow Me* / Not About Us (extended version) (Virgin GENDX15)
(*acoustic versions recorded with Ray Wilson) (CD single)
○ Not About Us (radio edit) / Anything Now / Sign Your Life Away /
Run Out Of Time (Virgin GENSD15) (CD single)
○ Shipwrecked / No Son Of Mine* / Lovers Leap (from Supper's Ready)* /
Turn It On Again* (Virgin GENDX14)
(*acoustic versions recorded with Ray Wilson) (CD single)
○ Shipwrecked / Phret / 7/8 (Virgin GENSD 14) (CD single)

1999:
- The Carpet Crawlers 1999 / Follow You Follow Me / Turn It On Again (Virgin) (CD single)

U.S. Singles:

1969:
- The Silent Sun / That's Me (Parrot 3018)

1973:
- Watcher Of The Skies (single version) / Willow Farm (Charisma 103)
- I Know What I Like / Twilight Alehouse (Charisma 26002)

1974:
- The Lamb Lies Down On Broadway / Counting Out Time (Atco 7013)

1977:
- Ripples (edit) / Entangled (edit) (Atco 7050)
- Your Own Special Way / In That Quiet Earth (Atco 7076)

1978:
- Follow You Follow Me (remix) / Inside And Out (Atlantic 3474)
- Go West Young Man (AKA Deep In The Motherlode) / Scenes From A Night's Dream (Atlantic 3511)

1980:
- Misunderstanding / Behind The Lines (Atlantic 3662)
- Turn It On Again (remix) / Evidence Of Autumn (Atlantic 3571)

1981:
- No Reply At All / Dodo (Atlantic 3858)
- Abacab / Who Dunnit? (Atlantic 3891)

1982:
- Man On The Corner / Submarine (Atlantic 4025)
- Paperlate / You Might Recall (Atlantic 4053)

1983:
- Mama / It's Gonna Get Better (Atlantic 89770)
- That's All / Second Home By The Sea (Atlantic 89724)

1984:
- Illegal Alien / Turn It On Again (live) (Atlantic 89698)
- Taking It All Too Hard / Silver Rainbow (Atlantic 89656)

1986:
- Invisible Touch / The Last Domino (Atlantic 89407)
- Throwing It All Away / Do The Neurotic (Atlantic 89372)

◦ Land Of Confusion / Feeding The Fire (Atlantic 89336)

1987:
  ◦ Tonight, Tonight, Tonight / In The Glow Of The Night (Atlantic 89290)
  ◦ In Too Deep / I'd Rather Be You (Atlantic 89316)

1991:
  ◦ No Son Of Mine / Living Forever (Atlantic 87571)

1992:
  ◦ I Can't Dance / On The Shoreline (Atlantic 87532)
  ◦ Hold On My Heart / Way Of The World (Atlantic 87481)
  ◦ Jesus He Knows Me / Hearts On Fire (Atlantic 87454)
  ◦ Never A Time / Tonight, Tonight, Tonight (live) / Invisible Touch (live)
    (Atlantic 87411)

Bootlegs:

Compiling a complete discography of Genesis bootlegs seems like an almost impossible task: Genesis is one of the most widely-booted groups in the history of rock and roll. So the following is just a sampling of the many titles available. Genesis bootlegs — like those of any artist — vary greatly in terms of sound quality and packaging, but they have provided a great deal of historical insight over the years. Without the bootleggers, fans would never have heard "The Light" or "The Silver Song" or numerous other hidden gems from Genesis' career . . .

A DEATH IN ANYTOWN
  (Recorded live at the Felt Forum, Los Angeles, 22 November, 1973)
    Watcher of the Skies
    Firth of Fifth
    The Musical Box
    Dancing With the Moonlit Knight
    The Cinema Show
    I Know What I Like
    Supper's Ready
    Horizons
    More Fool Me
    The Battle of Epping Forest
    The Knife

THE BEDSIDE YELLOW FOAM
  (Recorded live in 1974 — Side 1 in Britain, January 1974, side 2 in Canada)
  Dancing With the Moonlit Knight
  The Cinema Show
  Aisle of Plenty
  Supper's Ready

L'ANGE GABRIEL
  (Recorded live in Montreal, April 21, 1974)
  Dancing With The Moonlit Knight
  The Cinema Show
  I Know What I Like
  Firth of Fifth
  The Musical Box

AS THOUGH EMERALD CITY
  (Recorded live at the Shrine Auditorium, Los Angeles, January 1975, except *studio)
    Watcher of the Skies
    Lilywhite Lilith
    The Waiting Room
    It
    The Musical Box
    Happy the Man*
    Twilight Alehouse*

AWED MAN OUT (LP)
  (Recorded live at Wembley, 1975)
    Cuckoo Cocoon
    Back In N.Y.C.
    Hairless Heart
    Counting Out Time
    Carpet Crawlers
    Lilywhite Lilith
    The Waiting Room
    Anyway
    Silent Sorrow In Empty Boats
    Ravine
    The Light Dies Down On Broadway
    Riding The Scree

THE RAREST VOLUME1 (LP)
  (Recorded live in Montreal April 1974, except where indicated)
    Stagnation (BBC Session 1971)
    Get'em Out by Friday (BBC Session 1972)
    Twilight Alehouse (BBC session 1972)
    Dancing with the Moonlit Knight
    Horizons
    The Battle of Epping Forest

THE LAMB WOKE UP AGAIN (CD)
  (Recorded live at the "Six Of The Best" show and at Guildford Civic Hall, January 26, 1983)
    Back in N.Y.C.
    Dancing with the Moonlit Knight-Carpet Crawlers
    Firth of Fifth

176

The Musical Box
Solsbury Hill
Turn it on Again
The Lamb Lies Down on Broadway
Fly on Windshield-Broadway Melody of 1974
In the Cage
Supper's Ready
I Know What I Like
The Knife
Here Comes the Flood*
Solsbury Hill*
Reach Out(I'll be There)*
I Know What I Like(In your Wardrobe)*

THROUGH THE LOOKING GLASS
  (Recorded live in Genova, Italy, August 1972)
    Watcher Of The Skies
    Bye Bye Johnny
    The Fountain Of Salmacis
    Seven Stones
    The Musical Box
    The Return Of The Giant Hogweed

THE SHEPHERD
  (BBC sessions 1970-1972)
    The Shepherd
    Pacidy
    Let Us Now Make Love
    Stagnation
    Looking For Someone
    Twilight Alehouse
    Watcher Of The Skies

SWELLED AND SPENT
  (Recorded live in Birmingham, May 1975)
    Intro
    The Lamb Lies Down On Broadway
    Fly On A Windshield
    Broadway Melody Of 1974
    Cuckoo Cocoon
    In The Cage
    The Grand Parade Of Lifeless Packaging
    Back In NYC
    Hairless Heart
    Counting Out Time
    The Carpet Crawlers
    The Chamber Of 32 Doors
    Lilywhite Lilith

The Waiting Room
Anyway
Here Comes The Supernatural Anaesthetist
The Lamia
The Colony Of Slippermen
Ravine
The Light Dies Down On Broadway
Riding The Scree
In The Rapids
It

TRICK OF THE TAIL OUTTAKES
(Alternate / instrumental versions from *A Trick Of The Tail* sessions)
Beloved Summer (longer version of It's Yourself)
Dance On A Volcano
Indians (instrumental version of Squonk)
Robbery, Assault & Battery
Los Endos
A Trick of the Tail
Ripples Part 1
Ripples Part 2
Mad Man Moon

JUST A POOL OF TEARS
(Recorded live in Detroit, 1976, except *studio)
Dance on a Volcano
The Lamb Lies Down on Broadway
Fly On A Windshield
The Carpet Crawl
Cinema Show
Robbery, Assault & Battery
White Mountain
Firth of Fifth
Entangled
Supper's Ready
Squonk
I Know What I Like
Los Endos
It
Watcher of the Skies
Happy the Man*
Twilight Alehouse*

ALL WE NEED'S A HIT
(Recorded live at Earls Court, June 1977 and Manchester, January 1977)
Squonk
One for the Vine
Your Own Special Way

Inside and Out
Carpet Crawl
Afterglow
Eleventh Earl of Mar
I Know What I Like
Dance on a Volcano
The Lamb Lies Down on Broadway
The Musical Box

LIVE AT THE THEATRE ROYAL 5/4/80 (2 LP set)
Dancing Out With The Moonlit Knight
Carpet Crawlers
Behind The Lines
Duchess
Guide Vocal
Squonk
Turn It On Again
Ripples
Medley: In The Cage / Colony Of Slippermen / Afterglow / Follow You, Follow Me /
I Know What I Like (Stagnation)
The Knife

MUSICA
(Recorded live at the Lyceum Ballroom, London, 1980)
Deep In The Motherlode
Dancing With The Moonlit Knight
The Carpet Crawlers
Squonk
One For The Vine
Behind The Lines
Duchess
Guide Vocal
Turn It On Again
Duke's Travels
Duke's End
Ripples
The Lady Lies
In The Cage
Afterglow
Follow You Follow Me
Dance On A Volcano
Los Endos
I Know What I Like
The Knife

... AND THEN THERE WAS NUERNBERG
(Recorded live in Nuernberg, 1981)
Behind The Lines

Duchess
The Lamb Lies Down On Broadway
Dodo
Abacab
Man On The Corner
Who Dunnit?
The Carpet Crawl

THE INVISIBLE CAGE
(Recorded live in Mannheim, 1987)
Mama
Abacab
Domino: In the glow of the night
Domino: The last domino
That's All
The Brazilian
In The Cage / ... in that quiet earth
Afterglow
Land Of Confusion
Throwing It All Away
Home By The Sea / Second Home By The Sea
Invisible Touch
Drum duet / Los Endos
Turn It On Again (with medley)

SUMMER NIGHTS
(Recorded live at Knebworth, 1992)
Land Of Confusion
No Son Of Mine
Driving The Last Spike
Old Medley
Throwing It All Away
Fading Lights
Jesus He Knows Me
Home By The Sea / Second Home By The Sea
Hold On My Heart
Domino Part I
Domino Part II
Drum Duet
I Can`t Dance
Tonight, Tonight, Tonight
Invisible Touch
Turn It On Again

STRICTLY MECHANIC (2 CD set)
(Recorded live at Stuttgart, 1998)
No Son Of Mine
Land Of Confusion

The Lamb Lies Down On Broadway
Calling All Stations
Alien Afternoon
Carpet Crawlers
There Must Be Some Other Way
Domino
Shipwrecked
Firth Of Fifth
Congo
Home By The Sea
Second Home By the Sea
Dancing With The Moonlit Knight
Follow You Follow Me
Lovers Leap
Mama
The Dividing Line
Invisible Touch
Turn It On Again
Throwing It All Away
I Can`t Dance

The Hit Singles:

Britain:
- I Know What I Like, 1974 [No. 21]
- Your Own Special Way, 1977 [No. 43]
- *Spot The Pigeon* EP, 1977 [No. 14]
- Follow You Follow Me, 1978 [No. 7]
- Many Too Many, 1978 [No. 43]
- Turn It On Again, 1980 [No. 8]
- Duchess, 1980 [No. 46]
- Misunderstanding, 1980 [No. 42]
- Abacab, 1981 [No. 9]
- Keep It Dark, 1981 [No. 33]
- Man On The Corner, 1982 [No. 41]
- *3 x 3* EP, 1982 [No. 10]
- Mama, 1983 [No. 4]
- That's All, 1983 [No. 16]
- Illegal Alien, 1984 [No. 46]
- Invisible Touch, 1986 [No. 15]
- In Too Deep, 1986 [No. 19]
- Land Of Confusion, 1986 [No. 14]
- Tonight Tonight Tonight, 1987 [No. 18]
- Throwing It All Away, 1987 [No. 22]
- No Son Of Mine, 1991 [No. 6]
- I Can't Dance, 1992 [No. 7]
- Hold On My Heart, 1992 [No. 16]

- Jesus He Knows Me, 1992 [No. 20]
- Tell Me Why, 1993 [No. 40]
- Invisible Touch (live), 1993 [No. 7]

Canada:
- Follow You Follow Me, 1978 [No. 19]
- Misunderstanding, 1980 [No. 16]
- No Reply At All, 1981 [No. 4]
- Abacab, 1982 [No. 8]
- Paperlate, 1982 [No. 14]
- Mama, 1983 [No. 38]
- That's All, 1984 [No. 10]
- Invisible Touch, 1986 [No. 4]
- Throwing It All Away, 1986 [No. 20]
- Land Of Confusion, 1987 [No. 13]
- Tonight Tonight Tonight, 1987 [No. 39]
- In Too Deep, 1987 [No. 15]
- No Son Of Mine, 1991 [No. 3] (radio airplay chart)
- I Can't Dance, 1992 [No. 7]
- Jesus He Knows Me, 1992 [No. 5] (radio airplay chart)
- Hold On My Heart, 1992 [No. 5] (radio airplay chart)
- Never A Time, 1992 [No. 6] (radio airplay chart)

U.S.A.:
- Your Own Special Way, 1977 [No. 62]
- Follow You Follow Me, 1978 [No. 23]
- Misunderstanding, 1980 [No. 14]
- Turn It On Again, 1980 [No. 58]
- No Reply At All, 1981 [No. 29]
- Abacab, 1981 [No. 26]
- Man On The Corner, 1982 [No. 40]
- Paperlate, 1982 [No. 32]
- Mama, 1983 [No. 73]
- That's All, 1983 [No. 6]
- Illegal Alien, 1984 [No. 44]
- Taking It All Too Hard, 1984 [No. 50]
- Invisible Touch, 1986 [No. 1]
- Throwing It All Away, 1986 [No. 4]
- Land Of Confusion, 1986 [No. 4]
- Tonight, Tonight, Tonight, 1987 [No. 3]
- In Too Deep, 1987 [No. 3]
- No Son Of Mine, 1991 [No. 12]
- I Can't Dance, 1992 [No. 7]
- Hold On My Heart, 1992 [No. 12]
- Jesus He Knows Me, 1992 [No. 23]
- Never A Time, 1992 [No. 21]

Resources:

Steve Hackett's official web site (www.stevehackett.com) offers not only all Steve's CD's for sale, but all the remastered Genesis CD's, and solo efforts by other Genesis members. It also provides a wealth of information about Steve and his solo career.

The official Genesis site (www.genesis-web.com) includes information about the group's recent activities and an extensive section on the Archive box set. At the time of writing, the site was unavailable so it's future — like that of Genesis itself — seems to be in doubt. There are numerous other Genesis sites on the Web, too many to list, but easily found through a quick search.

For information on Daryl Steurmer and his new CD, ANOTHER SIDE OF GENESIS, point your browser to www.darylstuermer.com.

Gary Best's excellent site, The Way They Walk . A great source of Genesis news and information (http://www.congo.demon.co.uk/genesis.html).

Although his first solo album didn't appear until seven years after his departure from Genesis, Anthony Phillips has since proven to be one of the most prolific ex-Genesis members. His solo catalog is well worth investigating, and the following CD's are available by mail order from:

- BP201CD Phillips, Anthony Anthology
- BP202CD Phillips, Anthony Private Parts & Pieces I
- BP203CD Phillips, Anthony Private Parts & Pieces II
- BP204CD Phillips, Anthony Private Parts & Pieces III
- BP205CD Phillips, Anthony Private Parts & Pieces IV
- BP206CD Phillips, Anthony Private Parts & Pieces V
- BP207CD Phillips, Anthony Private Parts & Pieces VI
- BP208CD Phillips, Anthony Private Parts & Pieces VII
- BP209CD Phillips, Anthony Fingerpainting
- BP210CD Phillips, Anthony Sides
- BP211CD Phillips, Anthony Invisible Men
- BP212CD Phillips, Anthony Private Parts VIII
- BP213CD Phillips, Anthony Slow Dance
- BP218CD Phillips, Anthony The Living Room Concert
- BP219CD Phillips, Anthony Tarka
- BP229CD Phillips, Anthony Private Parts & Pieces 9
- BP272CD Phillips, Anthony Missing Links 3
- BP279CD Phillips, Anthony Archive Collection vol. I
- DM31502 Phillips, Anthony & Cazenave, Guillermo Live Radio Sessions
- RES102CD Phillips, Anthony Sail the World
- BP189CD Phillips, Anthony & Williamson, Harry Gypsy Suite

Look for these other books from Collector's Guide Publishing Inc.

20th CENTURY ROCK AND ROLL PROGRESSIVE ROCK
By Jerry Lucky

For progressive rock aficionados and all lovers of classical rock music, this book highlights the 50 most influential and important progressive rock bands, past and present, from around the world.

Exploring the artists and their music, from its origins to current prog music, the history and discography are presented in knowledgeable detail.

Veteran author Jerry Lucky shares with us his vast experience in the Progressive Rock world detailing the development of Prog by looking closely at the players as well as their music.

Progressive rock music combines and transends the various music genrés to a greater extent than possibly any other type of music. This book will take you straight to the very best that Prog has to offer and make you comfortable with its roots and where it's going next.

THE PROGRESSIVE ROCK FILES
By Jerry Lucky

After years of research, musicologist and broadcaster Jerry Lucky has created a definitive guide to Progressive Rock music.

Everything from the history and the critical thrashing, to the complex development this musical genre has gone through from it's beginnings in 1967 to the present day.

Included are definitions of virtually all popular musical styles and for the first time a definition of what Progressive Rock actually is...and it's probably not what you think.

Also included is a comprehensive A-Z listing of over 1400 Progressive Rock bands each with a brief musical description and recored discography to aid in your discovery of this challenging and adventurous musical art-form.

Jerry Lucky is a broadcaster and musicologist with a love of Progressive Rock music. He has authored articles on such diverse interests as music, marketing and drag racing. His work on The Progressive Rock Files began in 1983 while hosting a Prog radio show called Exposure. He currently resides in Victoria, BC with his family and an ever growing collection of Progressive Rock albums and CDs.

For more information visit us at **www.cgpublishing.com**